ce

THE HISTORY OF THE CARRIAGE

THE HISTORY OF THE CARRIAGE

by

LÁSZLÓ TARR

TRANSLATED BY ELISABETH HOCH

ARCO PUBLISHING COMPANY, INC.
New York

First published 1969 in the United States by
ARCO PUBLISHING COMPANY, INC.
219 Park Avenue South, New York, N.Y. 10003
© 1969 by Vision Press, London and Corvina Press, Budapest
All rights reserved
Library of Congress Catalog Number 69—14248
ARCO Number 668—01871—2
Printed in Hungary
Bound in Great Britain
MCMLXIX

Contents

5

the East-Roman Empire — The Theodosian Code — The load-carrying capacity of the carriages — Other types of Roman carriages — Street traffic — Funeral processions — Triumphal processions — Chariot races — The *tensa* — The circus chariot races and the drivers — Technical innovations to the Roman carriage — Thracian carriages — Pannonian carriages — The Adamklissi victory memorial

The Middle Ages

Modern Times

Illustrations by László Lakner and his associates

The origin and ancestors of the carriage — Theories concerning the development
of the wheel — The main components of the wheeled vehicle

Who invented the carriage? Inventions do not spring from the
inventor's head like Pallas Athene, full-grown from the head of
Zeus. Most inventions are collective in character, even if belief
or encyclopaedias associate them with individual names. However, the further we trace an invention back into the past, the
fewer names we find, and there is a point—somewhere about the
beginning of our era—beyond which no names are recorded,
except perhaps in mythology where inventions are often attributed to some legendary god. In Johann Christian Ginzrot's *Die
Wagen und Fahrwerke der Griechen und Römer und anderer alten
Völcker* (The Carriages and Vehicles of the Greeks and Romans
and Other Peoples of the Antique World), published in 1817, the
list of names associated with the invention of the carriage is
headed by Adam and followed by a host of gods, demigods and
heroes.

The inventor of the carriage cannot be identified with any one
person, since the development of this vehicle—as that of every
implement—was inevitably a gradual process. Improvement
followed improvement until, at the beginning of the twentieth
century, the carriage reached its peak of perfection. But if we
retrace our steps along the paths of human progress and strip the
carriage of the innumerable technical improvements added to it
during the ages, we find before us a simple loading-platform on
wheels: the ancestor of the carriage (Fig. 1).

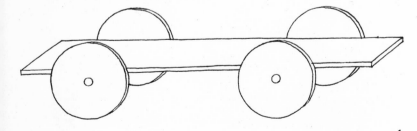

1

The wheeled vehicle as an implement. There is no doubt that
the wheeled vehicle or, to be more precise, the two-wheeled cart

1 Platform on wheels

9

and the four-wheeled wagon, came into existence at an advanced stage of evolution, with the use of developed tools and implements. The appearance of the wheeled vehicle on the scene was part of the development of productive forces: when prehistoric man had to carry relatively heavy loads over long distances, he set to thinking how he might make his task less arduous. The wheel and the axle-tree—now common objects, taken for granted—were the fruits of hard brain-work which should not be belittled in the perspective of time. To realize their significance one must appreciate the social and economic circumstances under which they were contrived. Ethnographic analogies help to form a picture of the production conditions ruling at that time; they prove beyond doubt that an implement serving to carry heavy loads over long distances was required only after man had settled down to hoeing and reaping, with relatively well-developed stone tools. This mode of living is associated with the neolithic period, that is, the later Stone Age.

The ancestors of the carriage. In trying to find an easier way of transporting his burdens, prehistoric man did not immediately hit upon the use of a vehicle. The wheeled vehicle was, in fact, preceded by other, simpler methods of conveyance, the most primitive of which was to tie up the easily sliding burdens of lesser weight with plaited bark rope into a compact bundle and to drag it by the rope along the ground. In a work entitled *A szorgalmatos mezei gazda* (The Industrious Farmer. Pest, 1791), János Nagyváthy, a Hungarian agronomist, says: "The nearer the stack-yards and granges are to the hayfield, the better, for it

2

10

makes the gathering in of the hay easier, and very handy means may be employed for this purpose, as for instance the chain which the Hungarians tie round the stacks for hauling them together." Indeed, in some parts of the Hungarian Plains the peasants have used this method of dragging home the haycocks up to the early twentieth century.

The bough—the ancestor of the sledge. The next innovation was to place the load on a bough cut for this purpose. Our illustration (Fig. 2), based on a photograph taken before 1914, shows this slightly improved method of transport. Its use was observed in 1912 by the German ethnographer Weule in Olonec, a province of Russia inhabited by Finns. According to his description "The parent-form of the sledge is the bough on which our ancestors dragged the kill back to their camp... the peasants of the Russian province Olonec still convey heavy loads over stretches of marshy land on slide-cars of this type, and our own peasants [meaning in this case Germans] also drag their ploughs home on a simple forked branch." In 1907 Ferenc Pávay Vajna, geologist and amateur ethnographer, observed and photographed in Transylvania the loading of haycocks on freshly cut hazel sticks; the pile was then drawn to the haystack by oxen.

2 Hay-transport on a bough
3 Fisherman with his sledge
4 The hide sledge of the Västerbotten Lapps

3

The hide sledge. A similarly primitive mode of transport was to pull the slaughtered animal or other burdens home on a kind of sledge made of hide or the bark of a tree (Fig. 3). The hide sledge is still used by Laplanders, Eskimos and North American Arctic Indians (Fig. 4). However, its widespread use in the northern geographic regions does not imply that it was common in ice and snow-bound countries only.

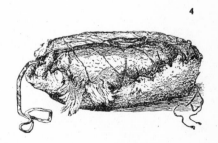

4

The sledge. Another ancient transport device is the sledge. There is an account tablet of 3000–2800 B.C. from the Ininn

11

5

6

Temple of Uruk, Mesopotamia, showing the clearly recognizable picture of a sledge with a small body covered by a gabled roof on the top (Fig. 5). This pictographic symbol shows that the sledge had been used five thousand years ago in the valley of the Two Rivers where snow is known only from hearsay.

It is generally accepted that the ancestor of the simple, box-like wagon without a pivoted front part was the sledge. Works on ethnography, archaeology and the history of technology indicate that the four-wheeled wagon is but a sledge put on wheels. This assumption is also borne out by the fact that, as well as the Ininn Temple pictograph, there is another symbol indicating beyond any doubt a wheeled conveyance, a kind of covered wagon or caravan (Fig. 6).

The slide-car. So far it appears that transport developed along two different lines: one started from the sledge and progressed towards the carriage, the other arose from the implement called the slide-car. According to experts, the latter was based on entirely different technological principles and developed quite independently from the sledge. It consisted essentially of two poles tied to one or two draught-animals—dogs, reindeer, horses or oxen—at one end with the other dragging along the ground (Figs. 7–11). The burden was loaded on these poles. Various types of slide-cars are known, distinguished from one another in the first place according to the number of draught-animals used.

The single-animal slide-car. If the slide-car was drawn by a single draught-animal, the two shafts were usually attached to the animal's side (Fig. 7), occasionally to its collar (Fig. 8). The

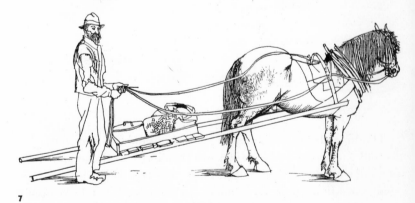

7

itinerant Indians of the North American prairies tied their tent poles to the back of the draught-animal. The Spanish writer Coronado de Castañedas recorded that as early as 1540 the Indians tied poles in the form of a capital A to the back of the dog, used as a draught-animal at that time. Some North Amer-

12

ican Indians still use this ancient form of portage, but with horses (Fig. 9).

Similar slide-cars were used by the Ukrainians, the Bashkirs, the Kazakhs, the Zyryans (Komis), the Ostyaks (Khantis), the Letts, the Esthonians, the Norwegians, the Swedes, the Finns, the Scots, the Welsh and the Irish. The Irish slide-car was in use in certain regions of Ireland, particularly in the Antrim valley, up to quite fairly recent times (Fig. 10), and it is not long since the Scots and the Welsh abandoned this means of transport. In the First World War the slide-car was used at first-aid stations on the Balkan front to transport the wounded.

The slide-car with paired draught. Another type of slide-car was that drawn by a yoked pair of animals. The earliest evidence —rock drawings dating from the early Bronze Age (second millennium B.C.)—were found in Val Fontanalba, Liguria (Fig. 11). They show oxen seen from above, dragging a ladder-like imple-

5 Sumerian pictograph of a sledge
6 Sumerian pictograph of a covered wagon
7 Slide-car
8 Slide-car in the Ukraine
9 Slide-car in Banff
10 Slide-car for turf-transport

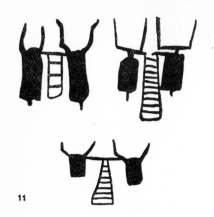

11

ment attached to their large horns by a yoke. For a long time the implement was thought to form part of a harrow or sledge. However, the German ethnologist H. Kothe refuted this and explained that "the implement can be neither a sledge nor a harrow, for in either case it would lie on the ground at full length. Since, however, one end of it is attached to the yoke and the other trails on the ground, it could not have lain flat, but must have been a slide-car with shafts and a yoke" *(Jochstangenschleife)*.

The 'chaasak'. Another example shows a slightly modified structure called the *chaasak* which was used by the Tartars of Crimea as late as around 1800. Peter Simon Pallas, the German traveller, drew a picture of the *chaasak* he saw in Alupka, a village of the Crimean peninsula. Fig. 12 shows this device used by the Tartars for carrying timber from the mountains.

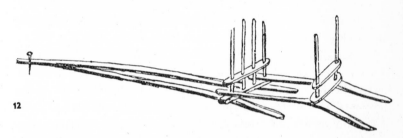

12

The origin of the two-wheeled cart. The cart with shafts developed from the H-shaped slide-car, that with a single pole developed from the A-shaped one, says the French ethnologist Haudricourt. He refers to Indian examples, for the two-wheeled cart still widely used in India can be clearly identified as originating from the A-shaped slide-car (Fig. 13). Regarding the

11 Pairs of yoked oxen drawing slide-cars
12 The chaasak
13 Slide-car from India
14 Carts with ladder-shaped chassis
15 Diagram of the development of the carriage

13

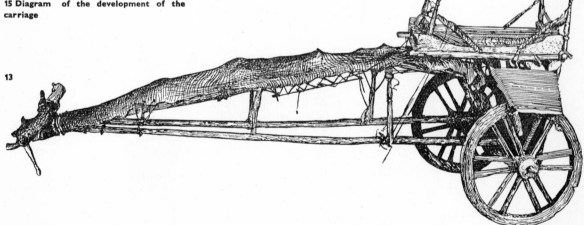

14

cart developed from the H-shaped slide-car, a prehistoric rock drawing at Los Buitres near Penalsordo in Spain, dating from the second millennium B.C., shows an H-shaped slide-car with wheels and a ladder-shaped chassis, viewed from above (Fig. 14). The wheels appear to have spokes, and one of them, the left wheel of the right cart which seems to be strengthened with a transverse strut, is reminiscent of an H-type wheel. However, it is improbable that wheels with cross-bars were used at that time. They may well have been solid wheels consisting of several parts. The drawing shows no harness, and it appears that the vehicle was drawn or pushed by man, like hand-carts today.

14

The development of the wheeled vehicle. On the basis of the generally accepted theory of Haudricourt, we may summarize: — The precursor of the wagon was the sledge, i.e. a piece of wood or hide drawn along the ground; the cart with a pole developed from the A-shaped, the cart with shafts, from the H-shaped slide-car. Haudricourt's sketches illustrating this process of development are reproduced here with slight alterations (Fig. 15), showing also how the wagon evolved—a combination of the two types of carts, with a pivoted front axle which enables the vehicle to be manoeuvered easily.

Theories regarding the development of the carriage. Since there is no carriage without wheels, we must consider the various theories about the origins of the wheel. It is perhaps best to consider first the views advanced on the subject by the purely theoretical scholars who at times further the solution of the question with some sound deductions, but as often make one smile at their fabrications.

15

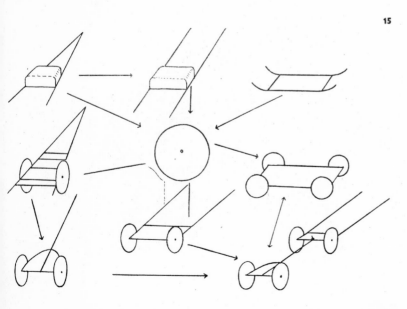

The roller theory. One well-known theory concerning the development of the carriage, the 'roller theory', gained ground in the nineteenth century. It was advocated also by Johann Christian Ginzrot who has already been mentioned, and who was Royal Bavarian Inspector of Carriage-Building. He assumed that originally prehistoric man transported his burden with the aid of a thick, trimmed branch or tree trunk which he hauled by one end. It may be presumed, says Ginzrot, that when these branches happened to turn sideways—which they easily did—primitive man discovered the advantages of rolling: all he had to do was to put his burden on the rolling timbers (Fig. 16). Thence it was only a step to cutting two disks from the trunk and fixing a shaft between them. Actually, it could hardly have been so simple. But though it is obvious now that the roller could not so easily have developed into the wheel, yet many nineteenth-century scientists concerned with kinetics and traffic techniques accepted this theory of evolution. They all regarded the trimmed timber as the ancestor of the wheel, on the grounds that the roller is still being used for the transport of heavy loads today, but it is a cumbersome method.

Ernst Mach, the Austrian physicist, suggested that prehistoric man prevented the sliding of the rollers from under the load by tying cross-bars or trunks under the platform (Fig. 17), which probably led to the use of the axle later.

17

In theory it appears easy to make wheels from a tree trunk: take a thick, trimmed timber and slice it as required, like a sausage (Fig. 18). However, in practice this was not so simple, not only because of the lack of suitable tools, but also because these cross-cut slices break easily. Planks have to be cut lengthwise so that they do not crack (Fig. 19).

Mystical explanations. Hahn, Forestier and Forrer sought the origin of the carriage elsewhere. Their theories were based on chance and even on mystical explanations instead of practical economic functions. Hahn and Forestier attributed great importance to the whorl in the development of the wheel. The whorl was a small ring made of some heavy material which, put on the spindle, permitted faster spinning. As spinning was known in very ancient times, prehistoric finds often include whorls in large numbers (Fig. 20). They are similar to small solid disc-wheels, and Eduard Hahn, German economic historian, probably based his whorl-wheel theory on this similarity.

Hahn's theory is a typical example of how a scholar with a rich imagination may get entangled in unfounded theories if he omits to take into account the laws of social evolution. According to Hahn, the invention of the wheel and the carriage was not related to the satisfaction of man's everyday needs, but had a cult origin. His theory—which he elaborated in detail and defended for decades with a zeal worthy of a better cause—associated the invention of the carriage with the ancient cult ceremonies of the Babylonian people. According to him, an idle priest of the sun worshippers watched the whorls until the idea occured of putting two of them on a small stick (Fig. 21). He then placed this structure on the ground and set it rolling. Having thus invented the wheel, it was only natural that he desired to turn it to religious use: the idols were put on wheels to increase

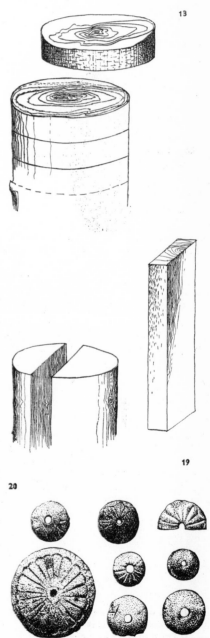

13

19

20

17

21

22

the splendour of the processions of sun worshippers. So much for Hahn's version of the problem.

While Hahn was still defending this theory at the end of the nineteenth century, Forestier, Chief Inspector of Bridges and Roads in France and lecturer on the subject, published his work entitled *La Roue* (The Wheel). In this he, too, attributed the invention of the wheel to mere chance with the only difference being that he assigned the part of the inventor to a mother, instead of to a priest. The rest of the story runs almost the same: "A prehistoric mother, wanting to amuse her child while spinning, put a whorl each on the two ends of a spindle, cast the toy to the ground and lo! the wheel was born." Hahn naturally welcomed Forestier's book with immense enthusiasm as a confirmation of his own theory.

In spite of devastating criticism by Kaj Birket-Smith, the Danish ethnologist who called the argument chimerical, Hahn's theory was adopted by one handbook and encyclopaedia after another, despite the obvious mistakes in his reasoning. For first of all, he failed to realize the scope of knowledge of primitive man: he presumed that man, five to six thousand years ago, was able to perceive interrelations between technological phenomena as easily as the man of our age. Further, he forgot the economic function of the wheeled vehicle as a working implement. Hahn's story of the invention of the wheel was not only arbitrary, but also contradictory to evolutionary principles.

A later theory based on errors similar to these advocated by Hahn, put forward by the Saxon archaeologist Robert Forrer in a study published in 1932, appears to be somewhat more realistic. The work deals with the origin of the wheeled vehicle used for religious purposes which Forrer also associates with the sun worshippers' myth. According to him, a priest of the creed made an image of the sun which he believed to be a revolving disk; he probably used some hard material (wood, clay or perhaps even gold) for this purpose and, to imitate the rotation of the sun, pierced the disk with a stick (Fig. 22). This solitary wheel—Forrer believes—was the ancestor of the carriage. In basing his theory on a cult origin, Forrer followed in the wake of Hahn, yet he attempted to approach the subject from a more realistic angle. Although evidently an odd wheel does not make a carriage, we may accept from Forrer's theory that the priests of sun worship played some rôle in the cult use of the wheeled vehicle, for they were interested in supporting religious beliefs by every suitable means. Regarding the origin of the carriage, however, the modern mind can accept only a realistic theory based on the fact that the wheeled vehicle was primarily a working implement developed by economic necessity.

21 Two whorls joined by a stick
22 Disk pierced by a stick
23 Two men before a sun disk

18

The essential components of the primitive wheeled vehicle are the wheel, the axle-tree, the carriage-body and the pole or the shafts. The first question arising about the wheel is similar to the old problem of 'the chicken and the egg': which was first, the carriage or the wheel? One would believe that the reply is simple: both are of the same age. But this is not the case. For when we talk of the wheel, we have before our mind's eye the real wheel revolving round an axle. This wheel is the fruit of man's technological ingenuity. However, there exists besides this another wheel, a symbolic one, similar to the real wheel, yet not connected with the latter at all.

The symbolic wheel. The prehistoric man liked to draw and engrave various figures and symbols—including circles—on smooth rocks or slabs (Fig. 23). The question arises: what did he

23

want to depict with the circle? No doubt, the sun in the first place, as the life-giving source of heat. The crosses he drew inside the circle may have represented the warm rays, though they deceptively resemble the spokes of a wheel. However, this symbol has nothing to do yet with the real spoke. Besides, the circle as a symbol means the infinite, something that has neither a beginning nor an end.

The real wheel is no doubt the result of a different way of thinking than that which gave rise to the symbolic wheel. It is just as likely that the symbolic wheel was invented by magicians and priests, as it is evident that the real wheel could have been contrived only by men endeavouring to ease the burden of their work.

What was the first real wheel like? This question is relatively easy to answer: — It was not a spoked wheel by any means. All remains of early wheels which have come down to us unequivocally point to the fact that the first wheel used in practice was a solid one (Fig. 24), and the laws of logic also lead us to the same conclusion. But to make a solid wheel—whether cross-cut or lengthwise—one needs to saw as thick a piece of timber as the wheel requires. Practically, such solid wheels are still usable and are actually used in some parts of the world, but they have the great disadvantage that they break very easily. In any case the solid wheel was still used at the beginning of the century in the Caucasus (Fig. 25). However, just because of its fragility, this primitive type of solid wheel was soon superseded by the wheel constructed in a rough way from two or more parts. The Sumerians generally used three pieces of plank for this purpose. In one of the earliest precise representations of the wheel which

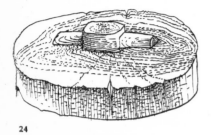

24

25

has come down to us, in the sacrificial plaque (Fig. 46), the middle part of the wheel is plum-shaped, with a waning and waxing crescent-shaped part attached to the right and left sides, respectively (Fig. 26). Such thinner, but still solid wheels were reinforced with cross-bars, the use of which may have been discovered while patching up broken wheels. Some of the oldest representations show tripartite wheels in which the three pieces of plank are fixed parallel to each other with the axle-hole bored in the middle part (Fig. 27). In fact, solid wheels pieced together from two parts were also made (Fig. 28).

The roughly constructed disk consisting of two or more pieces of plank is the most common form of the solid wheel. Its geographically widespread use is illustrated by Figs. 29–32, showing a Chinese cart, a Vietnamese large-wheeled cart, a Norwegian cart and a New Mexican 'Angel of Death'. These are also good examples of how certain forms have defied the passing millennia; they persisted, not because man hung on to them by sheer force of habit, but rather because living under more or less similar economic conditions for ages, he solved his technical problems in similar ways.

The above example shows that the classification of wheels according to type would prove an endless task. Similarly, if one tried to set up a sort of 'genealogical theory' based on chronological order, it would soon turn out that such systematization is impossible because many ancient types of the wheel have survived from the earliest period of the wheeled vehicle to today. In these circumstances no serial order can be established by trying to trace back one type to another. But let us now consider the other parts of the carriage.

The axle-tree. At the beginning, the axle-tree rotated together with the wheels, that is to say, the wheels were solidly fixed to it. The wheel held in place by a pin, but moving freely on the axle-tree, was a later, but still ancient achievement.

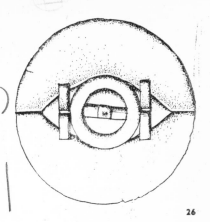

26

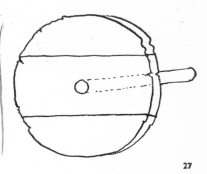

27

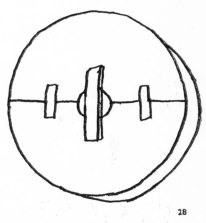

28

29

24 Wheel made from a solid piece of wood
25 Cart with solid wheels in the Caucasus
26 Wheel made from three pieces of solid wood
27 Three-section wheel
28 Wheel made from two pieces of solid wood
29 Chinese cart

The **carriage-body** probably consisted originally of a simple wickerwork floor; later this may have been superseded by a roughly hewn wooden platform. The box-shaped carriage-body and other structures imitating the chair, the stool or the saddle appeared only later; these were followed by carriage-bodies with rounded front and of various other forms.

The **pole and the shafts.** The development of this part of the carriage from the slide-car has been discussed, and its special forms will be dealt with later.

30 Vietnamese large-wheeled cart
31 Cart with solid wheels
32 'Angel of Death' sitting on a solid-wheeled cart

The yoke. Although strictly speaking the yoke does not form part of the wheeled vehicle, it is felt that the rôle of this device should be discussed at this stage. In addition to the solid wheel, another well-known characteristic, common to all the earliest wheeled vehicles, was the yoke for paired draught. It is present on every carriage and cart, whether it has come down to us in the form of a material archaeological find or only as a contemporary representation. The ancient form of the yoke (Fig. 33) for paired draught was a short bar placed crossways at the end of the pole and tied to the neck or the horns of each animal (Fig. 34).

32

33

A pair of draught-animals—oxen in the beginning, but later asses, onagers (the wild ass of Central Asia), and finally horses—were yoked to the vehicle on either side of the pole, so that the yoke rested on and was tied to their neck or withers. This way of harnessing a team is still usual today.

The yoke represented the most important prehistoric technical invention for transport besides the wheel, as it helped to exploit the traction-power of animals. At present it is used only with draught-oxen, but in olden times the ass, the mule and the horse were also put to the yoke as no other way of harnessing a draught-animal was known.

The two ancient methods of harnessing were either to put a pair of draught-animals under the yoke or a single animal between the shafts. The geographic distribution of the two different methods is amazing and leads to very interesting conclusions, for the Eurasian Continent may be divided almost with precision into a one-pole yoked-pair area and a double-shaft single-animal area. The boundary line starts from the Baltic Sea, runs in a southern direction and, diverting gradually to the east, crosses the Caspian Sea, continues along the Altaic Mountains to the southern frontier of China. To the left of this line on the map the paired-draught type, to the right the single-draught type have prevailed in usage.

In other words, in Northern Eurasia animal traction-power was transmitted with the aid of shafts on one animal; in South Eurasia with that of a pole hitched to the yoke on two animals. This division existed as early as 1000 B.C. and has undergone but little change up to recent times. The lively mutual cultural

34

influence of the two vast areas has hardly affected the vehicle. While in Europe the one-pole wagon and cart drawn by yoked pair is the dominant animal-drawn transport device, the steppes and deserts are the land of one-horse carts with shafts; each type is regarded as the standard traffic and portage device in its respective area, and deviations, if any, from their traditional forms are the result of a more recent cultural influence.

Summing up what we know of the ancient carriage—or 'proto-carriage'—we may state the following: (a) it ran on tripartite solid wheels; (b) the number of wheels used was two or four; (c) the draught-animals, when more than one, were hitched together with a double yoke; (d) the four-wheeled vehicle arose probably from the sledge; (e) the ancestor of the two-wheeled cart was presumably the slide-car.

Chapter II

The carriage: an invention of the nomads? — Sumer — Elam — Various types of carriages

Nomads and the origins of the carriage. Without roads the primitive wheeled vehicle—the wagon and the cart—could not compete with the human porter or the pack-animal over long distances, but it must have been suitable for transport over flat land with short-stemmed and thinly growing vegetation. Obviously, both the ancient wagon and the cart could be used only in areas where mountains, mud or desert sand, high vegetation or thick jungle did not obstruct its progress. The grassy steppe was the ideal terrain: here the carriage ran easily over the wide plains even if there was no road. The steppe, once a vast, but now a gradually shrinking bare open plain dividing Eurasia in two, was the native land of the nomadic pastoral tribes. However, stock-breeding on the steppe—that is, the rearing of reindeer, cattle and sheep—demanded continuous migration to fresh pastures, and on such occasions the shepherds had to move not only their tents and personal belongings, but also the implements and utensils they needed for tending and milking the animals. It was for this purpose that they contrived—and still use—the herdsman's cart. A clever shepherd must have discovered that, instead of seeking refuge in a hastily pitched tent against the vicissitudes of weather, it was much simpler to put a roof over his cart and take cover under that. This is probably how the covered wagon was invented.

Could the nomads have invented the carriage? The question has been raised by many, and others may also guess that the carriage was a product of nomadic culture and not of urban origin. The answer is that the Central Asiatic nomad tribes contributed many a brick to the structure of civilization; for instance, the domestication of the horses was the work of the nomads. The problem is one of those for which the history of technology has not yet provided the final answer. It is generally believed that we owe the carriage—as so many other feats of civilization—to the Sumerian people. However, there are opinions also to the contrary, based on the assumption that economic and cultural relations had existed between the Sumerians and the nomad

26

tribes of the Central Asiatic steppes, as early as the fifth and fourth millennia B.C., that is, when the Sumerians supposedly still inhabited Central Asia, before migrating to Mesopotamia. Under these circumstances it is possible that the Sumerians— the oldest people we know for certain to have used the wheeled vehicle—did not invent, but only adopted the use of this transport device from the nomads. According to Birket-Smith, the Danish ethnologist, we have absolutely no ground for regarding Mesopotamia as the country of origin of the carriage; on the other hand, the Central Asiatic steppes "seem to have been created for this very vehicle". The well-known ethnologists Wilhelm Schmidt and Koppers, and after them Oswald Menghin, the Austrian palaeologist, consider it possible that civilization owes the invention of the wheel, and consequently that of the wagon, to the nomad herdsmen of Central Asia.

Unfortunately, these statements do not bring us any nearer to the solution of the problem, and the fact that there were other peoples capable of having invented the wheeled vehicle renders the question only more complicated.

Tell Halaf. There are strong reasons for supposing that Mesopotamia was indeed the original home of the carriage, and that the peoples of Mesopotamia were its inventors. For while the claims of the latter are supported by archaeological finds, not a single linchpin has survived from the supposed carriages of the nomads. The inhabitants of Tell Halaf, for instance, also belong to the possible inventors. Who were these people? The civilization created and disseminated by them from Ras Shamra to Nineveh and Tepe Gawra—put by archaeologists in the Uruk IV period—is named after their ruined urban centre, Tell Halaf. This town was situated in the area now occupied by Syria; here the German archaeologist Max Freiherr von Oppenheim excavated about 1911–13 the cup (Fig. 35), 3½ inches (nine centimetres) high, on which also other archaeologists believe to have discovered the earliest representation of the wheeled vehicle. The cup being broken, its glazing badly damaged and the drawing poorly defined, it is difficult to interpret the enframed scene which once decorated its outer surface. Still, Hubert Schmidt, the German archaeologist, associate of Oppenheim, claims to have solved the problem: having discovered some relations between the tracing near the figure of the man with uplifted arms and the uncertain lines a little further, he believes that the circle represents the wheel of a vehicle, and the lines, the dashboard of the latter. According to him, the picture shows a man standing in front of a two-wheeled cart, and, if we accept this assumption, little imagination is required to regard the detail above the dashboard as the outlines of a horse.

35

35 Design on the Tell Halaf cup

The spoked wheel—did it exist in the fourth millennium B.C. ?
At the same place and from the same layer that yielded the cup, Oppenheim and his associates recovered also the clay model of a two-wheeled vehicle with spokes painted on the wheels. Hubert Schmidt ranged the clay cart with the painted-pottery period of Tell Halaf, dating from the middle of the fourth millennium B.C., and immediately risked the assumption that the Sumerians inherited the carriage from the Tell Halaf people. (The painted-pottery period of Tell Halaf preceded in time the earliest evidence of the Sumerian carriage.)

In a book entitled *Altertumskunde des Zweistromlandes* (The Archaeology of the Land of the Two Rivers) published in 1940, V. Christian—also an excellent archaeologist—rejects Schmidt's early dating and puts the find at five hundred years later. The comments of the British archaeologist Gordon V. Childe include the remark that the find in question cannot be assigned to the Halaf period with absolute certainty; as regards the cross traced in the circle which Schmidt took to be spokes, he advanced the view that they were only decorative elements.

In the circumstances the first carriage and wheel theories should be accepted with reserve. Besides, the scrawl on the cup in question can be considered as a cart only with the aid of a bold imagination; the figure of the man with arms raised may be in worshipping attitude, and if so, why should not the circle next to the figure represent the sun? In this case the picture is but a cult scene. As regards the painted spokes seen on the cup and on the model cart, they hardly fit in with the logical and generally accepted theory of evolution, according to which the primitive solid wheel could have been followed by the spoked wheel only centuries later. For one must bear in mind that—with the single exception of the doubtful Tell Halaf find—on all carriages dating from periods before the third millennium B.C., whether drawings or material remains, only solid wheels can be seen.

If Mesopotamia is regarded as the possible country of origin of the wheeled vehicle, then either Tell Halaf or Sumer may claim credit for having been the first to use this transport device although the rôle of Tell Halaf is, as we have seen, rather doubtful in this connection, and evidence is in favour of Sumer. Sumer was situated on the territory of present-day Iraq, in the valley of the Tigris and the Euphrates, called Mesopotamia. The valley of the Two Rivers has been recognized long since as the land of the earliest civilizations. The fertility of its soil was legendary; if we give credit to the reports of Herodotus and Strabo, we have to believe the unbelievable, as according to them the seeds sown there returned two hundred or three hundred-fold in crop. But even if we reduce these factors to a rational and credible level, they still remain high enough to explain the rela-

28

tively high density of population and the remarkably developed culture of Mesopotamia.

Regarding the existence of Sumer, documentary evidence is available from about as early as 3500 B.C. The excavations of the last sixty years and the recently solved cuneiform writing have cast further light on the cultural achievements of this highly gifted people, so that, instead of Egypt, Sumer is today regarded as the native land of the first civilizations of the world. According to widely accepted scientific opinion, the Sumerians were beyond doubt the first to use the wheeled vehicle. This was the natural outcome of their growing agricultural production which involved an increasing demand for transport facilities; further, the ruling 'royal' families and temple dignitaries required vehicles for ritual purposes, and the ruins of the vast temples indicate that vehicles had played a considerable role also in the religious ceremonies.

The written history of the Sumerians is a mixture of myth and tall-tales, dished up with childish naivety. The King-Lists, for instance, begin with the statement that A-lu-lim reigned for 28,000 years; A-la(l)-gar, for 36,000 years. No wonder that under the circumstances the Sumerologists prefer to rely on tangible remains which are also abundantly present there.

The country of Mesopotamia is an inexhaustible mine of information for the archaeologists excavating, legally or illegally, on her territory. The ruins of ancient towns and vast quantities of monuments documenting the history of long past millennia have been brought to light from its various strata. The archaeological congress held in Baghdad in 1929 resolved to name the different and clearly distinguishable civilizations of Mesopotamia after the places where the most characteristic finds have been excavated first.

Accordingly, the earliest periods are called:
Samarra–Tell Halaf (about 3500–3250 B.C.)
al'Obeid (about 3250–3000 B.C.)
Uruk (about 3000–2800 B.C.)
Jemdet Nasr (about 2800–2700 B.C.)
Further Sumer periods:
The Mesilim period (about 2600 B.C.)
The early dynasties were:
The First Dynasty of Ur–Lagash (about 2500–2350 B.C.)
The Akkad period (about 2350–2150 B.C.)
The new Sumerian period (Third Dynasty of Ur) (about 2150–1920 B.C.)
From the Samarra–Tell Halaf period the only existing relic is the doubtful cup referred to above. There is no find or—to put it more precisely—no reliable find from the al'Obeid or Uruk periods, but scanty finds are available from the period called Jemdet Nasr.

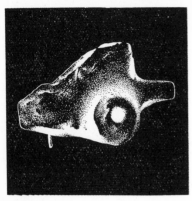

36

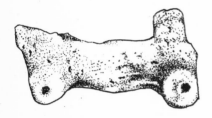

37

The Jemdet Nasr period (about 2800- 2700 B.C.). The clay model of a chariot dating from the same period and found in the oldest layer (VIII) of Tepe Gawra yields some precise information: this chariot is two-wheeled; it is open at the front and closed at the back, with a kind of foot-board at the rear (Fig. 36). The frame and the foot-board bear evidence to a certain technological skill; however, the hole bored for holding the axle points to primitive construction, for if the model is a true replica of the original vehicle, its wheels must have rotated together with the axle-tree.

The Tepe Gawra excavations have brought to light a total of eighteen clay model carts, half of which were, however, in such fragmentary condition that they hardly permitted any conclusion. But the other half guide us through the layers of six settlements (VIII–III) of Tepe Gawra, that is, they represent vehicles used over a period of about thousand years. In addition to the aforementioned clay model excavated from layer VIII, another find recovered from the same layer, that is, from the Jemdet Nasr period, is the model of a four-wheeled terra-cotta wagon probably used for agricultural purposes (Fig. 37). Although only clay models, these relics prove that the two main types of the wheeled vehicle, the cart and the four-wheeled wagon, already existed in this early period.

The idea one may form on the basis of these models is completed by the Sumerian pictograph (Fig. 6) which proves that the wheeled vehicle was a developed and widely used transport device in the Jemdet Nasr period, since otherwise no special pictographic character would have been used to designate it.

The Mesilim period (about 2600 B.C.). The first material remains of a real wheeled vehicle date from this period. These were recovered by L. Ch. Watelin in the course of his excavations at Kish in 1928. Kish was one of the many Sumerian city-states which competed with each other for hegemony. In this competition Kish advanced the 'weighty' argument that the right to rule had been bestowed upon it directly by God himself. It was from the graves of their 'kings of divine origin' that the remains of the first real carriages came to light: the one yielded a four-wheeled vehicle, the other—as far as it can be established from the fragments—three two-wheeled carts. (It is possible, however, that the latter find represents the remains of a two-wheeled and a four-wheeled vehicle, as the only certain thing is that six wheels were present.) Only in grave No. Y 237 did Watelin find a relatively complete specimen of a four-wheeled wagon. It rested on two axles, and a pair of horse-like animals may have been harnessed either side of the 117-inch (three-metre) long pole which protruded well forward. At least five human skeletons lay scattered around the wagon which, according to Watelin, are probably the bones of human sacrifices, men who had accompanied their 'God-sent ruler'—voluntarily or non-voluntarily—on his last journey. The wagon was found almost completely decayed, but the imprints of its wooden parts on the ground supplied precise information as to its size and structure.

What was the earliest wheeled vehicle like? Imagine a hand-cart with a pair of unwieldy, solid wheels—disks measuring $19^1/_2$ inches (50 centimetres) in diameter, roughly fabricated from planks—rotating on each of the two axles of only $35^1/_{10}$ inches (90 centimetres) length, and a chassis $17^3/_5$ inches (45 centimetres) wide resting on the latter. The precise length of the chassis could not be established owing to the decayed condition of the plank forming this part of the vehicle. The chassis was semicircular at the rear bound with copper and having on the sides two carved beams which were formed of bent rods (Fig. 38). Such was the magnificent vehicle which carried the 'divine' ruler of the all-powerful city-state of Kish on his last journey.

But even this primitive vehicle shows the signs of improvements on the drawbacks of former structure, discovered in practice. Thus, for instance, its wheels do not rotate with, but on the axle and are built up from more than one plank; the rim is fitted with a leather tire fixed with copper nails $1^3/_5$ inches (four centimetres) long. However, the vehicle seems to have retained the primitive structural solution peculiar only to our perambu-

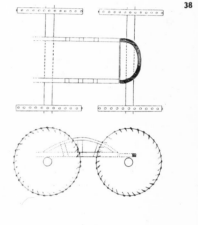

38

39

36 Clay model of a chariot
37 Terra-cotta wagon
38 Diagram of a wagon
39 Imprint of a cylinder seal
40 Clay model of a two-wheeled chariot

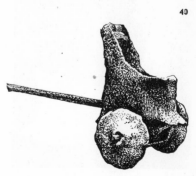

40

lators today; it could change direction only with one pair of the wheels either raised from the ground or made to slide in the desired direction. As the carriage could easily have lost its balance on such occasions, its centre of gravity was placed very low, and the chassis made use of only half the width of the axle to prevent capsizing.

31

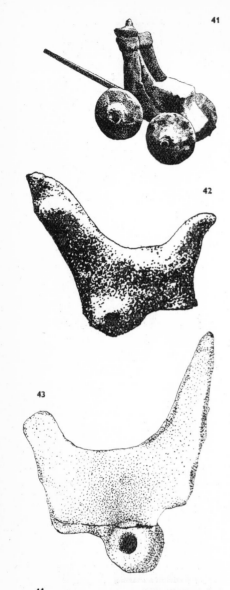

41

42

43

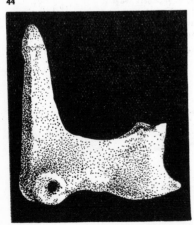

44

We know of another cylinder seal, dating back to the Mesilim period, which represents a war-chariot of a vague type (Fig. 39). Whereas the way of harnessing can be seen clearly enough on it, the components of the carriage and the studs of the wheels pose another riddle.

Fortunately, the clay model vehicles—present in abundance throughout the country—fill in the gaps which written records have left in the history of the carriage during the Mesilim period (Figs. 40–44). The most important information we may gather from the models found in Kish and Tepe Gawra is that of the four-wheeled wagon.

What purpose did the clay models serve? Although the occurrence of clay model vehicles is a regular concomitant of all excavations carried out in Mesopotamia, the rôle of these objects still requires definite elucidation. Some archaeologists hold the view that they were small-scale replicas of 'divine' carriages, that is, of vehicles used for cult purposes; some are of the opinion that they represented votive gifts such as it is customary to offer at places of worship; others again believe that the models were mere toys. From the historical point of view the question is of no consequence, for whichever theory proves correct, the fact remains that the models were meant to imitate the real carriages of the age. Still, considering that technical reasons must have forced the model makers to neglect various details, the clay vehicles cannot be accepted as documentary evidence at their face value. Reduced to such a small size, models of clay cannot possibly be true to scale. The wheels, for instance—if extant at all—appear to be made of a single piece; however, this does not exclude the possibility that the real wheels were built up from three parts or were of the cross-bar type, only these details could not be reproduced in the model.

The chariot scene (Fig. 45) decorates a black and red urn, dating from the Mesilim period, found at Khafaje. Unfortunately, the illustration does not show the number of wheels clearly enough, but the studs on the rim are very likely made of copper and are meant as substitutes for a tire. The assumption that this vehicle was destined for warfare or hunting is justified by various arguments: (a) the warrior or hunter standing on the chariot has a quiver of arrows within easy grasp; (b) the main figure is holding a spear in his right hand; (c) the chariot is drawn by a horse-like animal and not by oxen, zebus or donkeys. The smaller figure behind the first one is presumably the beater; obviously, the artist wished to express the social difference between the two figures by representing the driver as half the size of his 'master'. The reins are passed through the top edge of the dashboard, which is a characteristic feature of the Sumerian wheeled vehicle.

32

I

II

iii

I Detail of the 'standard' of Ur
iI Sumerian king riding a chariot
III Cylinder seal from Babylon

41 Clay model of a wagon
42 Fragment of the clay model of a carriage
43 Clay model of a carriage
44 Clay model of a carriage

IV

IV Carrying of Sharrukin's throne-chariot
V Alabaster relief with warriors on chariots
VI Syrians paying tribute

VII

VIII

IX

X

VII The work of the carriage-builders
VIII Detail of a painted wooden chest
IX Pharaoh Seti I on his war-chariot
X Lion-hunters on chariot

XI

XI Coloured clay model of a quadriga carrying a goddess
XII Indian state-cart
XIII Two-storied temple with the 'wheel of the doctrine'
XIV Prince Vishvantara roaming in the forest

XII

XIII

XIV

XV A wagon-shaped clay vessel
XVI Remains of a four-wheeled Scythian
wagon
45 Chariot scene on a Sumerian urn from
Khafaje

XV

XVI

46 Sacrificial limestone plaque from Ur
47 Cart used in Sardinia in the 19th century
48 Cart used in Formosa in the 19th century

A different type of vehicle may be seen on the sacrificial plaque dating from the Mesilim period (Fig. 46), excavated by Sir Leonard Woolley at Ur. The relief decorating the plaque represents beyond doubt a religious scene. The extant lower part shows servants carrying food and drink—on foot and by a wheeled vehicle—to the holy feast represented in the broken upper part. The vehicle is not a cart properly speaking but rather a kind of saddle on wheels; it is covered with fur and has a curving pole; a bundle of javelins can be seen in the front. The wheels are particularly interesting as the three clamped parts forming each one are represented with perfect precision.

When Woolley published this relief, another excellent British archaeologist, E. Mackay, reproved him in a friendly way, stating that the cart would have deserved greater attention than Woolley had devoted to it. In the same article Mackay compared the 'saddled' cart with the type still used in Sindh (Pakistan). The wheels of the latter are also built up from three parts, and the saddle-like upper structure of the vehicle is fixed to the axle by pins in the same way as seen on the relief found at Ur. It may be inferred from these details that the axle of the Ur cart also rotated with the wheels; the wheels of the Sindh cart rotate between wooden pegs extending from the bottom of the body downwards, and Mackay believes that the axle of the Ur 'saddled cart' was of a similar construction. This type of vehicle is called the 'creaking cart'. It is certain—says Mackay—that the Sumerian cart must have made a terrific noise, just as the Sindh carts do even today. But the early Chinese carts were also favoured for their clatter because it scared the enemy.

The persistence of old forms. The parallel drawn by Mackay also proves how persistently the old forms withstood every change. The 'creaking cart', whose main characteristic was that its axle rotated between wooden pegs, has been current in comparatively modern times, not only in Sindh but in some parts of Europe. The Italian scholar La Marmora saw a cart of similar structure in the eighteen-twenties in Sardinia; its picture (Fig. 47)

47

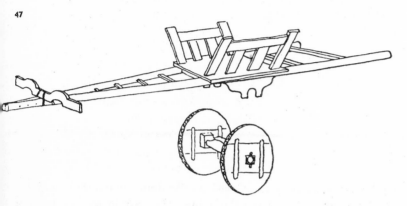

clearly shows the position of the axle between the pegs extending from the bottom of the body. Similar carts were in use in Taiwan (Formosa) (Fig. 48). The Portuguese cart depicted in Ginzrot's work (Fig. 49) made a noise which—the author says—

48

could be heard from half an hour's walking-distance. In the drawing it only appears from the rectangular, that is, not cylindrical axle-tree that the wheel and the axle must have rotated together. The cart was anyhow a poor piece of structure; for travelling over muddy ground it had to be pulled by six oxen.

35

49

In a style typical of the German schoolmaster, Ginzrot adds to
his description that if the Portuguese did not insist on the old-
fashioned structure, two oxen were enough to draw the cart, but
—he says (and one can imagine him waving his hand in resigna-
tion)—in such countries prejudice triumphs over common sense.

And indeed, the creaking of the cart resounded not only in the
Portuguese but also in the picturesque Spanish Cantabrian hills
and in the mountain paths along the shores of the Atlantic
Ocean even a century later. Professor Telesfero de Aranzadi says
that the creaking noise produced by the friction of the axle-tree
and the linchpins has a definite and unmistakable pitch, and that
in the narrow mountain paths, with room for only one track, its
far-sounding tone has the practical advantage that it warns the
carts wishing to pass in the opposite direction to step aside in
good time. The Spanish carter does not regard the creaking of
his cart as unpleasant in the least; on the contrary, he even
waters the axle-tree "that it should sing nicely".

> *Si queres qu'o carro canta*
> *Mollal'o cixo n'o rio*
> *Que dempois de ben mollado*
> *Canta com'un asubio,*
>
> (If you want your cart to sing,
> Wet the axle in the river,
> When it is sodden,
> It will sound like a pipe,)

says the Galician folk-song.

There were some Spanish towns in which it was forbidden to drive a creaking cart through the streets. The owners of such vehicles used cart-grease to damp the noise while passing through the town, but as soon as they left the last house behind, they got off the cart, scraped off the grease and poured water over the axle or smeared it with resin to make it sound again.

The First Ur period. One of the main centres of Sumerian civilization between 2500 and 2350 B.C. was the town of Ur. It was situated on the banks of the Euphrates, near the sea at that time. (Today, owing to alluvial deposits in the bay, the ruins of Ur lie deep in the continent.) The excavations conducted by Sir Leonard Woolley in 1927–28 have thrown light on the dramatic rites performed at royal funerals several millennia ago; the precision of detail and the authenticity of his report on the subject is regarded as unparalleled in archaeology.

The funeral of King Abargi. Passing over the archaeological description of the excavation, which the reader may peruse in detail in Woolley's books, the story of the funeral of Abargi, king of Ur, may be summarized in the form of an 'on-the-spot account' as follows: —

The dowager-queen and the court paid their last tribute to the deceased ruler with great funeral pomp. Hosts of court dignitaries, ladies-in-waiting, royal concubines, body-guards, drivers and grooms followed the King into death 'to continue serving him in after-life'. The four-wheeled hearses were buried with the King. The reins, encrusted with lapis lazuli and silver beads, were held by the drivers, and the two keepers of the oxen joined the latter in their journey to the next world (Fig. 50). Shub-ad, the

49 Portuguese 'creaking cart'
50 Reconstruction of King Abargi's funeral at Ur
51 Ground-plan of the grave of King Abargi

51

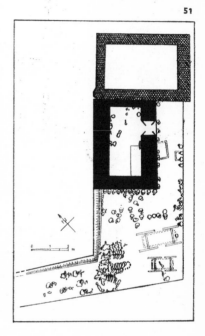

50

37

dowager-queen who—heaven knows why—did not choose to die a voluntary death, gave orders that when her hour would come—at some indefinite time later—she was to be buried in a vault to be built next to her husband's (Fig. 51). When the Queen died a natural death, the masons began building her vault and soon reached the brick roofing of King Abargi's grave. As they well knew what treasures lay buried under it, they cut a hole in the vaulting, stole a good part of the treasures and, very pleased with themselves, covered up the opening with a chest Shub-ad wished to take with her to the next world. (Woolley discovered this about 4,500 years later!)

52

The funeral of Shub-ad took place as follows. The body of the Queen, dressed in state, was put on a sledge-chariot (Fig. 52) in sitting position; the vehicle was drawn by onagers. The corpse was then placed in the inner crypt of the vault, with one of the Queen's waiting-maids crouching at her foot, another at her head, while a third lay down a little further. The door to the crypt was then walled in. Meanwhile the members of Queen Shub-ad's court and girls playing the harp and the lute settled down in the passage of the shaft leading to the vault; the sledge-chariot was also placed there with the driver in place and the groom standing at the head of the onager. Everyone held a cup, from which they drank a deadly potion.

The measurements of Abargi's hearse were established by Woolley on the basis of the imprints the decayed wooden components had left in the ground. According to these, the diameter of the front wheels of one of the vehicles was 24 inches (60 centimetres); that of the rear wheels, $31^1/_5$ inches (80 centimetres); the length of the axle was $27^1/_3$ inches (70 centimetres); the width of the carriage-body, $22^2/_5$ inches (56 centimetres). The other vehicle was larger: the diameter of both its front and rear wheels was $39^2/_5$ inches (one metre); the length of the axle, similarly $39^2/_5$ inches (one metre); and the width of the carriage-body, the half of this measurement, the same as with the smaller vehicle. The poles measured 117 inches (three metres) and $105^1/_3$ inches (two metres seventy centimetres), respectively. The long poles were obviously required on account of the low-hung body of the car, as one end of the pole was fixed to its bottom at half a metre height from the ground, the other end was attached to the neck of the draught-animal, at about $58^1/_2$ inches (one metre fifty centimetres) height. The makers of the vehicle probably preferred a longer pole to a steeply rising one; this naturally made the manoeuvering of the vehicle only more difficult, though it could not have been an easy job with the rigid pole, anyhow.

The 'standard' of Ur. Another famous find of Woolley's at Ur was the 'standard' which is one of the most valuable documents of the history of the carriage. The mysterious object in question was given the name 'standard' because Woolley found it next to the skeleton of a man whom he believes to have been the king's standard-bearer. The excavated 'standard' does not look like a real standard at all, but rather like a panel, with two sides decorated with coloured mosaic in about 19¹/₂ inches (50 centimetres) length and 8³/₅ inches (22 centimetres) height. According to Woolley this ensign was carried fixed to a pole in the same way as standards are carried in processions nowadays. One side of the Ur 'standard' represents a peaceful scene, the other, a scene of war. We are concerned with the war scene only, as it includes wagons, and five of them at that! The representation is arranged in three rows. In the uppermost row the empty chariot of the king is seen; it is drawn by four animals, harnessed abreast; the reins are held by a driver walking behind the chariot (Fig. 53). The lowest row shows the chariot 'in action' (Pl. I). While the driver is handling the reins, the warrior stands ready to throw his spear. The vanquished enemy soldiers are lying under the feet of the animals.

Some riddles of the 'standard'. Ignorant of the rules of perspective, the artist of the 'standard' had left posterity a puzzling picture of the vehicle of Ur. On closer examination it immediately strikes the eye that—according to the modern notion of perspective—some of the details are represented as if twisted at ninety degrees. The dashboard with the rein-rings, for instance, should be perpendicular to the length of the pole, but rendering a side-view in perspective was a technique still unknown at that time, so the artist simply reduced these 'spatial' elements to a (two-dimensional) plane and represented the dashboard as the fore-part of the side-panel. This assumption may be easily verified by comparing the picture with the 'shields' of the clay models. But

53

39

the riddle of the wheels is less simple to solve. There can be no doubt about their structure: they are tripartite disks beyond dispute, similar to those seen on the relief of the sacrificial plaque of Ur; but their number is intriguing, and the question arises: how many wheels are there to the chariot? At first sight perhaps only one out of a hundred thousand would doubt that the vehicle in question ran on four wheels; however, the few who say it had but two include such recognized experts as Lefebvre des Noëttes and Freiherr von Oppenheim; they insist that the chariot was a two-wheeled vehicle; only the artist, unable to draw in perspective, but desirous to represent both wheels (the nearer and the farther one), found no other solution than the one seen on the standard. They are of the opinion that only people unable to escape from the conventional notion of perspective regard the chariot in question as a four-wheeled vehicle. Lefebvre des Noëttes supports his views by a further argument which should not be lightly dismissed: he says that the prehistoric war-chariot was bound to be a two-wheeled vehicle because, with the rigidly fixed axle then in use, a four-wheeled chariot would have been most cumbersome to manoeuvre. Indeed, from the tactical point of view, a drawback of this nature must have been of decisive importance in warfare, especially if the army had to retreat before the enemy.

It is interesting to compare the type of chariot represented on the 'standard' of Ur with that on the cylinder seal shown in Fig. 54. There is a striking similarity between the two: both have

54

the same type of dashboard with cross-ties in the top edge; the number and position of the wheels are also identical, only the poles show some difference, and while the chariot on the 'standard' carries a driver and a warrior, that on the seal is mounted by a driver alone. This, however, does not represent a structural difference.

40

The vehicle that vanished . . . Woolley also discovered the remains of still another real vehicle: the hearse in the necropolis of Ur, or rather its imprints, for the wooden parts have mouldered beyond recovery. Only the wheels of one side of the carriage have left clearly visible marks in the ground. The diameter of these was $85^4/_5$ inches (two metres 20 centimetres); they were similar to the wheels seen on the relief of Ur. Their rims were probably studded with nails. According to the imprints all the four wheels in question were tripartite in structure, and it is presumed that they rotated freely round the axle. The remains of a chariot brought to light at Kish are similar (Fig. 55).

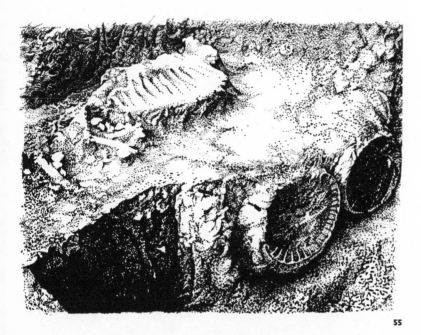

55

Some representations dating from the same period also survive, but, unfortunately, offer little or no basis for extending our knowledge on vehicles.

The Stela of the Vultures. One fragment of this famous monument represents the standing figure of a king riding a chariot (Pl. II). Another part of the same stela, showing vultures feasting on the corpses of fallen warriors (hence the name of the stela), was found by the French archaeologist de Sarzec in 1876 in the ruins of Tello (the modern name of the ancient town of Lagash). De Sarzec did not then know, but it has been clarified since, that the stela had been erected by Eannatum, king of Lagash, to record his victory over the neighbouring town of Umma (2500 B.C.). The figure in the chariot is the conqueror king himself, advancing at the head of his army. The fragment betrays little about the structure of the vehicle, as only the top part of its

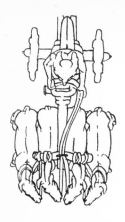

representation survives; from the extant small pieces it may be inferred, however, that the vehicle of Eannatum was similar to those represented on the 'standard' of Ur.

The Tell Agrab chariot. This model chariot from about 2500 B.C. (Fig. 56), brought to light at Tell Agrab, north-east of Baghdad, is again similar to the saddled wheels seen on the sacrificial plaque of Ur (Fig. 46, Page 34) dating from the Mesilim period. The copper model gives an extremely realistic idea of the vehicle, the driver and the harnessed animals. The bearded figure is represented driving the four animals in what seems to be a standing, rather than a sitting position.

56

The Akkad period. In the middle of the twenty-fourth century B.C., Sharrukin (Sargon), king of the city-state of Akkad, situated north of Sumer, conquered and ravaged Sumer, and united under his suzerainty the territories of Mesopotamia and Elam, and part of Syria and Asia Minor advancing as far as the Persian Gulf, 'to wash his weapons in the sea.' The era beginning with this conquest—subjugating the Sumerians to Akkad rule for two hundred years—is called the Akkad period (2350–2150 B.C.). The monuments of the Akkad period do not show any progress in the field of transport; in fact, the period is generally characterized as one of stagnation.

The Gudea period. Gudea, the *patesi* (priest-ruler) of Lagash at the turn of the third and second millennia, reigned in Sumer at the time of the Guti conquest and probably collaborated with the conquerors. In a clay cylinder document he reports on the chariot of Ninigirsu, the patron god of Lagash, which—he states —was drawn by "four strong-voiced asses coming from a well-known stock". Documentary evidence dating from Gudea's time proves that vehicles were used also for the transport of burdens: the extant fragments of two stelae show the conveying of loads on a four-wheeled w.. on and a two-wheeled cart, respectively.

The diffusion of the Sumerian civilization. Obviously, a civilization of such vitality and high standard as that of Sumer could not but exercise a powerful influence on the evolution of the neighbouring peoples. According to archaeologic evidence, close trade relations had existed between Sumer and the countries of Hither Asia as early as in the third millennium B.C. It may be assumed that in the commercial deals—documented amongst others by the cylinder seals of Cappadocia (eastern part of Asia Minor)—the Sumerian party included the wheeled vehicle, a rare and therefore valuable article, among the items exchanged.

56 Copper model of the chariot from Tel Agrab and its drawing from aerial view
57 Cylinder seal from Cappadocia

57

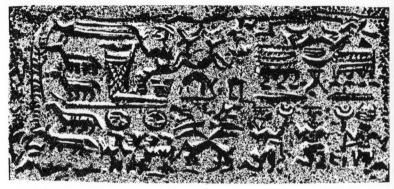

58

59

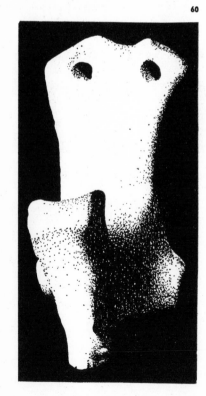

60

The cylinder seals of Cappadocia. The so-called Cappadocian cylinder seals (Figs. 57–58), excavated from among the ruins of Kaneshatti, at about thirteen miles (twenty-one kilometres) distance from present-day Kayseri, exhibit chariots very similar in appearance to those seen on the 'standard' of Ur and the cylinder seal of Kish (Pl. I and Figs. 53–54). Although their style and structure are of local character, they are provided with the same type of dashboard with cross-ties (also represented twisted at ninety degrees), and even if the impression on the top of the dashboard is not round or curved but angular, this difference is probably due only to the artist's style of representation. The clay model chariot dating from about 2000 B.C. (Fig. 59), found at Assur, represents a further analogy; it is, in fact, an especially good example, as it shows the same type of stool as that figuring on the cylinder seal. The two holes seen on the dashboard may be regarded as a mere variation of the cut for the reins.

The texts of the so-called Cappadocian clay tablets make frequent mention of the four-wheeled wagon—the *erreqqu*—whose deep tracks are still visible in the pavement of the streets of Karum, in Kanesh, today; they also make reference—though only in one instance—to the horse-drawn fast-moving war-chariot, the *narkabtu*.

Elam. The civilization of Elam, the country situated between the mountains of Zagros and the Persian Gulf, also developed under Sumerian influence; as a result of this, the Sumerian and Elamite vehicle relics show a close relationship, and archaeology assigns both to the same period. The earliest Elamite relics (clay model chariots, Figs. 60–63) were unearthed at Susa, once the capital of Elam, by Jacques de Morgan, during the excavations he started there in 1897. The finds included the two main types of Sumer vehicles: the war-chariot with dashboard, driven in standing position, and the saddled wheels with the driver sitting. Another extremely interesting relic—the fragment of a piece of

44

painted pottery, representing a cart from the Mesilim period (Fig. 64)—was also brought to light in Susa. It shows a throne-like structure, different in shape to all other known vehicles of the period. The curve of its pole is baffling at first sight, but there is an explanation for its use: it did not hinder the movement of the draught-animals when the vehicle was manoeuvered—a task performed anyhow with great difficulties, owing to the rigidly fixed axles in use at that time. On the left side of the picture a structure similar to a *ziggurat* (a stepped temple-tower) is seen, on top of which a deity stretches his hands in blessing towards the figure seated in the carriage. It appears logical to conclude from this representation that the vehicle was used for cult purposes.

A real wheel was excavated at Apadana, in Susa (Fig. 65). As it appears from our illustration, it was fabricated from three parts and bound by a rim of $1^4/_5$ inches (four and a half centimetres) thickness.

Types of carriages. A large number and a great variety of carriages have come down to us both in original and in authentic representations, all of which bear witness to the fact that the new invention had been continuously improved upon; by incessant experimenting and repeated innovation, man strove to render this transport device more and more serviceable as time went on. The carriages occurring most frequently among the finds may be divided into the following types: —

(a) The most common kind was the 'plank on wheels', like the vehicle shown in Fig. 38. This type was used also for the transport of burdens—an assumption borne out by the presence of supporting bars on the two sides of the vehicles of Kish.

(b) The wagons seen on the 'standard' of Ur and other vehicles of a kindred type represent an important category, for they served also as war-chariots (Pl. I and Fig. 53); there is at least no doubt about this in the case of the vehicles depicted on the 'standard' of Ur.

61

62

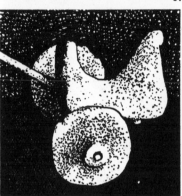

63

64

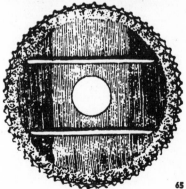

65

45

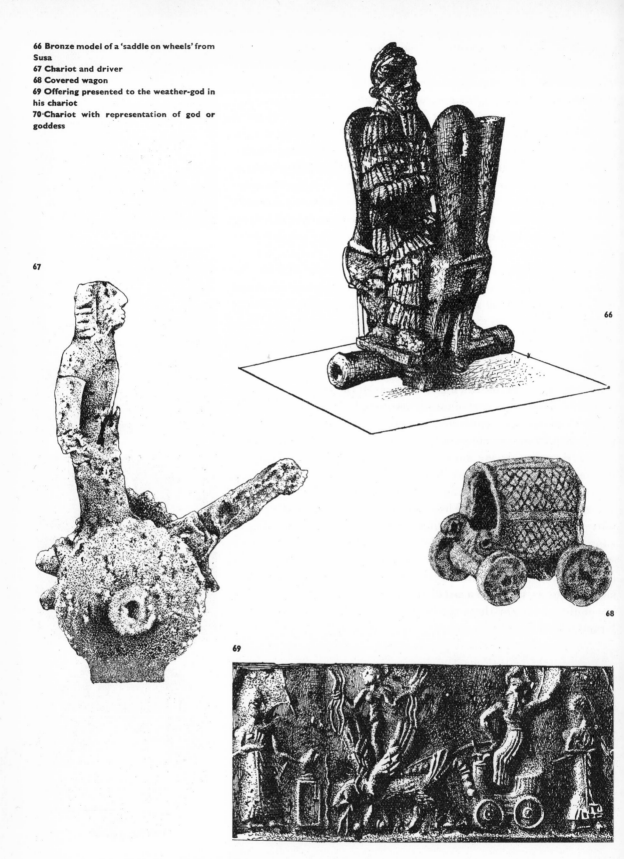

66 Bronze model of a 'saddle on wheels' from Susa
67 Chariot and driver
68 Covered wagon
69 Offering presented to the weather-god in his chariot
70 Chariot with representation of god or goddess

67

66

68

69

46

(c) The 'saddle on wheels' may be studied best on the sacrificial plaque of Ur (Fig. 46) and on the copper model chariot of Tell Agrab (Fig. 56). Another interesting specimen is the bronze model found at Susa (Fig. 66). This type of vehicle could not have been of much practical use; they probably owed their existence to the then prevailing love of splendour. Maybe it was also meant to imitate horse-riding in a comfortable and safe way. Just as the first railway carriage was actually a mail-coach on rails, and the first motor-car—bashfully hiding its motor under the seat—was in form the slavish imitation of the horse-drawn carriage, the Sumerians may have preserved the saddle for use on wheeled vehicles: by putting the saddle on wheels, they could ride the 'carriage' as if it were a horse. True, that the earliest evidence that horse-riding had been known in Sumer dates from only about 1900 B.C., and the 'saddled wheels' go back to the middle of the third millennium, that is to more than half a millennium earlier, yet it is felt that the above assumption cannot be ruled out from among the possible explanations of the development of this type of vehicle.

(d) The clay model excavated at Kish, whose dashboard approaches the horizontal (Fig. 67), may be regarded as a further variant of the above type of vehicle.

(e) Perhaps the most interesting relic of this sort found in Mesopotamia is the covered wagon (Fig. 68)—a vehicle prophetic of the American West pioneer wagons. The model had been unearthed at Tepe Gawra from layer VI. (Its excavator, E. A. Speiser, assigns the find to the middle of the third millennium.) Speiser pointed out that the excavated covered wagon was a stranger among the real vehicles, model carriages and carriage pictures deriving from Mesopotamia. It represents a foreign type which—in his opinion—must have been imported from some place either beyond the Caucasus or beyond the Caspian Sea. Thus the find may be a proof that relations were maintained at that time between these territories.

In addition to these general types, several vehicles of special forms have also been brought to light. While on some of the recovered representations the deities are riding in four-wheeled wagons (Fig. 69), on others they are seen on two-wheeled carts. In most cases they are crouching on a kind of stool, but some finds represent standing gods, and there is one type of chariot in which the god or goddess is represented in relief on the high back-wall of the carriage-body (Fig. 70). The clay model of a wagon excavated from the temple of Sin at Khafaje (Fig. 71), resembling a tower rather than a carriage, represents another interesting specimen of the four-wheeled vehicle used in cult ceremonies.

70

47

Herewith closes the second important chapter of the story of the carriage, with the Sumerians in the principal rôle.

After the fall of the Third Dynasty of Ur, around 2000 B.C., the Sumerians disappeared from the theatre of history. The peoples succeeding them in their geographic place inherited the Sumerian traditions of vehicle-building and developed them further, as described in the following chapter.

71

Chapter III

Ethnic groups of the Middle East — The spoked wheel — Babylon — The Kassites — The Hurrians — Mitanni — Assur, the Assyrians — Urartu — New Babylonia — The Persians — Egypt — The war-chariot in the Sahara — The Hittites — The post-Hittite city-states — Phoenicia — Cyprus — Syria — Palestine — The Bible and the carriage

After the fall of the Third Dynasty of Ur, the Middle East disintegrated into small parts. Owing to the continuous migration of the peoples taking the place of the Sumerian–Akkad state, its political map underwent frequent changes, reacting to each move like the pattern of a kaleidoscope. Since the migrants wandered through the vast territories of the Middle East in organized tribes, with families and chattels, the cart or the wagon probably played some rôle in their nomadic life. (This is naturally a supposition only, as they might have transported their baggage with the aid of pack-animals, on the backs of asses, oxen or zebus.) The use of metals began to spread around the same time. The technological revolution which followed resulted in the modernization of the instruments of production, among them in that of the cart and the wagon. A major improvement on these vehicles was brought about by the advent of the spoked wheel.

The spoked wheel. The first traces of the application of spokes date from the eighth century B.C.; they were found—first on terra-cotta wheels—in Babylonia. (This is without taking into consideration the dubious Tell Halaf find, allegedly representing spoked wheels.) Babylonia had territorial ambitions, the realization of which demanded the replacement of the clumsy, old-fashioned solid-wheeled chariots by more up-to-date war-vehicles. The tactics of warfare called for increased speed, which the Babylonians first tried to reach by reducing the weight of the wheels; the application of spokes appeared to be an extremely suitable means to this end. Secondly, they replaced the slow oxen and the still not agile enough mule by the more nimble horse which was also easier to steer. According to almost unanimous scientific opinion, the spoked wheel and the harnessing of the horse date from the same time and place.

However, the spoked wheel proved more costly than the solid wheel, as its production was more complicated and demanded the competence of a skilled wheelwright. The spoked wheel consists of the following parts, each of which must be fashioned with

49

meticulous care and great precision: the hub with the axle-hole, the felloes with dowel holes for the spokes and finally the spokes themselves (Fig. 72).

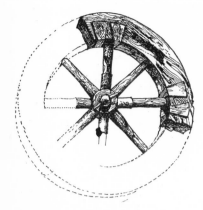

The development of the spoked wheel. Some people believe that the spoked wheel was an independent invention, with no antecedents; others hold that it was developed gradually. According to the latter opinion, the initial step towards the spoked wheel was prompted by the necessity to reduce the weight of the disk-wheel; to this effect the three-part wheel was first assembled with gaps between the planks. The next innovation was to leave only a rim round the edge and to tie it with cross-bars; these bars are said to have given rise to the spokes later. But these are only assumptions. There is no documentary evidence that would throw light on the early development of the spoked wheel; the archaeologic finds representing transitional forms date from a millennium later, from about 1000 B.C. However, more recent specimens demonstrating analogies between the disk-wheel and the spoked wheel are available in abundance. The cart in Fig. 73 comes from

73

Branosera (Palencia, Spain). The explanation of the archaic form is that Branosera is a secluded farm situated in a valley cut off from the outer world by huge mountains. A similar cart—coming from Mexico—(Fig. 74) is preserved at the Smithsonian Institute in Washington D.C. It dates from 1865 and was drawn by two oxen. The structure is obviously of Spanish origin; it must have been introduced into Mexico by the colonizers, and the primitive economic and social conditions of the country permitted it to persist there for centuries.

72 Construction of the Assyrian spoked wheel
73 Cart from Branosera
74 Mexican ox cart

50

The modernization of harnessing. It was only through the harnessing of the horse that the light chariot could develop into a formidable war-engine. However, this was no simple matter. At the beginning, the horse was also yoked, but the shoulder-blades of this animal being less broad than those of the ox, the yoke did not rest on them firmly enough. The yoke put on the withers of the horse was therefore held in place by a 'breast-band' passing in front of the throat (and not the breast) of the animal. Thus the horse was forced to draw the carriage with its neck. This ancient way of harnessing—the only one employed for centuries—is called ancient harnessing. More modern methods of harnessing appeared only at the beginning of the Middle Ages. According to Lefebvre the ancient harnessing was but an infantile experiment, a temporary solution of the problem. Harnessing is the more effective, the more it helps to exploit the traction-power of the animal. With ancient harnessing the horse had to pull with its neck and could hardly have drawn anything heavier than a light war-chariot.

Hammurabi. In the eighteenth century B.C., Hammurabi succeeded in uniting almost all of Mesopotamia around Babylon as a centre. However, his famous Code, inscribed on a stela, now preserved in the Louvre, makes no mention of the carriage. The most obvious explanation of his silence on the subject is that, although carriages existed at that time, they were still very scarce and therefore of minor economic importance, not liable to involve any legal problem.

Under the soft-handed successors of Hammurabi, from about the seventeenth century B.C., new peoples streamed into Mesopotamia and crushed the Babylonian empire. The invading highlanders brought not only ruin but innovations as well: they reorganized the military forces or, to be more exact, developed the chariot into a new arm.

The Kassites (Kasshu) infiltrated into Babylonian territory from the mountains of Iran; part of them entered into military

51

service and became the lords of the country in the sixteenth century B.C. It is said that horse-breeding—a prerequisite of the chariot—was introduced into Babylonia by the Kassites. This assumption is supported only by indirect philological and logical arguments.

The philological reasoning is based on the fact that in the Sumerian language, used also in Babylonia, the horse was named 'mountain ass' *(anshu kura)*, that is, they distinguished the newly domesticated animal—the horse—from the ass by adding an adjective to the name of the latter, indicative of the horse's origin, in the same way as certain negro tribes had named the horse 'the white man's cow'. The other argument is that the horse was first mentioned in Babylonian records under the rule of the Kassites only, consequently the Babylonians had not known the horse until then. This argument is supported by a letter of the Hittite king Hattushili III (1282–1250 B.C.), asking Kadash-man-Enlil II, king of Babylonia (1277–1271 B.C.), for horses. "In my brother's country [meaning Babylonia] there are more horses than stalks of straw," wrote Hattushili, and this florid style was meant to express in a veiled form his innocent desire to acquire some horses by free gift on the grounds that where horses ran about in such large numbers, a few could make no difference. It may be concluded from the above that Babylonia was by then known as a country rich in horses (Pl. III).

The war-chariot as a weapon and a symbol of power. With the aid of the horse the war-chariot became a really important arm and, at the same time, an attribute of power and dignity. That this rôle of the war-chariot originates from Babylonia is proved by the fact that Amenhotep IV, Pharaoh of Egypt, requested and received horses for his grand war-chariot from the Babylonian king Burnaburias II. The concluding words of courtesy used in the correspondence of dignitaries, kings and overlords of the Middle East, are extremely characteristic of the great esteem entertained for the war-chariot and the horse at that time: "Best wishes to thee, to thy country, thy household, thy wives, children, horses and chariots..."

The war-chariot—what it looked like. The axle of the war-chariot was fixed usually right at the back, at the rear part of the carriage-body; in some cases, however, it was nearer the front, somewhere about the middle of the carriage. There are some interesting data available regarding the weight of the war-chariot; according to these about 18 pounds (8 kilograms) of bronze was used for eight spokes. (This applies no doubt to a royal state-chariot.) Two other written Kassite records indicate the weight of the bronze spokes as 62 and 68 pounds (28 and 31 kilos), respectively. The apparent contradiction between the different data is probably due to the fact that war-chariots of various weight were in use.

Northern Mesopotamia. Although the development of northern Mesopotamia was not furthered by the same favourable geographic and climatic conditions as those ruling in southern Mesopotamia, in the Bronze Age the north succeeded in catching up with the more fortunate south. One of the northern states was formed by the Hurrians, whose role in the dissemination of the war-chariot was most significant, in fact, they may have been the very inventors of the new arm. It is presumed that they spread from the territory of the present-day Armenian Soviet Socialist Republic in a southerly direction. Their state, Mitanni, developed after the nineteenth or eighteenth centuries B.C. Beside the Hurrians—or rather above them—another ethnic group of Indo-European tongue inhabited the country. In the language of the Hurrians they were called *Marianis*. The *Marianis* were great masters of the war-chariot and bred horses, and revolutionized military technics throughout the Middle East.

The Hurrians. In archaeology the Hurrians were formerly bracketed with the Hittites; their archaeological monuments were 'pooled' under the comment that, in addition to the Hittites, a number of other ethnic groups, difficult to define—but including the Hurrians—also contributed to what at present is understood by Hittite art and civilization. However, on the evidence of more recent excavations, the Hittite and Hurrian

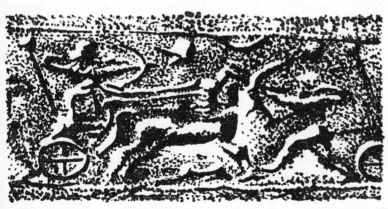

75

peoples, and their respective civilizations, can be clearly distinguished. The carriage, and in particular the war-chariot, appear already on the early seals recovered from Hurrian settlements. Figure 75 shows one noteworthy cylinder seal from Mitanni, dating from 1750–1500 B.C.

53

Mitanni had reached the peak of her power around 1400 B.C. under the rule of King Tushratta (1420–1380 B.C.) who was related to the then reigning Pharaoh dynasty of Egypt by numerous family ties. It appears that Tushratta appreciated the truth of the saying that "Small gifts deepen friendship", for he was liberal in sending rich fraternal presents—including carriages—to his Egyptian kin. Thus in one of his letters to Amenhotep III, after expressing his best wishes to the Pharaoh's horses and chariots, he continues saying: "Hear, my brother, that from the booty I took at Hatti I have sent thee a chariot, two horses, a youth and a maiden. My fraternal gift to thee includes also horses for five carriages . . ." In another letter he mentions the gilding of the chariots. They were not thrifty with the use of gold, for—as we know from other sources—320 *shekels*, over five pounds in weight, were used for the gilding of a single carriage.

Assur. The state known in history by the name of Assyria developed in northern Mesopotamia along the main trade routes, around Assur. After the fall of the Third Dynasty of Ur, Assyria set up a well-developed army to ensure her control over the caravan routes. The organization of the troops was no difficult task as the Assyrians were a people of strict military discipline who regarded war almost as their national calling. Be it said in their excuse that the geographic situation of the country attracted and even forced them to follow this course. The army was based on two services: the chariotry and the infantry. The important military duties of the charioteers could not be performed without liberal material support from the king, for the keeping of horses and the purchase of chariots cost a small fortune, and the training of the animals, drivers and warriors also consumed piles of money besides requiring immense trouble. All these factors set limits to the number of the war-chariots. Initially, they were used chiefly for pursuing the enemy, but their significance increased gradually not only in war but also as a symbol of power: hardly any of the Assyrian reliefs show the king or higher officers otherwise than standing in their chariots.

The chariots of Assur and Assyria. The quantity of written records and artistic monuments Assyria had left us is enough to fill an encyclopaedia on the ancient history of the carriage. Even a quick survey is sufficient to increase our knowledge with many valuable data. To mention but a few: Shamshi-Adad (1749–1717 B.C.), the ambitious king of Assur, asked his son, the Prince Jasmach-Adad, who was engaged in the breeding and breaking-in of horses for chariots, to send him most urgently some stately chariots with horses to match that they might increase the splendour of the New Year procession in Assur. This information points to the important role the chariot played on ceremonial occasions as a symbol of power. The same is evident from the gifts exchanged between ancient eastern rulers: we know of a letter Ashur-Yuballidh, King of Assur (1480–1341? B.C.), addressed to Amenhotep IV, advising the Pharaoh of the despatch of a fine royal war-chariot and two white horses.

Tukulit-pal-E-saria (Tiglath-Pileser) I (1116–1090 B.C.) multiplied the number of the Assyrian war-chariots. But, light and elegant as these vehicles were, without suitable roads, it was difficult to proceed with them in warfare. Consequently, in his campaign against Elam, Tukulit-pal-E-saria was obliged to provide also for road-builders to cut paths for his vehicles and advancing troops. "I got into my war-chariot, and, with my warriors rallied around me, I had paths cut with bronze pickaxes through the high mountains and steep slopes to make them passable for my war-vehicles and troops..." says the King's report on the campaign. However, he appears to have made use of his chariots not only in war but in hunting, too: "Commanded by my patron Ninurta I killed with courageous heart 120 lions afoot and 800 from my chariot in heroic fights..."

The chariot of Ashur-nasir-pal II (883–859 B.C.) shows some difference in structure, compared to other chariots of the period. There is a quiver-like case for arrows and spears on the outside of the carriage-body, and a shield decorated with a lion's head appears in the middle of the rear part of the vehicle. This chariot may be studied best on the reliefs from his palace at Nimrud, excavated by Austen Henry Layard, the famous British archaeologist and diplomat, in 1848. A double row of reliefs running frieze-like at eye-level in the main room (B) of the palace shows the King in battle and in hunting scenes (Fig. 76). From the many vehicles represented in the relief we learn details about the war-chariots of Ashur-nasir-pal II. Some of them were drawn by three stallions, two of which were yoked, the third ran along as a trace-horse. The animals were decorated with rich feather head-dress and tassels. Between the carriage and the horses a second pole can be seen above the normal one; it was probably destined to fix the lower pole. (According to certain opinions it is not a second pole at all but a sort of fender meant to ward off the rising dust.)

Shalmaneser III and the gates of Balawat. Shalmaneser III (859–824 B.C.) gives a terse summary of the annual events of his thirty-five years' reign, inscribed on an obelisk. The chronicle for the eighteenth year includes the following passage: "In the

55

76

eighteenth year of my reign, I crossed the Euphrates sixteen times. Xaza'el of Damascus dared enter into war with me. I took 1,121 of his chariots and 470 of his horses, with his complete camp..." It may be inferred from these dates that the number of chariots thrown in at battles had increased considerably.

Shalmaneser III recorded the outstanding events of his wars in the relief decorating the bronze gates of Balawat (Fig. 77). These give a clear picture of the war-chariots and of the weapons used for the storming of fortresses.

76 Lion-hunt of King Ashur-nasir-pal
77 War-chariot
78 Captured women and children carried away in carts

77

The reforms of Tukulit-pal-E-saria III. Tukulit-pal-E-saria III (745–727 B.C.) introduced important military reforms in the Assyrian army. Amongst other innovations, he was the first to employ cavalry, in addition to chariots, in warfare. This reform was carried out because the chariot was growing obsolete and began to lose its importance as a weapon.

The representations available for the carrier carts of the age are perfectly clear and precise; in fact, one could not wish for any better. The loads they transport in Fig. 78 is human merchandise: the women and children, carried off from a captured city, are being taken to the slave market.

78

In the palace of Sharrukin (Sargon) II (722–705 B.C.) (Dur Sharrukin), a series of reliefs illustrated the events of the King's campaigns against Musasir. Of his seventh campaign Sharrukin left an account told in the first person singular; it is a precise report on the events of his expedition addressed to the god Ashur. According to this, the King proceeded to the battle by war-chariot; where the lack of roads prevented his progress, he had paths cut in the rocks with bronze pickaxes. Later he learned through his spies that Ursa—known also as Rusa—king of Urartu, wanted to attack him from an ambush. "Taking only my own chariot and my mounted body-guards, who in foreign and hostile lands never leave my side, I broke in upon the enemy with Sinamusur's company, like an invincible spear, and put them to flight." And Ursa? "To save his life, he got on his chariot and escaped with his troops." Sharrukin pursued him, but the path was so narrow that the men had to carry his chariot on their backs; he himself was finally obliged to proceed on horseback. He then looted Musasir. From the temple of the supreme deity he took, amongst other booty, 33 silver-mounted war-chariots.

Sharrukin had still another special chariot: it was a kind of throne whose picture has come down to us in the relief of the Khorsabad palace. Its wheels were small, and consequently the carriage-body was low. There is no doubt that it was drawn by man, with the aid of the handle seen on the pole (Pl. IV).

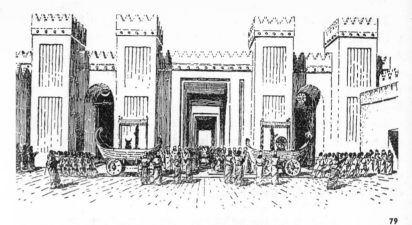

79

The conquest of Sennacherib (Sinaheeriba) I. During his first campaign against Babylonia, Sennacherib I (705–680 B.C.) took 7,200 horses and mules and 11,073 asses, the greater part of which must have been draught-animals. The booty included also war-chariots and two-wheeled carts. Sennacherib looted Babylon and razed the town to the ground, yet he was not content with his material booty: wanting Marduk, the Babylonian god, to serve Assyria, he extended his conquests to the deities of Babylonia. He had a special road built in Assur, similar to the one which served for worshipping Marduk in Babylonia. It was used for the religious procession celebrating New Year, when the divine statues left their temples and, following strict funeral rites,

80

made a symbolic infernal journey along a branch of the Tigris, to the festive house built on the bank of this river. Here they stayed for twelve days, after which they were 'resurrected' and, placed on an ark on wheels, returned to their temples, accompanied by far-sounding gay music and singing. Exulting men danced at the head of the procession, and crowds delirious with joy surrounded the majestically rolling, unwieldy vehicle (Fig. 79).

81

In the streets the king generally travelled about in his chariot. He could hardly have walked, as the streets were covered with puddles, putrid gutters and mud. When he went out from his palace or went hunting, he stood with two others in his chariot. Besides, the driver, the highest court official, originally called 'the king's third', was by then also included in representations of the royal carriage. The members of the court ran in front of and behind the vehicle as couriers. The higher the rank a courtier held, the nearer the carriage he was allowed to run. It was regarded as a special royal favour if one was permitted to hold the shaft of the vehicle; even visiting foreign princes were obliged to prove their loyalty by 'running with the wheels of their lord.'

The reliefs of Nineveh. Sennacherib was not only fond of war and hunting but was also a great patron of the arts. He had a magnificent palace built at Nineveh, in the citadel now called Kuyunjik, whose walls were almost completely covered with reliefs. These were also excavated in 1845 by Layard who was the first to set eyes on the masterpieces which had been buried in sand and ruins for about 2500 years.

One relief presented here (Fig. 80) shows the transportation of colossal statues: two loaded carts can be seen, besides the men working with ropes and levers, and the *lammashu* (bull colossus) on the sledge. The other relief (Fig. 81) represents the carterage of ropes and cranes, obviously for the performance of jobs similar to those illustrated by the first relief.

59

82 Ashur-bani-pal in his state-chariot
83 Ashur-bani-pal in his hunting-chariot
84 Assyrian soldiers escorting prisoners and
transporting women in a cart

83

Ashur-bani-pal (Ashurbanaplu) (668–628 B.C.) had left a vast
number of reliefs to posterity in his palace at Nineveh, which
like veritable 'picture-books' illustrate the different types of
chariots and other vehicles of the period. In addition to the conventional forms, they show various innovations; the range of the
vehicles represented is varied in every respect. His state-chariot
is decorated with a sun-shade (Fig. 82). Besides his driver only

84

85 Umanaldashi II, King of Elam, is led to prison
86 Elamite prisoners beside carts
87 Elamites in escape

an eunuch is shown standing in the chariot. (That the second figure is an eunuch is betrayed by his unbearded face.) The hunting and battle scenes generally repeat the old motifs (Figs. 83–87), but they show a few interesting new characteristics deserving special attention. The Elamite carts in Figs. 84 and 87, for instance, have no box, the draught-animals are not controlled with reins, and the wheels are twelve-spoked. Note also Fig. 85, interesting as a human document: it shows the captive King Umanaldashi II, conveyed by carriage, his hands held by an Assyrian soldier. Pl. V shows an alabaster relief presenting a battle scene with warriors fighting on chariots in the top corner and with prisoners of war in the lower row. Parts of the latter are shown separately on Fig. 86. The subject of Fig. 88 is the crossing of a river.

85

86

87

63

88 Assyrian soldiers crossing a river
89 Detail of a bronze helmet
90 Clay model of a covered cart

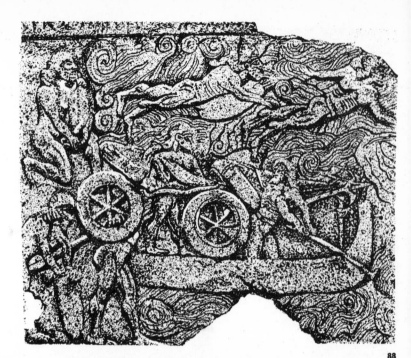

89

88

The end of the Assyrian empire. The mastery of military organization and modern arms could not remain the monopoly of the Assyrians for long. The peoples of Urartu, Babylonia and Elam soon learned the tactics of the Assyrians. In 605 B.C. the Assyrian empire was definitely overthrown in the battle of Kargamish.

Urartu. Beginning with the ninth century B.C., Assyria had to fight bitter wars against the tribes of North Urartu, inhabiting the mountainous regions now belonging to the Armenian Soviet Socialist Republic, southern Georgia and eastern Turkey.

The carriage finds which have come down to us throw light on the uses of the chariot in that country. Assyrian sources also contribute to our knowledge on the subject, and a triumphal stela betrays that King Ishpuini and his fellow-ruler Menua (810–781 B.C.) mobilized the following army for a battle fought east of Lake Van: 106 war-chariots, 9,374 mounted warriors and 22,704 infantrymen.

Some of the metal objects which have come to light in abundance also depict chariot scenes, for example, the bronze quiver excavated from the ruins of an Urartu fortress on the hill of Karmir-Blur (Armenian Soviet Socialist Republic) and a bronze helmet (Fig. 89) which belonged to King Arghishti (781–760 B.C.), similarly recovered at Karmir-Blur.

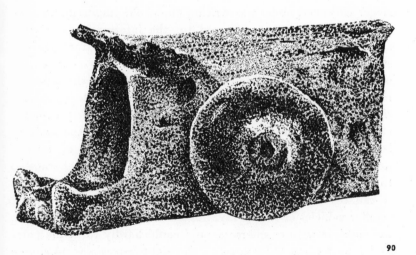

90

Although the two further model carriages of the tenth and ninth centuries B.C. presented in Figs. 90 and 91 are not directly related to Urartu, their illustration here is justified by the fact that they come from a neighbouring geographic region: they were found at Mingechaur (Azerbaidzhan Soviet Socialist Republic), along the lower part of the river Kura, and may be added to our list of carriages as a further new and unusual type.

65

New Babylonia. After the collapse of the Assyrian Empire, political supremacy in the Middle East was again seized by Babylonia. The new Babylonian vehicles do not show any novel features; they brought neither structural nor any other essential innovation to the field of transport. The war-chariots and hunting-carriages were horse-drawn as before; not so the vehicles used for carterage—unless by the special command of some god, as in the exceptional case of King Nabonidus (555–538 B.C.) who was bidden by the gods to build a temple of bricks cartered by his horses. Nabonidus is known also as an archaeologist and excavator: he brought to light—amongst other things—the ancient carriage of the god Lugal-maradda in the temple of E-igi-kakalamma, which he restored and decorated with silver, gold and precious stones.

The Persians. A little more information is available on the vehicles used by the Persians who conquered Babylonia in Nabonidus' lifetime (538 B.C.). Persian culture created new forms of expression replacing the style peculiar to the privileged chariotry by that of the rising new army, the cavalry.

Some interesting inventions. The Greek historian Xenophon, writing about the Persian King Cyrus II (558–529 B.C.), recorded some interesting data bearing on the history of the carriage. However, as he was writing about one hundred and fifty years after the events referred to, the information conveyed should be accepted with reservations. Xenophon states, for instance, that the cruel arm called the 'mower' was an invention of the Persians. The 'mower' was a vehicle with sharp blades mounted on its wheels; when in rotation, the blades simply slashed the enemy in battle. Another invention, the four-poled chariot, is attributed by Xenophon to Abradates, the military leader. It is said that Abradates had advised Cyrus to use one hundred vehicles of the new type, drawn by eight horses harnessed to the four poles, in the battle against Kroisos, king of Lydia. Abradates hoped that the heavy chariot would sweep away the smaller vehicles of the enemy, but his experiment failed because the chariots were cumbersome and could hardly turn, the poles broke easily, and the control of the eight horses was no simple matter either. Abradates himself fell in the battle, victim of his own invention. The only use of it was that—as Xenophon tells us—Cyrus developed the four-poled chariot further by inventing the eight-poled wagons; these he used for the transport of towers eighteen feet high, each sheltering twenty archers or slingers whose task it was to support the fighting troops in battle.

91

66

Darius I. The well-known seal of Darius I (522–486 B.C.) (Fig. 92) shows the King standing in his chariot, just placing the third arrow into his bow. In this representation the body of the vehicle is longer, and the pole is straight. (With the Assyrian war-chariot the pole curved upwards at the end nearer to the carriage-body.) In this seal the King is still represented in his chariot, but as the chariot grew more and more obsolete, it was replaced on later seals by a more modern setting: the King was shown on horseback or even afoot.

The relief of Persepolis. The long relief beside the staircase of the magnificent palace of Xerxes (Xshayarsha, Ksajarus, 484–465 B.C.) at Persepolis shows the King receiving tribute from the defeated Syrians (Pl. VI). We present here only the part of the relief, in which grooms are leading up an empty chariot. The vehicle exhibits some novel features again: its carriage-body is a simple box, without any decoration of arms. The ancestors of the tyre, the studs, are clearly visible on the wheel.

Written documents on Darius III. The numerous records which have come down to us from the time of Darius III (335–330 B.C.) cover the campaigns of Alexander the Great. Curtius Rufus writes that, in the battle Darius fought against this great king, he also used 200 'mowers'. It appears that Curtius Rufus, as well as Xenophon, also described this cruel weapon. According to him: —

Spears stood out at the end of the poles and three swords, each projected from the side of the yokes; spits were fitted between the spokes of the wheels, and some scythes stuck out from the felloes. When Darius arrayed his troops, he lined up 50 four-horsed war-chariots, behind which the 'mowers' were let loose on the enemy. They gave rein to the horses and succeeded in causing confusion among the first lines of the hostile troops. But the Macedonians soon recovered their wits and, keeping their spears close to each other, thrust them into the groins of the horses from both sides. The animals galloped madly forward. Then the enemy surrounded the chariots and pulled down the warriors. The battlefield was covered with the corpses of animals and fallen warriors. The drivers lost control over the shying horses, which shook their necks until they freed themselves of the traces, often overturning the carriages...

In another passage Curtius Rufus says that when Darius marched to the field, his train included the holy chariot of 'Jupiter', drawn by ten selected fine horses of equal size. The beautiful chargers were called 'solar horses'. Close behind them followed ten chariots richly decorated with silver and gold reliefs. In writing about the carriage used by Darius, Curtius Rufus states: —

> The two sides of its body were embellished with pictures of deities in silver and gold; diamonds glittered on the yoke which was decorated with two golden statues about an ell in height. Between them a golden eagle—a holy symbol—spread its wings. The carriage of Darius' mother, Sisygambis, followed at a stadium distance; another vehicle carried his wife Statira; this again was followed by fifteen *harmamaxas* with the King's children, their tutors and a band of eunuchs. (The *harmamaxa* was a four-wheeled covered luxury wagon with upholstered sides.) Behind them came the carriages of the three hundred and sixty concubines of the King.

In conclusion we have to add that—according to historians—the glory of Darius ended on a cart: after his defeat he was captured, shoved on to this ignominious vehicle covered with dirty hides and was killed by his own men.

The war-chariot reaches Egypt. The war-chariot was introduced into Egypt in about 1670–1570 B.C., with the Hyksos conquest. In the Old Kingdom, burdens were either carried on shoulder or transported by sledge; however, the Egyptians first got to know the carriage not as an implement of labour but as one of war. It is common knowledge and practically every manual and text-book tells us that the Hyksos conquerors—a people of mysterious Middle Eastern origin—vanquished the Egyptians around 1670 B.C. with the aid of light war-chariots. In any case, there is no doubt that the chariot came into Egypt from Syria; this theory is supported also by the fact that the Egyptian words for chariot and its component parts, as well as for the horse and the harness, are all of Semitic origin. The elements of decoration used on the carriage-body, the palmettes and animals facing each other, are also of Asiatic provenance.

The first Egyptian written record on the carriage dates from the time of the king Kamose. Referring precisely to the Hyksos people, it states that, vanquished after a rule of nearly a hundred and fifty years, "they took to flight in their chariots". Thus the first reliable data regarding the use of this vehicle on Egyptian territory (though not by the Egyptians themselves) dates from about 1580–1557 B.C. Thothmes I (1506–1494 B.C.) recorded the capture of only one chariot, which indicates that this fighting-

93

vehicle was still very rare in his time. We also know from Thothmes I that he had received a horse and a carriage as a feudal gift
from the upper regions of the Euphrates.

The chariot becomes conventional. The Egyptians soon realized
that to combat the war-chariots they needed such fighting-
vehicles themselves. Thus chariots became characteristic of the
New Kingdom. It is assumed that the Pharaohs spent on the
equipment and training of the chariotry not only out of military
considerations but also because the new arms were spectacular.

94

Arrayed in units of twenty-five, the brightly coloured and richly gilded chariots with the ornately harnessed, ostrich-plumed horses presented a dazzling sight indeed. The war-chariots carried a crew of two. The driver slashed a whip whose handle was often a masterpiece of art; the warrior was armed with a bow, arrows and spears.

The chariot of the Pharaoh. From Dynasty XVIII onwards, the ceremonial importance of the chariot increased steadily. The Pharaoh used it for riding to the temple, and the higher officials also travelled by chariot when calling on the Pharaoh or the viziers for an audience. It appears, however, that the vehicle was not used for longer journeys. Thus, for instance, the governor of Kush had his chariot transported on his large boat when travelling to Thebes. On the other hand, it was frequently used in hunting; various game, water fowl and ostriches fell in heaps killed by arrows shot from chariots.

The battle of Megiddo. The annals of Thothmes III (1490–1436 B.C.) give a detailed account of the battle of Megiddo. According to this, on the morning of the event, Thothmes III gave orders for his war-chariots to line up in battle array; he himself stood in the middle of the field in his resplendent carriage. The enemy troops took up their position on a great plain so as to be able to use their chariots to better advantage. "But, no matter where they stood," say the annals, "Thothmes led his army to victory. He took 2,238 horses and 924 war-chariots, including the gilded carriages of the two hostile leaders." A tidy booty, indeed!

The carriage-builders. Some very interesting mural paintings show the work of the carriage-builders (Pl. VII). Those found in

95

70

the grave of Menche-perre-seneb (c. 1475 B.C.) illustrate the building of a war-chariot as on a moving band; the carriage-body and the pole are being made in our illustration.

What was the Egyptian war-chariot like? The series of mural paintings and reliefs illustrating the outstanding events of the Pharaohs' reign include a good many hunting and war-chariots; the horse and the light hunting-carriage figure in Egyptian art throughout the period from Dynasty XVIII to Dynasty XX

95 Hunting scene
96 Relief from the tomb of Kha-em-chet
97 Chariot from the tomb of the parents-in-law of Amenhotep III

96

(Figs. 93–96). The changes in the structure of the vehicle may be also observed in the pictures: the four-spoked wheel, for instance, was gradually replaced by the eight-spoked one.

Even more interesting than the pictures is the actual chariot (Fig. 97) excavated from the tomb of the parents-in-law of Amenhotep III. On the basis of this vehicle and the mural representation referred to above, it is now quite easy to form an idea of the shape and structure of the Egyptian war-chariot. Its main

97

71

98

98 State-chariot from the tomb of Tutankhamen
99 Ostrich feathers fan from the tomb of Tutankhamen
100 War-chariot from Thebes

feature was that it was extremely light; another, that it was built up from an extraordinary large number of component parts; an Egyptian poem enumerating these mentions fifty, but it does not exhaust the complete inventory. And if we examine the way the components are assembled, we hardly know what to admire more: the incredible precision of the structure or the ingenious choice of the material used. The latter was not subject to whims or directed by a desire for ostentatious display; the cartwright's only concern was to use the most suitable material for each component: one kind of wood for the straight parts; another, for the bent ones, and so forth. Great care was taken with the fixing of the spokes. To make them less rigid, they were composed of two pieces of wood glued together lengthwise. The felloe, too, generally consisted of several parts fixed together with wooden nails, pins and gluing, but the felloe bent by vapour was also known. For better hold, the tenons of the spokes were fitted into the felloe and the hub wound in hider or bast; the wheels were provided with leather tyres. The carriage-body itself was made of wood, metal or bark-matting; it was open at the back and rested directly on the axle, either so that its centre of gravity fell approximately in line with the axle, or the axle was near the rear part of the carriage-body. The sides of the carriage-body were covered with wooden panelling, leather or—in the case of royal carriages—with stucco. A quiver for arrows and spears and a sheath for the bow were attached to the sides. The yoke was

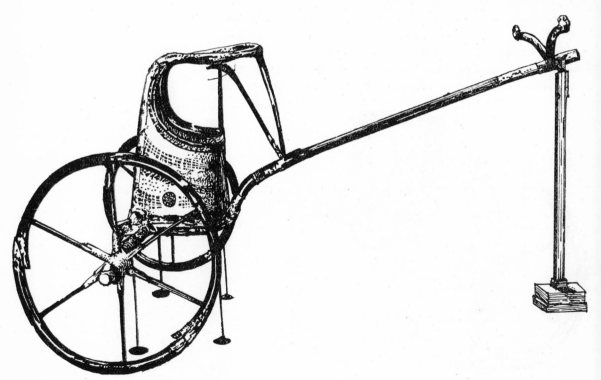

fitted cross-ways to the end of the firmly-fixed shaft stretching from the front of the carriage-body.

No wonder that such a masterpiece of a war-chariot counted as an article of luxury. Besides the king, only a few of the notabilities or the wealthy could call such a vehicle his own. But everyone longed to possess one and envied the fortunate owners. "Thou climbeth into thy carriage with a golden whip in thy hand; thou hast new reins; Syrian ponies are harnessed to thy vehicle; negroes run before ye awaiting thy orders..." wrote an Egyptian poet.

Tutankhamen. Among the Pharaohs who followed Akhenaton on the throne, Tutankhamen is no doubt the one best known to the general public. The excavations carried out by Howard Carter have brought to light the treasures—and among them the chariots—of this short-lived Egyptian ruler almost intact. In the ante-chamber of his tomb the working parts of five dismantled chariots were found, one of which—a gilt masterpiece of handicraft (Fig. 98)—was inlaid with semi-precious stones and stained glass. The carriage-body, the pole, the wheels, down to the smallest components, were all made of wood. A small wooden chest, also found in the tomb, containing the King's festive robes, sandals and other wearing apparel (Pl. VIII), bore pictures of war-chariots. Three sides of the chest were decorated with painted hunting and battle scenes. In one of them Tutankhamen is shooting lions, in the other he is fighting the Syrians; on the top picture he is seen pursuing ostriches. A magnificent

99

100

73

gilded fan, whose edge still holds the stumps of ostrich feathers, also shows a scene of ostrich-shooting (Fig. 99).

The Egyptian war-chariot in the Florence museum (Fig. 100) had been unearthed also intact from a *mastaba* at Thebes exactly one hundred years before the opening of Tutankhamen's tomb. It formed part of the material brought to light by the French–Tuscan scientific expedition of 1828–29. Though the chariot broke to pieces in the course of the excavation, it was successfully reassembled afterwards, with every bit in its original place, excepting the pole, part of which had to be replaced. It occured to the Italian Egyptologist Rossellini to have the chariot examined by botanists to establish what kind of timber the Egyptians had used for its construction. They stated in general that the timbers in question were not of Egyptian origin but "came from the north". Since then more modern scientific methods—discovered about fifty years ago—have enabled the botanists to come to a more precise opinion. According to more recent tests the timbers used were holm-oak for the axle and the spokes, elm for the pole, ash for the felloes, the chassis and the dashboard, hornbeam for the yoke and birch bark for wrapping and for joining the spokes with the felloes and the hub.

The obscure statement that the chariots were made of timber "of northern origin" gave rise to a plausible legend. Though the word 'northern' meant in this case only countries situated north of Egypt, some imaginative scientists began to refer to Scandinavia and Germany as the original home of the Egyptian chariot. Actually, it may be taken for granted that the wooden material of the Egyptian chariots came from the Caucasus. This is proved by the inscription figuring next to a mural drawing of two such vehicles in Kenamun's tomb at Thebes, stating that the timber they were built of had been imported from the mountains of Naharina which, we know, also includes the Caucasian mountains.

'Genre' scenes. Some of the Egyptian reliefs and mural paintings represent *genre* scenes of everyday life. One was excavated from the tomb of Horonemheb. The driver makes the best of his time: while the master is watching the harvesters, he is having a good nap under a tree, with the overseer sharing his idling (Fig. 101). The wall paintings found in the tomb of Huie, governor of Kush, show a Nubian princess in an ox-drawn carriage (Fig. 102); the driver in this picture is also a woman—the first represented in this position. The female slave caressing the oxen is also a new figure, occurring for the first time in Egyptian drawings.

The Pharaohs apparently did not want posterity to know them from peaceful scenes. The artistic monuments from their reign illustrate battles and hunting. Seti I and Rameses II had covered

101

101 Relief from the tomb of **Horonemheb**
102 **Wall painting** from the tomb of **Huie**
103 The battle of Kadesh

102

103

75

the walls of temples and halls with monster reliefs. Seti I had a fascinating relief 164 feet long, carved in the hypostyle hall at Karnak (Pl. IX); it represents chaotic episodes from his life in an elaborate style. Rameses II had the battle of Kadesh recorded in relief at Karnak, Abu Simbel, in the Ramesseum at Thebes, at Luxor and at Abydos (Fig. 103). The event had been described also by the Egyptian chroniclers in detail, approximately as follows: —

The battle of Kadesh. When Rameses II waged war on Kadesh, deserters or—as it turned out later—sham deserters of the enemy fooled him with the fake rumour that his foe, the Hittite king Muwatallis, had taken to flight, leaving Kadesh unprotected. Rameses was taken in by the false information and—leaving the bulk of his army rashly behind—proceeded in pursuit of the enemy with his chariots at an increased speed. This was just what the cunning Muwatallis had been waiting for. While Rameses, unapprehensive of the guile, advanced with his chariots on the one side of Kadesh northward, he pressed forward with his vehicles on the other, in southern direction, taking good care to keep the city all the time between them to conceal his operations. He thus succeeded in outflanking and surrounding the weak detachment led by Rameses II, who found himself cut off from the main body of his army. Eventually, however, Muwatallis' cunning was of little avail, for the Pharaoh managed with difficulty to escape and even to gain foothold on the battlefield.

104

The reason for this unexpected turn in fortune was that Muwatallis did not trust his infantrymen who were at loggerheads with the haughty aristocratic charioteers; he therefore led only the latter into action, but they proved unable to decide the outcome of the battle which eventually was celebrated by both parties as a victory.

By this time the development of the war-chariot had already reached its peak; later specimens of this vehicle show no further improvement.

The war-chariot in the Sahara. The use of the war-chariot spread even to Central Africa. Whether it got there from Egypt or the Sudan, or from some other territory (for the latter possibility cannot be ruled out either), is still a matter for speculation. In any case, it created great sensation when on the rocky plateau of Tassili-Ahaggar, somewhere halfway between Tripolis and the Niger-bend, red and violet-coloured line drawings, including the pictures of galloping war-chariots (Fig. 104), have been discovered. Judging by these representations, the war-chariot of the Sahara was adapted to the special character of the desert. It appears to have had an extremely light structure. Its weight was reduced by shrinking the carriage-body to a mere platform; the driver stood right on the pole where it emerged from the chassis, so that the centre of gravity of the whole structure was transferred to the fore-part of the carriage.

How the chariot may have reached the Sahara. Although civilization flourished in the Central African steppes and savannahs as early as the beginning of the first millennium B.C., the ethnic groups inhabiting these regions were not acquainted with the carriage in any form. The carriage or, specifically, the war-chariot must have come to these parts from outside. But the question is: where from? There are various theories current in this connection. According to one, the mercenaries taking part in the fights between Libya and Egypt around 1200 B.C. may have been the first to use the new vehicle. Another opinion is that the charioteers of the desert were identical with the Garamantic warriors so often referred to by Herodotus, while a further theory is based on the assumption that the lively trade which existed between North Africa and the Sudan—the latter a region rich in gold—was directed through routes crossing the western part of the Sahara which therefore must have been highly frequented by freight vehicles. The most creditable explanation is, however, the one given by H. Lothe, an outstanding expert on the subject: he associates the rock drawings and the representation of the war-chariot in them with the Aegean migration, stating that one of the home-seeking coastland peoples must have settled temporarily in Central Sahara, and the rock drawings are relics of their passage. In any case, it is interesting to note that the black ethnic groups of North Africa, although they had seen the carriage, did not attempt to imitate it because the economic conditions for the use of draught-vehicles were lacking in the regions inhabited by them.

The direct recipients of the Middle Eastern traditions of carriage-building were the Hittites.

The Hittites. The original home of the Hittites was in the eastern part of Asia Minor, but the Hittite empire formed there in the seventeenth century B.C. extended its sway to northern Syria as early as in the sixteenth century B.C. Following their Syrian conquests, the Hittites also invaded Babylonia and thus came into direct contact with the Mesopotamian peoples, rich in carriage-building traditions.

The Hittite empire became a great military power whose army consisted of chariotry and heavy-armed infantry.

The Hittite war-chariot is known to us not only from reliefs and cylinder-seals but also from written records. A document dating from the seventeenth century B.C. indicates, for instance, that Anitta, king of Kussar, a Hittite city-state, took a booty of forty war-chariots and forty pairs of horses when defeating a rival city sovereign. In the songs glorifying the feats of the Hittite kings Hattushili I and Murshili I—who in the seventeenth and sixteenth centuries B.C. piled victory upon victory—eighty chariots are mentioned. It may be inferred from these data that the number of war-chariots thrown into battle at a time could hardly have exceeded one hundred. In the fourteenth and thirteenth centuries B.C. the Hittites conquered Syria and Palestine and have thus reached the territories which scientists once believed to have been the original home of this people. They owed their success to the exemplary training of their charioteers. The earliest work on hippology, dating from the fourteenth century B.C., was written by one Kikkuli of Mitanni in the Hittite language for use by the Hittites. It is an extremely detailed and precise description of the method of horse-training for war-chariots, specifying the daily routine for one hundred and seventy days. The ratio between the war-chariots and the infantrymen may be deduced from the data, according to which Murshili II obliged the vanquished king of Kizzuwatna to raise one thousand infantrymen and one hundred harnessed horses for his army in case of war; this means that there was one chariot to twenty infantrymen (a hundred horses taken in pairs were for fifty chariots). On another occasion, however, the Hittites threw fourteen thousand infantrymen and forty chariots into battle, which corresponds to a ratio of 1 : 35.

105

Fig. 105 illustrates an interesting Hittite cylinder seal: it represents the weather god in an ox-drawn chariot, driving to his holy nuptials. The goddess, emitting jets of water from her body, receives him 'attired in veils'.

The decline and fall of the Hittite empire. The Hittites gradually lost the leading position they had attained in chariotry and its inseparable concomitant, horse-breeding. In the letter to Kadash-man-Enlil, referred to earlier in this work, the Hittite king Hattushili III all but implored the Babylonian ruler to send him horses: "So I speak to my brother. Send me horses and let them be shapely colts. The stallions thy father hath sent me were of good stock but are old nags now, lacking in strength. It is very cold in Hatti, and old horses do not live long. Send me, brother, young stallions, for nags I have enough in my land; just ask, brother, thy ambassador, and he will confirm that it is thus." So the tables have turned: the centre of horse-breeding shifted to the south, to Babylonia.

The Assyrian, Hittite and Hurrian traditions were upheld by the city-states of Asia Minor.

106

79

The chariot finds of Arslan Tash, Handatu by its old Assyrian name, originally fit into Assyrian development, for the palace of Tukulit-pal-E-saria III stood just in this place. One of its ornaments was the relief that represents the King in his chariot (Fig. 106).

Kargamish. The chariot scenes (Fig. 107) from the so-called 'long wall' of Kargamish represent part of the ritual procession of gods and warriors illustrated on this wall, measuring 124 feet and 5 inches (37 metres) in length. The motif of the scenes—the warrior or hunter standing in his chariot—is not new; yet on closer examination it appears that the chariot figuring in the Kargamish scenes differs to some extent from the types which occured so far: the carriage-box does not rest directly on the axle (which may of course be due to the artist's negligence); the side of the carriage-body exhibits a round-shaped decoration, probably a relief; the back of the carriage-body bulges out shield-like; between the yoke on the horse's neck and the front of the carriage-body, a second pole can be seen, similar to the one found on the Assyrian vehicles, only in a somewhat simplified form. The provincial style of the reliefs, the naive representation of the small, ungainly horses recalling the rocking-horse, and of the trampled army, is very characteristic.

Malatya. The chariot appearing in this libation scene (Fig. 108) looks as if it were built one thousand or two thousand years

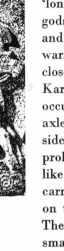

107

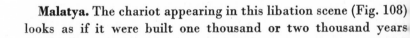
108

earlier; its obsolete solid wheel recalls the tripartite wheel of the Sumerians. Why these archaic features? The explanation is simple: because the vehicle carries a god! In every religion and myth gods and mythical characters are represented in archaic clothes and with obsolete implements, almost without exception! Another definitely provincial-style Malatyan relief (Fig. 109) which, however, bears witness to a highly developed sense for the decorative shows a hunting-chariot, although unfortunately only in a sketchy way. It can be discerned, however, that the body of the vehicles rested on the axle now with its middle part, now with its rear part; a spear was struck into the back of the carriage, and two quivers lay crosswise on its side.

Senjirli. The carriage in the Senjirli relief (Fig. 110) is similar to the one seen in the Kargamish vehicle (Fig. 107), and both are reminiscent of the carriages in the hunting scenes from the time of Ashur-nasir-pal II (883–859 B.C.), so that certain common characteristics of the vehicle enable us to date the relief. Both the Kargamish and Senjirli war-chariots have a round shield at the back with a boss in its middle and a pike or a lion's head. The spear is stuck in slantwise, with the spear-head stretching upwards. The same features may be observed in the chariot scene of Ashur-nasir-pal II.

Sakça-Gözü. In a relief from Sakça-Gözü (Fig. 111) we find again the characteristic component of the Assyrian carriage, referred to on several occasions earlier, namely 'the second pole' (present also in the Kargamish relief). This, too, helps to determine the age of the relief and the carriage: both may be assigned to the ninth century B.C.

107 War-chariot from a battle scene
108 King Sulumeli's sacrifice to the water-god
109 Relief with a lion-hunt

109

110 Relief with warrior and charioteer from Senjirli
111 The sun-god comes on his chariot to the help of god Temb
112 Hunt

110

Tell Halaf. The dating of the special style exhibited by the Tell Halaf stone reliefs has been the subject of many arguments between archaeologists for a long time (Pl. X). It is now generally accepted that the reliefs are datable from the ninth-eighth centuries, for the stylistical marks which had induced certain experts to consider the works as antique turned out to be only the marks of provinciality. Unfortunately, the chariots are even more 'sketchy' on them than on the Malatyan relief.

The cultural sway of the Mesopotamian states spread gradually over Phoenicia, the isle of Cyprus, Syria and Palestine.

111

The main city-state of Phoenicia was Ugarit. The library of clay tablets excavated at Ugarit (Ras Shamra) is a regular mine of information on the subject of war-chariots. The tablets contain numerous administrative instructions regulating the registration and maintenance of the chariots, horse-furniture and wheels. From among the Ugarit finds we present here the drawing of a decorative gold plate (Fig. 112) dating from the fifteenth century B.C.; it shows a hunter in his chariot, shooting wild bisons and gazelles.

112

Cyprus. As the Cypriot civilization developed under Phoenician sway, naturally the vehicles found in Cyprus also bear witness to Phoenician influence, both direct and indirect in character, for the Phoenicians themselves were the transmitters of various other cultures, as appears from their own vehicles. No actual carriage has been found in Cyprus, but the clay models and ivory gaming-chests supply us with information on a wide range of wheeled vehicles, including the four-wheeled wagon, the two-wheeled cart and various other types of carriages (Pl. XI, Fig. 113).

Palestine. In the second millennium B.C., the two-wheeled chariot was not yet used as a fighting-vehicle in Palestine but only

83

113 Ivory gaming-chest with relief of a hunting scene
114 Prisoners of war paying homage to a king

113

as a symbol of power meant to increase the splendour of the court. However, a Megiddo ivory carving dating from 1350–1150 B.C. (Fig. 114) shows already some prisoners of war tied before the horses of a chariot to render homage to the king of Palestine. Unfortunately, the part showing the front of the chariot is broken, but the quiver and the spear at the back are clearly discernible in the carving. Towards the end of the thirteenth century B.C., a Hebrew tribal community, bearing the name of Israel, seized power in Egypt. The Israelites invading the country from the desert knew the freight vehicle but not the war-chariot, as they had not yet mastered the new military technique. However, they soon adopted the mercenary chariotry as a weapon and increased their chariot park by vehicles seized from the conquered city-states.

114

The Bible and the carriage. The Bible also supplies data regarding the Palestine history of the horse and carriage. Though the patriarchs figuring in the Old Testament are surrounded by a haze of myth, the Books contain numerous useful references to the carriage, acquainting us at least with the contemporary uses of this implement. In the Books of Moses, for instance, the cart and the carriage occur in several passages. Thus Moses or Joseph "made ready his chariot" (Exod. 14.6); further on we find that the Pharaoh "took six hundred chosen chariots, and all the chariots of Egypt and captains over every one of them" (Exod. 14.7). In the well-known myth of Israel crossing the Red Sea, we are told that "Pharaoh's chariots and his host hath he cast into the sea" (Exod. 15.4). The references to the cart and carriage contained in the Book of the Judges are connected with quite a variety of events. Jabin, king of Canaan, sent his host against the children of Israel. Sisera, the captain of the host, "had nine hundred chariots of iron", but when he saw that the fortunes of war had turned against him, he "flew down off his chariot and fled away on his feet." Sisera then fled to the tent of a woman named Jael, who smote a nail into his temples while he slept. "The mother of Sisera" who waited in vain for the return of her son, "looked out of a window and cried through the lattice: Why is his chariot so long in coming? Why tarry the wheels of his chariots?" (Judg. 5.28.) A characteristic recurring sentence in the Old Testament refers to the social importance of the carriage: Samuel, Absalom and Adonijah equally regarded the carriage and the "men running before it" as a symbol of power and welfare. The biblical king Solomon "had four thousand stalls for horses and chariots, and twelve thousand horsemen; whom he bestowed in the chariot cities..." (Chron. II.9.25), and he "gathered together chariots and horsemen; and he had a thousand and four hundred chariots and twelve thousand horsemen." (Kings I.10.26.) The Bible informs us even about prices, in saying that "A chariot came up and went out of Egypt for six hundred *shekels* of silver, and a horse, for a hundred and fifty; and so for all the kings of the Hittites and for the kings of Syria did they bring them out by their means." (Kings I.10.29.)

The rôle of the war-chariot in the history of the Ancient East. From the second millennium B.C. onwards, the war-chariot marks the ancient history of the East. After the sixteenth century B.C., the discipline of the mercenary charioteers and the skill of the horses trained especially for warfare have rendered chariotry an invincible arm, deciding the outcome of the battles. The chariot alone would have been of little avail without the well-trained drivers, archers and lancers, or without the systematically drilled horses and the thorough exercising of the precisely planned military operations. Thus chariotry as a weapon demanding expensive equipment and training, and disciplined troops, was peculiar to the military monarchies based on privileged warrior classes; its development and employment fits in with the social evolution of the various peoples.

The first users of the 'modern' war-chariot of the light, spoke-wheeled and horse-drawn fighting-vehicle were the Hittites, the Hurrians and the Kassites. Which of them was the very first is a question still requiring elucidation.

Asiatic culture in Europe. The Hittites played an important rôle in uniting, developing and preserving the culture of the Middle East; in addition to this, they maintained friendly relations with the people of the Aegean Islands and, through this, formed as it were a bridge between Asia and Europe.

The Hittite written records from the time of Shuppiluliuma and Murshili II often refer to a country called Ahhiyawa, and we also know that the princes of Ahhiyawa got the mastery of charioteering at the court in Hattusa. It is assumed—and not without reason—that the inhabitants of Ahhiyawa were identical with the Achaean people. The Achaeans again are identical with the Greeks of the Mycenaean culture, with the inhabitants of Greece prior to the Doric migration. And if these presumptions are correct, the chariot could have easily crossed from Asia to Europe through the bridge formed by the above connections.

Chapter IV

The Indus civilization — The *Rig Veda* — The conquests of Alexander the Great — China: legend and history — The origin and the earliest examples of the European carriage — Züschen, Storozhevaya mogila, Budakalász — Central Asia — Tri Brata, Znamenka, Minusinsk and Pazirik — The Scythians and the nomads

Let us turn our attention now to the Indus valley, China and the steppes of Central Asia and look around in India first.

India. Not so long ago it was still a generally accepted scientific view that the Indian peninsula owes all her feats of civilization —including naturally the development of the carriage—to the Indo-European tribes which invaded Punjab in the second half of the second millennium B.C. and spread thence to further territories later. However, the excavations carried out at Harappa (Punjab) and Mohenjo-Daro (Sindh) since 1921 proved that an independent native culture had flourished in India as far back as in the early part of the third millennium B.C. The assumption that the wheeled vehicle existed under what is now termed the Indus civilization has been borne out partly by the fact that model carriages have come to light in those regions and partly by the excavation of streets among the ruins at Mohenjo-Daro. Considering that in many cases they measured even 32 feet 10 inches (10 metres) in width, it is but logical to suppose that they had been built for carts and wagons. Moreover, at Harappa the pavement of the excavated streets were marked by ruts of 41 inches (1 metre and 5 centimetres) gauge.

The earliest known Indian carriage (Fig. 115) is assigned to the third millennium B.C., i.e. is presumed to be about as ancient as the first Sumerian carriage finds. Its frame looks like a bent three-stepped ladder. The copper models found at Chanhu-Daro are also from the same age. Their light carriage-body is covered, and the passengers must have sat in it back-to-back (Fig. 116). It is interesting to note that vehicles of this type can still be seen in India (Pl. XII).

After these early carriage finds, there is a blank for several millennia. The lack of further relics may be due to the fact that the actual carriages, made of wood, decayed in the process of time. No works of art have come down to us either, as the peoples inhabiting the Indian peninsula during the ages in question were not acquainted yet with the art of stone-carving, and the objects

they modelled in clay or wood also fell victims to the ravages of time.

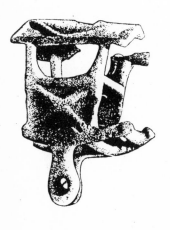

116

The 'Rig Veda'. The British scientist Stuart Piggott endeavoured to fill the gap with quotations from the *Rig Veda*. This Hindu literary relic describes the structure and dimensions of the war-chariot of the second millennium B.C. with a precision sufficient even for actual reconstruction. It gives the measurements of the pole, the yoke and the axle in '*angulus*' (= one inch = 2.54 cm). Thus we know that the length of the axle of a war-chariot was almost 78 inches (2 metres), that of the pole more than $136^1/_2$ inches (3 metres and 50 centimetres), while the yoke measured $62^1/_2$ inches (1 metre and 60 centimetres). The carriage-body was open at the back and rounded off in shape; the warrior had a seat, but the driver had to stand.

There are no data regarding the diameter of the wheels, nor any bearing on the spokes, but on the basis of a literary simile it is assumed that heat-bending had been applied to the felloes.

The other *Vedas* simply swarm with carriages. Every respectable god—with Indra, the supreme deity, in the first place—travels by chariot. A hymn to Indra says that "The horses were harnessed betimes to his magnificent new chariot which had four yokes, ten whips, seven traces and ten wheels." Although technologically this description is hardly convincing, one has to appreciate the munificence of its author. According to another passage, Indra's chariot was drawn by two golden-haired steeds "as swiftly as falcons wing their flight." Savitri, personifying the sun, rode now in a golden chariot, now in a high, gaily coloured one, inlayed with mother-of-pearl and fitted with a golden pole.

In old Hindu literature the carriage is often used in symbolic comparisons. In the *Riksanhita*, for instance, we read that Indra unites heaven and earth as an axle unites two wheels, and the two worlds roll in his trail like wheels after a steed.

The symbolic meaning of the wheel. From the sixth century B.C. onwards, the symbolic meaning of the wheel was enriched with further traits by the Buddhist religion. The 'wheel of life', full of sufferings, is represented in the clutches of the demon of instability. The 'wheel of the doctrine' (Pl. XIII) reminded the devout of Buddha's sermon in the garden of the gazelles at Benares with which the divine teacher "sent off the redeeming doctrine like a rolling wheel." Of Buddha himself it is said in a figurative sense that he "kept the wheels of the doctrine turning." Buddha's wheel forms part of India's coat of arms (Fig. 117). In the Buddhist religion the wheel symbolizes the law of rebirth, but at the same time it represents also the transience of all that is worldly. The Sanskrit word *ratha* which in the *Rig Veda* meant 'carriage' lived on in the European languages, in the Latin word *rota*, the Celtic *roth*, the German *Rad* and the Lithuanian *ratas*— all meaning 'wheel'.

117

Alexander the Great extended his conquests also to India (334–326 B.C.). Arrianos and Curtius Rufus inform us about his wars and exploits there. According to Arrianos' report on the preliminaries of the battle of Sangala, the troops of Alexander camped on the hill where they arrayed their chariots in a triple defense line. In May 326 B.C., Alexander the Great reached the river Hydaspes (now called Jhelum). Porus gathered his troops to stop the conqueror. Curtius Rufus reports that he threw a hundred chariots and four thousand cavalrymen into action against the Macedonians. Each chariot carried a crew of six warriors; two of them held the shields, while two others were shooting arrows, and two drove the vehicle, but the drivers were not without arms either: when it came to hand-to-hand fights, they threw javelins at the enemy. The battle was in full swing when it took a turn which eventually led to the victory of the Macedonians. The report of this fight of the fourth century B.C. runs as follows:

...as mentioned above, the unusual downpour made the terrain slippery and unsuitable for the cavalry; the heavy chariots, almost incapable of movement, stuck in the mud and pot-holes. But Alexander got along easily with his light and mobile vehicles. The Indian chariots soon wobbled about in the field without their drivers.

The Indian road-system and the army. Only a few decades later, around 280 B.C., the Greek historian Megasthenes went to India as the ambassador of Seleucus Nicator. His work is a source of interesting information on the carriage and the war-chariot.

115 Clay model of a cart
116 Copper model of a carriage-body
117 India's coat of arms

Although Pliny warns us not to take it too seriously because of the many contradictions contained therein, and Strabo goes as far as to call Megasthenes a liar, yet the book—known to us only in fragments through its later users, including Strabo and Arrianos—is not without value, for Megasthenes was a careful observer. His data concerning the ancient Indian road-system may be considered the more reliable as the royal chancellor Quantilya gave a similar account on the subject. According to these sources the royal road leading from the border to Palibothra (Pataliputra), the capital of the country, was marked with milestones at intervals of ten stadia, indicating also the by-roads and distances. The care of the roads was organized by a special staff of officials, and their maintenance was prescribed even by religious laws, for Buddha bade every devout soul to tend the roads. Under the reign of King Ashoka, about 273–236 B.C., the communication system was developed further.

The early Indian representations of the carriage show an astonishing range of structures, especially if we consider that their development was a fairly isolated process. We find among them two-wheeled carts as well as four-wheeled wagons, open and covered, some drawn by a pair, others, by four draught-animals. One of the most interesting types is the caravan wagon (Pl. XIV), in which Prince Vishvantara, the last of Buddha's incarnations, is seen roaming with his household in the forests, after he had left his father's court to seek his salvation in seclusion.

Models found in Central Asia, south of the Kara Kum desert, on the territory of the present-day Turkmen Soviet Socialist Republic, indicate that the wheel and the carriage were known in these regions as early as 2250–2000 B.C. One of the sites was Anau Tepe, one of the oldest grain-growing and stock-breeding centres of Central Asia. The clay model wheels found in layer III of this site and also west of the locality, at Shah Tepe, near Ashkhabad, are similar to those recovered at Tepe Gawra, Kish and Shuruppaki; the hub of the wheels protrudes in the middle also on these finds. The model wheels prove beyond doubt that the actual wheels—and consequently actual carriages (carts or wagons)—had also existed in these Central Asiatic areas in the above-mentioned age.

Legendary China. To set up the chronological order of the wheeled vehicles on the basis of legends or to write the story of the carriage on the strength of such unreliable evidence would be an attempt doomed to failure. Still, let us record at this stage the data we are able to pick out from the Chinese myths relative to the carriage. It appears from these that wheeled vehicles had

90

been in use even before the Hsia dynasty (i.e. before 2000 B.C.); at least this is what we may infer from the legend, according to which Huang-ti, 'King of the Yellow Earth', led his clans into battle in chariots. His other name, Houan-yuan-shi, actually means 'from the clan of the draught-pole'. The Chinese annals attribute the invention of the solid wheel and the carriage to the Chinese emperor Huang-ti. The naive details of the legend tell how, walking in his gardens one day, the great emperor saw some plucked anemone blossoms rolling in the wind; the idea of the wheel struck him at the sight of them.

The *I-ching* (the Book of Changes) envelopes the invention of the carriage, its cult use and subsequent adoption for profane use in a mythological haze. It speaks of the thirty spokes of the mythic wheel (according to the number of days in a month) and

118

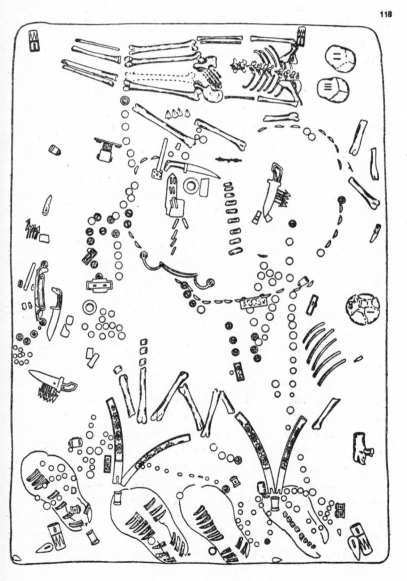

91

mentions two types of carriages: the slow, ox-drawn wagon and the fast, armoured war-chariot. Against this the legends referring to the establishment of the empire glorify Yu, the mystic hero, as the inventor of the ox-drawn cart and also as the first man to have harnessed a horse to a carriage.

The story of the State of Shang-yin is another source of information on the subject, for it appears that in the middle of the second millennium B.C., the Shang tribe, advancing gradually from the east to the west, was equipped with war-chariots. According to H. G. Creel *(The Birth of China)*, they adopted the vehicle from the Indo-European tribes which by that time had reached Central Asia. By 1300 B.C. the Shang tribe knew also the spoked wheel. The excavation in the fields of the village of Hiao-t'ung near Anyang, the last capital of the Shang-yin state, brought to light from grave No. M 020 the remains of a carriage (Fig. 118). The greater part of the wooden components were found decayed, but it was still possible to establish that the carriage-box measured $50^5/_6$ inches (one metre and 30 centimetres) in width and $39^2/_5$ inches (one metre) in length; the wheel gauge was $78^4/_5$ inches (two metres). At the bottom of Fig. 118 the skulls of the four horses can be seen; above them are the remains of the yoke, and still higher, but below the two human skeletons on the top, the outlines of the roughly round-shaped carriage are easy to discern. The ancient Chinese pictographs, dating from about the same period, include characters for the designation of the carriage, which implies that the vehicle must have enjoyed widespread use by that time (Fig. 119). Most of the pictographs—though not all—clearly show the carriage-body, the pole and the double yoke. The oracular inscriptions found incised in bones at Hiao-t'ung (containing the questions put and the answers received from oracles) also mention the pair-draught.

The Chou period (1027—223 B.C.). The Chinese not only knew and used the carriage but also built important road systems. Even before the Chou dynasty's rule, a highways commissioner was charged with the supervision and maintenance of the roads. At the turn of the second and first millennia, the Chinese began also to construct roads leading to the west. Along the westbound highway from Tun Huang to Lop-nor rest-houses were built. Under the Chou dynasty traffic required that prescriptions be set for wheeled vehicles as to standard weights and size; fast driving was prohibited, and at the busier crossings certain traffic regulations were introduced. Roads were classified into five grades: (a) pathways for man and pack-animals; (b) roads taking a vehicle of narrow gauge; (c) roads with room for broad-gauge vehicles; (d) roads wide enough for wagons to pass one another; (e) highroads taking three wagons abreast.

119

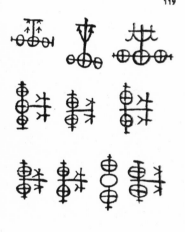

119 Ancient Chinese pictographs—the signs for carriages

The Chinese chariotry. Under the Chou dynasty the backbone of the army was formed by the vassals. They fought from war-chariots and were followed by lightly armed peasants marching afoot. In about 1150 B.C. Wu Wang, king of the Chou dynasty, defeated the house of Shang-yin and "restored the good government of old times" in China. When on his way home he had crossed the Yellow River, he let his war-horses loose to the four winds and sent his oxen grazing; he then smeared his war-chariots and armour with ox-blood and put them in his arms-store, demonstrating hereby that he never wanted to use them again.

From the eighth century B.C. onwards, China became a loose alliance of liege-lords who ruled under the nominal supremacy of the 'Son of Heaven', the king. Whenever it became necessary, it was incumbent on the liege-lord to send his vassals to war, but the organization and work involved was carried out by his official, a kind of minister of war who decided the number of chariots and horses, as well as that of the troops—charioteers and infantrymen—to be despatched. Each vassal was to equip a definite number of chariots, according to the estate and rank held by him.

How the Chinese charioteers went to war. The weapons of the warriors embarking on an expedition were smeared with blood; the supreme commander offered a sacrifice and invoked the gods; then the army set out to meet the enemy. The noblemen sat in their chariots playing the lute. The vehicles they used were short and narrow; they were open at the back and rested on two wheels. Two-wheelers were harnessed to a pole with two horses on either side of the pole. The inner reins of the ornate harness were tied to rings at the front of the carriage, the other six reins were held by the driver. The clattering ornaments and ringing bells made a terrific din under way, which may have exceeded even the ringing of the earlier sledge bells or the noise of the Sicilian carts. The driver stood in the middle of the carriage-box with the archer on his left—the chief place in the chariot—and the lanceman on his right to ensure the balance of the chariot. The body of the three men was protected by armour made of three layers of ox-hide; at the front of the vehicle they were sheltered by a light shield each. The quiver of the archer contained two arrows; the lanceman had fork-shaped thrusting-weapons at hand, but the long-shafted grappling-hook which served to pull the enemy off his chariot was perhaps the most important of the fighting-implements: once the enemy lay on the ground, the infantrymen took care of the rest.

When the army had a respite or advanced at a slow, dignified pace, the warriors—whose fatigue was only enhanced by the terrible jolting of the vehicle—rested on mats or tiger skins in

93

the carriage-box. Infantrymen marched on both sides of the chariot; the men on the right were to keep an eye on the poles, those on the left had to pick grass on the roadside to feed the horses.

Episodes from the life of the charioteers. Most of the chariot battles were naturally fought in dead earnest and were bloody affairs. Still, it was a military custom for the enemies to greet each other before entering into battle. Not on their knees, of course—for they were armed—but in any case they alighted from their chariots, bowed thrice, and if a general sighted an enemy of a higher rank, he even lifted his helmet. A liege-lord could be attacked by his equal only, for "anyone else touching him deserved punishment." Only men of equal rank could fight each other. Conventions demanded that a warrior "be courteous in fight". If, for instance, an enemy chariot was stopped and forced to surrender, and its occupant offered a ransom in homage on the spot, he was allowed to flee. "It is a noble gesture to spare the enemy's life in a chariot battle and a valiant thing to seek danger", teaches the slogan of the Chinese charioteers, "but the most sublime experience is if a soldier may sacrifice his life for his war-chief."

Wars with the nomads. From the eighth to the sixth century B.C., hardly a year passed without some barbaric tribe harassing the cities of the Chinese liege-lords. The assaults of foot-soldiers were fended off by the Chinese with chariots. Contemporary sources frequently refer to the Hiung-nu tribes, now generally identified with the Huns. Their penetration into China is described in an ode. "What excitement in the sixth month of the year!" exclaims its author. "The chariots are all prepared; four splendid horses are harnessed to each of them; they are equipped as only right. The Hiung-nus have invaded the country with fury and wrath."

The white dog's hide on the carriage-frame. In feudal China solidarity among the liegemen was obligatory. If the majority took a decision in some question, all the others had to accept it. Anyone maintaining an individual opinion to the contrary had to atone for his lack of loyalty. He had to renounce his country, which he left "with his face turned towards the deserted home, lamenting bitterly; he wore garments of mourning and sandals of untanned leather, hung the hide of a white dog on the frame of his carriage and left the hair of his horses uncut..."

The 'imperial roads'. The Emperor Ch'in Shih Huang-ti liked to travel up and down his land, so he had imperial roads built

in the regions of the Yellow River and in the valley of the
Yangtze. They were called the 'fast' or 'straight' roads, as the
Emperor had the hills levelled and the valleys filled up to make
them even. It is said that the width of these roads was 50 *pu*
(about 246 feet, 75 metres), and that they were flanked with pine-
trees. However, common people were not allowed to soil these
roads with their feet; they had to walk or drive through the
rough byroads.

'Ghosts' of chariots in the province of Honan. The chariots
unearthed at Liu Li Ko in 1950 date from the last period of the
Chou dynasty (fourth century B.C.). The remains of the vehicles
could not actually be excavated, for the wooden parts of the
poles, wheels and carriage-bodies were found decayed beyond
recovery; only the colour of the soil indicated their erstwhile
position. However, the tremendous patience and skill of the
excavators did not remain futile: they succeeded in reconstruct-
ing the vehicles on the basis of the traces they had left, as illustrated in Fig. 120. The chariots appear to have stood in two
rows, so that the poles of the vehicles in the back row stretched
into the body of those in front. In some cases the frame and the

120

121 Detail of the gate of the San-chi stupa
122 Battle on the bridge
123 Stone relief from a grave

sides of the body were varnished, which naturally helped to determine the place and shape of the vehicle. The chariots had probably formed a funeral procession. The horses were buried separately, but—contrary to the practice followed under the Shang dynasty—here the drivers survived the horses' funeral safe and sound. The grave of the dead individual, in whose honour the procession had been arranged, could not be found, although local inhabitants remembered that a grave had actually been discovered before World War II.

At the end of the Chou dynasty's reign, the Chinese forces consisted of a thousand chariots; each chariot was followed by 72 infantrymen and 25 attendants, so that, with the crew of three carried by the chariot, there were altogether one hundred men to each vehicle.

Under the Han dynasty, or perhaps even earlier, prior to the fall of the Chou dynasty, the chariotry and infantry gradually lost their superior position, while the more mobile cavalry gained ground. The wars against the 'barbarians' continued, but, to conclude them with success, the Chinese needed a fast-moving and well-equipped army. These circumstances practically put an end to the mobilizations required earlier from the liege-lords; their services were reduced to despatching occasional small numbers of chariots to the camps for a short time. The backbone of the imperial army was the permanent cavalry which did not shrink from lengthy campaigns on the steppes.

Cartage. While the glory of the war-chariot was waning, the heyday of the cart as a freight vehicle began. Though under the Han dynasty the only honourable work was agriculture, this outlook did not in the least prevent the populous class of craftsmen from drawing rich profits from the organization of the army. The soldiers needed clothing, arms and food; roads had to be built so that the troops might move along quicker. Willy-nilly, the emperors were obliged to support the activities of the army furnishers and carters. The number of vehicles possessed by some enterprising contractors ran to several hundreds.

The Chinese historian Sema Ts'ien depicts in sombre colours the situation prevailing in the country during the early Han period. "It was difficult to raise four horses of the same breed even for the state carriage of the Son of Heaven [the emperor]. The generals and high officials travelled by ox-drawn wagons, the same as the simple folk."

Some Chinese imperial carriages. According to the notions prevailing in Han China, the emperor embodied the universe; consequently, the imperial carriage was also part of the world: its body symbolized the earth; its round canopy, the sky; and

121

122

the flags decorating it represented the most important constellations. But this was not enough for Emperor Wu; he craved for even more extravagant carriages and practically emptied his treasury to ensure the services of Chao Wong, the great magician cartwright. True, what Chao Wong promised Wu was not to be

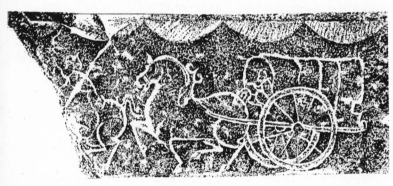

123

sniffed at, for he ensured the Emperor that—although it would cost the latter a tidy sum—he would design for the imperial household some very useful carriages indeed: their very irradiation would triumphantly repel all evil spirits. Incredible as it may seem, Chao Wong actually delivered the carriages he had promised (only we lack authentic information as to the results achieved with their aid in practice).

Shih Huang-ti, Emperor of the Ch'in dynasty, died on the shores of the Eastern Sea in 210 B.C. while searching for the elixir of eternal life. To nip the expected revolts of the pretenders in the bud, the Emperor's followers decided to keep his death secret. They wanted to take him back to the capital in the imperial chariot, behind drawn curtains, as if he were still alive, although this meant a journey of 1,650 *li* (about 594 miles or 950 kilometres). Meals were served to the dead Emperor as usual, the mandarins reported to him at regular intervals under way and even put questions to him, which were answered by the eunuchs behind the curtains. However, a small matter nearly prevented the execution of the plan: namely, in the hot summer weather the foul smell of the corpse became more and more unbearable around the imperial carriage. But the mandarins were too smart to be deterred from their plan by such trifles: they distributed a cargo of stale salted fish among the carriages of the suite, and the stench of this stifled every other smell.

124

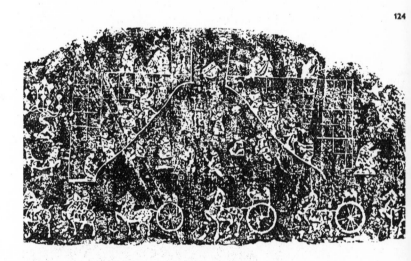

125

98

The cart with a pair of shafts. According to the Chinese characters (Fig. 119), carts with one pole and two draught-animals were known in China as early as the second millennium B.C. As already mentioned, this structure is clearly distinguishable in the pictographs. However, the carts and wagons figuring in the wall paintings, reliefs and cultic objects dating from the Han period and later, all have shafts (Figs. 121–126). Even two clay models (Figs. 127–128) represent vehicles with a pair of shafts.

127

One can tell at a glance that harnessing applied during the Han period differed from that used with the single-pole vehicles we have seen in the relics of prehistoric East. The bent thill shafts and special traces are characteristic features of the Chinese relics; they are the results of a perfectly independent development based on old Chinese traditions. (The thill shafts appeared in Europe only fourteen centuries later!) The difference between the European and Chinese way of harnessing to shafted vehicles was that while the Chinese horse was tied directly to the thill shafts, the European one was harnessed with traces or—at a more primitive stage—was tied direct to the vehicle or the swingletree.

128

Züschen. We have no authentic carriage from the European Stone Age, but some scholars regard as Neolithic the stone chest recovered at Züschen (Hessen-Nassau, German Federal Republic), one inside slab of which bears the extremely primitive engraved picture of a two-wheeled vehicle. According to the German archaeologist Jörg Lechler, the find dates from the first half of the

126

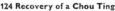

124 Recovery of a Chou Ting
125 Cart
126 Relief from a pedestal
127 Clay model cart and horse
128 Clay model cart

99

129

130

third millennium B.C. and represents a pair of long-horned yoke oxen, viewed from above (Fig. 129). Some may not find the fork-shaped figures very convincing, for they little resemble oxen seen from above, but the assumption is confirmed by the so-called Ligurian rock drawings. Fig. 130 shows one of the Val Fontanalba finds representing such long-horned oxen viewed from above. The dating of the Ligurian drawings—which fluctuates between the Late Stone Age and the Bronze Age—gave the archaeologists plenty of headaches. Real detective work has been carried on to throw light on the problem. On the basis of a number of similarly primitive drawings found more recently, some authorities on the subject now believe that the Ligurian rock drawings are Mesolithic (about 9000–5000 B.C.); others, however, suggest that they date from the middle of the second millennium B.C. because the drawing of a dagger resembling one of the Ligurian finds has come to light from the sixth shaft grave at Mycenae.

Malta. We have some indirect proofs of the Neolithic use of wheeled vehicles at Malta: tracks cut into rocks with a precision that may well amaze the modern spectator (Fig. 131) bear witness here to the Sisyphean work of Neolithic men. Themistocles Zammit, a Maltese historian, believes that the double tracks leading to the mountains were used in springtime to cart back to the slopes the masses of earth which the winter rains brought down into the valley. The carts used for this purpose have perished, but the tracks show beyond doubt that their gauge was four feet six inches (135 centimetres). It is also evident that they were two-wheeled vehicles as otherwise they would have got stuck in the tracks.

The earliest European actual carriage. The tombs of chieftains of the Andronovo civilization and the timber-lined cist-graves were often found to contain vehicles. The earliest European actual carriage was recovered from the second grave of the Storozhevaya mogila, a *kurgan* (grave-mount) south of Dniepropetrovsk, on the river Dnieper. The remains—consisting of a solid wheel of about 20 inches (50 centimetres) diameter, certain parts of the body and bits of the forked pole—are datable to c. 2200 B.C. The vehicle must have been a cart drawn by a single horse, as used by the stock-breeding tribes of the steppes who roamed with their herds between the Dnieper and the Volga.

The Budakalász carriage. This small clay model carriage (Pl. XV) was found in grave No. 177 of the cemetery at Budakalász, one of the Copper Age centres of Eastern Europe along the Danube, brought to light in 1953. The model—a toy-like, wagon-shaped vessel—lay in a cenotaph where it may have been

131

129 Oxen yoked to two-wheeled cart
130 Ligurian rock drawing
131 Ancient cart tracks in Malta
132 Plan of kurgan No. 9 at Tri Brata

buried around 2000 B.C. It is possible that the cenotaph was to preserve the memory of some distinguished member of a Danubian Copper Age tribe, who found his death in a way that prevented the burial of his corpse; he may have been torn to pieces by some wild beasts or drowned. It is presumable that in such cases the carriers of the Copper Age culture or, more specifically, of the Pécel culture, dug a cenotaph for the dead personage and placed the carriage in the pit to facilitate his journey to the next world. The model carriage in question rests on four wheels with slightly protruding hubs; lines scratched into the bottom of the model mark the axle; the carriage-body may be best compared to an upward-flaring quadrangular box whose four corners end in tips; the upper edge is decorated with a zigzag design. It may be assumed that—with the exception of the

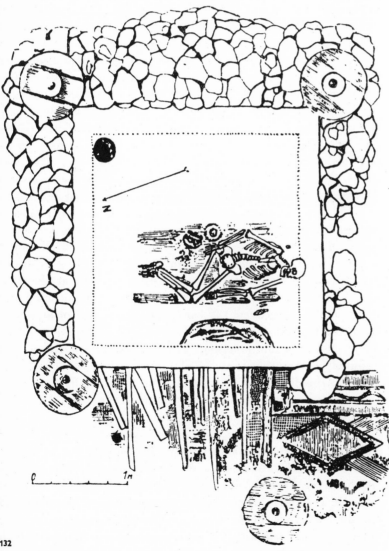

132

133

134

133 Clay model cart found in kurgan No. 9 at Tri Brata
134 Body of a model carriage
135 Stela from Znamenka, near the river Yenisei
136 Drawing on the Shuliek Rock
137 Remains of a carriage

135

pole which on the model is reduced to a lug—the small carriage is a comparatively precise replica of the type of wagon used by the Copper Age inhabitants of this Danube settlement. It represents at the same time an indirect proof of the fact that the agricultural settlers of this region, who at the beginning carried their burdens on their back or loaded them on pack-animals or boats, have reached a stage of evolution, at which cartage became normal: the raw materials or semi-finished products—practically in the nature of commercial goods—acquired by them at distant places were transported home in wagons. In other words: the vehicle which served as a model for the clay wagon was an implement of work.

The carriages of Central Asia and Siberia. The vast territories of Central Asia and Siberia, once inhabited by peoples of the Andronovo civilization and tribes which created the culture of timber-lined cist-graves, have yielded a wide range of extremely interesting carriages.

The covered wagon or caravan was a characteristic vehicle in these parts, evidently because of the pastoral life lead by the native population. Finds excavated near Tri Brata, a village in the Kalmyk steppes, from the later part of the timber-lined cist-grave civilization, bear witness to the Central Asiatic use of this type of conveyance. In *kurgan* No. 9, a small covered model carriage and four wheels were found (Figs. 132–133). The clay model, $6^2/_3$ inches (17 centimetres) high, is the replica of a cart, covered probably with felt or mat; its wheels and pole have perished (those seen in the drawing are reconstructed). Actual wheels, however, were also recovered from the same grave: in the middle of the *kurgan*, at the four corners of the seat round the pit, four 'real' wheels were found which must have belonged to two two-wheeled carts. The pole, with the yoke at the end, stretched forward from the front of the carriage. Although the yoke was found decayed, the excavators succeeded in making a mould of the imprints, so that its size and structure could be established with fair precision. This find confirmed the widely disputed presumption that the clay model (Fig. 134) excavated at Ul, in the district of Maikop, represented actually a covered carriage and not a model house or an urn in the shape of a house, as some experts maintained in the past.

Znamenka. The remarkable stela—a monument from the Andronovo civilization—excavated at Znamenka, near Bateni, on the river Yenisei (Fig. 135), plainly represents a covered carriage. The find is assigned to the Karasuk period, one of mutual cultural influence between the native inhabitants of South Siberia and the tribes immigrating into these parts from North

China. The close relation between the covered carriage represented on the stela and the vehicles seen on objects excavated near Anyang, the capital of Shang-Yin, bears witness to the cultural sway of the immigrants.

Minusinsk. Because of their geographical proximity and subject-matter, we have to mention at this point the rock drawing found opposite Minusinsk, and the other discovered on the river Yenisei; in addition to a variety of animals and equestrian figures, it shows the picture of a covered cart with a pair of shafts, drawn by a camel (Fig. 136).

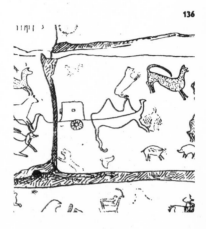

The Pazirik 'kurgans'. From among the large *kurgans* of the chieftains of nomadic tribes in the Altaic mountain regions, those in Pazirik are the most interesting from 'the carriage aspect'. In the valley of Ulagan, situated at an altitude of 5,250 feet (1,600 metres), several carriages were found dating from the middle of the first millennium B.C. It was established that all had been placed in the graves already broken up. Some of them were of the more primitive, solid-wheel type. Rudenko, the excavator of the graves, suggests that they served for carting the stones required for the construction of the *kurgan*. One vehicle, found in grave No. 5, differed in type from the others: it appeared to be a once-elegant state-carriage of fine workmanship (Figs. 137–138); its four multi-spoked high wheels had no tyres; the carriage-body—made of birch—was easy to dismember; the throne-like high seat was covered by a canopy of felt, decorated with swans cut out similarly from felt.

137

103

138 The same carriage reconstructed
139 Nomadic caravan, "as the Kunduran Tartars used it"
140 Clay model of a four-wheeled caravan

Nomadic tribes. In the first millennium B.C. the Eurasian steppes were inhabited by nomadic tribes or peoples just beginning to change over to agriculture. Owing to their similar way of living, involving constant migration, the classic authors often mix them up, so that what they state regarding one tribe usually applies also to all the others. Thus, for instance, Ammianus Marcellinus says that the Alans

had no huts and did not know the plough... they lived in travelling-carts covered by a curved bark roofing. These vehicles carried the tribes along the endless steppes. When a piece of good grazing-land was reached, they stationed their caravans in a circle and gathered food like wild beasts. Once the grass was fed down, the whole company set out to seek fresh pastures elsewhere. The caravan was the scene of their sexual life and the place of birth and growth of their offspring. It was their permanent abode wherever they went and meant 'home' to the members of the Alan tribe.

Similar descriptions recur in the classic historic works wherever the ancient nomadic tribes of the steppes are portrayed.

138

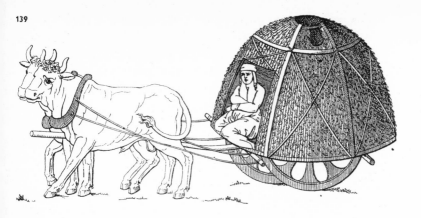

The Scythians. From among these migrating peoples, the Scythians are the best known to us; we have the most written reports on them, and the many archaeological finds relative to their carriages are particularly interesting. The word 'Scythian' is a collective denomination: it includes all the related tribes which in the seventh century B.C. took possession of the steppes in the northern regions of the tributaries of the Black Sea. Among other classical historians reporting on their life and customs, Herodotus, writing in the fifth century B.C., also tells us that their homes were hemispherical carriages which they covered with felt. A work attributed to Hippocrates gives a fantastic description of this vehicle. According to him, some of the wagons had two or even three 'rooms', they gave full protection against rain, snow and tempest; the smaller wagons had four wheels, the larger ones, six. This latter observation should, however, be viewed with a fair amount of doubt, for it is hard to imagine how such a long vehicle with a rigidly fixed frame could be steered even in the wide steppes. To complete this literary information we have to add here an imaginary graphic illustration according to Ginzrot (Fig. 139) which, in spite of its many anachronisms, has been reproduced in numerous works as an 'authentic' representation of the nomadic caravan.

The clay model (Fig. 140) dating from the third century B.C., excavated at Kerch on the Crimean Peninsula, constitutes a more reliable document and gives a better idea of the Scythian caravan. The nomadic life led by the Scythians remained for centuries the symbol of liberty in the steppes: "Far better live the Scythians of the steppes whose wagons haul their homes from place to place, as is their wont," writes Horatius.

Hearses. There are many other types of Scythian vehicles known to us, besides the caravan, and the most interesting among them is the funeral wagon. It was a Scythian custom to show the mourning tribe their dead chieftain in full pomp for the last time before he was buried. The hearse used for this ceremony was interred with the corpse. It was a richly painted and decorated four-wheeled wagon; bars terminating in bronze or iron were attached to the four corners of the box for the suspension of bells. In one of the more noteworthy Scythian *kurgans* excavated at Yelizavetina Stanitza (near the river Kuban), two hearses were found; on one of these the pale-blue, yellow and white paints could still be distinguished.

The caravan survives. Before ending here—at least for the time being—our review of nomadic caravan life, let us add that the force of habit and people's attachment to time-tested forms may be illustrated with numerous examples also in this field: the caravans and trailers of the modern holiday-maker or of those used by circus companies and gypsies permit us to follow the development of this type of vehicle to our own time, and ample data are available also to bridge the intervening centuries. To cite but one: the Flemish Franciscan monk Willem van Ruysbroeck (Rubruk) reports as an eye-witness that around 1255 the Mongolian nomadic tribes living along the lower reaches of the Volga advanced three to five miles (five to eight kilometres) daily with their cattle while dwelling in caravans.

The Scythians in the Carpathian basin. The thread we have followed leads us back to the Scythians. Although no written records are available on the subject, we know from archaeological finds that the Scythians crossed the Carpathian Mountains and settled in Transylvania around 600 B.C. Eighty years later another wave of Scythian immigrants reached the Hungarian Plain, bringing with them to their temporary new home their ancient funeral rites. At Szentes-Vekerzug, a village in the Hungarian Plain, they buried an actual four-wheeled wagon (Pl. XVI) in grave No. 13. Only the iron components of the vehicle, namely the tyre of the six-spoked wheel and the nave ring of the hub, survived; the carriage-body probably consisted of planks which rested on the axles.

At this stage we have to investigate more closely the question referred to on the preceding pages, namely, whether the wheeled vehicle came to Europe from the Middle East or was, so to speak, 'invented' here independently, as a result of an indigenous evolution. Both theories have numerous supporters. Those believing in the eastern origin of the wheeled vehicle designate two routes through which it may have reached Europe. One leads through the Middle East and the Caucasus, the other starts from Egypt and runs through the Aegean islands.

The Caucasian route. The archaeologist F. Hančar suggests that Transcaucasia—the territory of the present-day Georgian, Armenian and Dagestan Soviet Socialist Republics—constituted the 'bridge' through which Mesopotamian civilization in general, and the carriage in particular, crossed to Europe and Central Asia. We have to add, however, that this opinion does not enjoy the unanimous support of all scientific circles. The earliest Transcaucasian carriages (dating from about 2280 B.C.), unearthed at Shengavit Hill, near Yerevan, and at Shreshblur, Kyul Tapa (near Echmiadzin), are but solid wheels, made of clay, similar to those found in layer III at Anau Tepe and in layer II at Shah Tepe earlier, and—as we have seen—regarded almost common among the Mesopotamian finds. However, other finds also prove that around 1500 B.C. the Transcaucasian tribes were in contact with the more important centres of Middle Eastern serf civilization. Several vehicles have come to light in the central Georgian district of Trialeti, situated in the valley of the river Tsalka. The finest among them is the four-wheeled wooden carriage recovered intact, which is now the pride of the Tbilisi Georgian Museum of Fine Arts. Another carriage found in *kurgan* No. 29 shows that the chieftain buried there had been interred in his old-type wagon, together with his arms and treasures. The vehicle, 70 inches (1 metre and 80 centimetres) wide, had four tripartite wooden solid wheels of $44^1/_2$ inches (1 metre and 15 centimetres) diameter; since there was no sign of a pole, it is presumed that the vehicle was drawn by a rope. Apart from a few teeth, no other human remains could be discovered in the Tsalka valley graves. The probable explanation of their absence is that the tribes of these regions had adopted the funeral rites of the Hittite kings, according to which the corpse was cremated, and the carriage of the dead personage was placed in the middle of the grave. The adoption of this custom indicates that some intercourse must have existed between Trialeti and the Hittite Empire.

Further proofs of the Transcaucasian past of the carriage. The clay wheels found at Jemikent and the drawing of a carriage recovered at Berikey (both localities in the Dagestan Soviet Socialist Republic) represent further archaeological evidence in support of the early use of the carriage in Transcaucasia. The latter find (Fig. 141) was found, besides other engravings, on the inside slab of a stone chest of fine workmanship. It represents a cart, $19^1/_2$ inches (50 centimetres) long and $27^1/_3$ inches (70 centimetres) wide, viewed from above. The structure is clearly defined: the narrow carriage-body was rectangular, with rounded corners at the front; the axle was broad; the wheels had four spokes, and there was a yoke pegged to the pole.

141

141 Drawing of a cart

107

In the territory of the Armenian Soviet Socialist Republic, the Soviet scientist E. Lalayan excavated a large royal grave $124^4/_5$ inches (320 centimetres) long and $97^1/_2$ inches (250 centimetres) wide near Adiaman, on the southern shore of Lake Güekchay (Lake Sevan). The reason for its impressive size was that this pit contained also the skeletons of thirteen slaves or captive enemy soldiers; they lay scattered around the corpse of the royal personage buried with his arms, in full pomp. Although the carriage found in the same grave had rotted in the soil, its excavator made an attempt at reconstruction. He found three wheels in fair condition and assumed therefore that the vehicle had been a three-wheeled structure. This appeared the more probable as two of the wheels measured $29^1/_3$ inches (75 centimetres), and the third, only $23^2/_5$ inches (60 centimetres) in diameter. All the three were tripartite solid wheels. The reconstructed vehicle is presented here in Fig. 142; we have to add, however, that Russian literature on the subject does not accept the three-wheel solution.

142

The other route to Europe led through the Aegean Sea where the Isle of Crete filled the role of a 'relay station'. The narrow island of Crete is situated almost equidistant from Europe, Asia and Africa. Here, in the Middle Minoan period (about 1800 B.C.), the first four-wheeled wagon—the only form of vehicle known in this civilization—appeared in Palaikastro. It is presumed that similar vehicles had been used for the transport of building materials to the huge palaces constructed in Crete at that time. Two-wheeled war-chariots can be traced in Crete only after 1650 B.C.; no chariots figure in the hunting scenes before that date.

From among the Cretan war-chariots we present here only one find—the paired-draught chariot on a Prinian relief—which has a high, turned-up pole with a yoke pegged to its end (Fig. 143).

143

142 Carriage found in a grave near Adiaman
143 War-chariot on a relief at Prinia
144 Terra-cotta tablet with sign of a war-chariot and a horse

144

The Knossos terra-cotta tablets. The arms registers found on the terra-cotta tablets of the Knossos archives and listing swords, daggers, spears, armours, etc., mention also war-chariots. Further, the archives supply numerous interesting data relative to the use of wheeled vehicles. The frequent breaking of the wheels, for instance, appears evident from the fact that on one occasion the 'wheel-joiners', i.e. the wheelwrights, submitted a bill for the repair of 478 wheels. Similar data regarding vehicles and horses occur frequently in the records of the royal chancellery. One of the numerous tablets is shown in Fig. 144. (Note the schematic drawing of the war-chariot left of the horse's head.)

If we consider that the Mycenaean Greeks—who so to speak 'rocked the cradle' of Greek history—owed their civilization to the Cretans, we have the second route of the dispersion of the carriage clearly outlined before us. Its stations were: Egypt or the Middle East via Crete and Greece.

We cannot, however, rule out the possibility that peoples living under similar economic conditions in different parts of the world may have 'invented' the carriage independently. True, the wheeled vehicle appeared in Europe later than in Mesopotamia, but considering the isolated civilizations and the traffic conditions of the age, it is possible that the carriage was indigenous—if later—also in Europe.

It is difficult to foretell which of the current theories will be accepted by science as definitive in the future, as new archaeological remains may yet come to light; one thing is, however, certain, namely that the wheeled vehicle had rapidly gained ground in Europe and was so to speak 'lifted' by the cultural waves which surged through this continent. The wagon, and especially the war-chariot, were improved by the Greeks, the great promoters of European culture, in the first place. Greece is the next station of our journey in the wake of the development of the carriage.

Chapter V

The Greeks — The carriage of Homer's epic poems — The hearses — The Greek war-chariot — The cross-bar type wheel — Pleasure-driving — Chariot races — The Greek travelling-carriage — Roads and rut-roads — The diffusion of Greek culture — The chariot in Greek mythology — Western and Central Europe in the Bronze and Iron Ages — The stone chest of Kivik — Stonehenge, Trundholm, Skallerup, Peckatel, Milavec — Scandinavian rock drawings — Wheels — Carriages of the Hallstatt period — Representations on Pomeranian face-urns — Carriages of the La Tène period — The Dejbjaerg wagon — Britannia — The Celtic war-chariot — The Germans — The Goths

The Mycenaean Greeks who witnessed the birth of Hellas took over a great deal from the Cretan civilization and technology, although, compared to the luxuries of Cretan culture, life on the Greek mainland was much simpler. Many of the monuments which have come down to us from the Mycenaean period of Greek art, extending from the sixteenth to the twelfth century B.C., represent war-chariots (Fig. 145). They have been recovered from Mycenaean shaft-graves and probably illustrate chariot races, though some archaeologists are of the opinion that the stelae are marks of the religious belief that the personage buried in the grave had passed into the next world in a war-chariot proper to his rank and dignity. However, the chariot as a representational motif appears not only on stelae but also on carved gems, such as the one of *sardonyx*, shown in Pl. XVII.

Homer's epic poems also supply information on the carriage of the Mycenaean age. Despite the poetic style, the data contained in his works are perfectly realistic. In the *Iliad* we read, for instance, that Pandarus regretted bitterly that he had not brought with him to the campaign some chariots, although—as he says—eleven bright new ones stood in his father's royal palace. From this we may conclude with certainty that the chariot was an important and even indispensable implement of war, and that this was the number of chariots likely to be possessed by a royal personage. The part of the *Iliad* which begins with Hebe's fixing "bent wheels to her chariot, two eight-spoked bronze ones to the iron axle", although it refers to a goddess, actually illustrates a scene from everyday life; the description of the divine splendour —the golden felloes, the silver hub, the seat tied with gilded and silvered straps, the silver pole and gilded yoke—follows only thereafter. (The somewhat ambiguous reference to the strapped seat is regarded by some as the first sign of the suspended carriage-body.) The light weight of the war-chariots appears from the passage, in which Diomedes, accompanied by Odysseus, descends on the sleeping camp of the Thracian chieftain, Rhesos, and

145

145 Mycenaean stela representing a war-chariot
146 Detail of a Geometric vase
147 Detail of an amphora from Melos

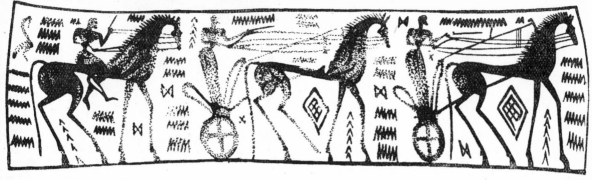

146

ponders whether he should draw the royal chariot away by its
pole or "lift it high and carry it off that way"—a procedure that
would have been impossible, had the chariot been heavy. According to Homer, a pair or, occasionally, three or four horses were
harnessed to a chariot, but even in the latter case only the pair
tied direct to the pole did the actual pulling. However, the references to vehicles in Homer's poems are not confined to the
war-chariot. We are told, for instance, that Priam went to
Achilles in his ox-drawn wagon to beg for the body of Hector,
and that it was a new and wonderful vehicle with a wicker cover.
In the *Odyssey* a road is mentioned, along which timber was
carted from the mountains to the castle of Lamos. In another
passage of the same work, Nausicaa also takes the washing to the
sea in a cart drawn by placid oxen, while in the *Iliad* we may
read of a chariot race and even learn about the ruses old Nestor
advised his son to use in the contest.

147

148

148 Detail of the so-called Chigi jug
149 Detail of a red-figured vase

149

XVII

XVIII

XIX Hydria with scene of harnessing from Vulci
XX Attican crater with representation of a quadriga
XXI Garden of the Hesperides with Heracles driving a biga

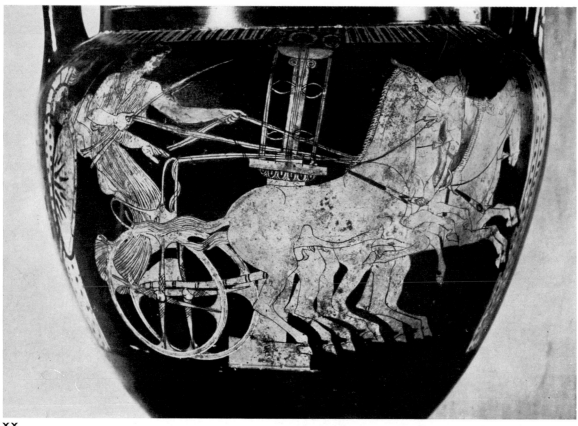

XX

XXII

XXIV

XXIII

XXV

XXVI

XXVII

XXXV

XXXVI

ΣΕVΣ ΟΡΑΝΙΑ

151

Hearses (Geometric style). Around 700 B.C. the chariot ceases to be an implement of war and from that time on is used only for hunting and racing. In turn, funeral wagons or hearses begin to appear on the Geometric sepulchral vases of the eighth century B.C. These large vessels with figured decorations were not buried with the corpse or used as urns but were placed on the graves to hold the sacrificial drink. On their outside surface the dead person was represented either on a hearse or a bier, but many of the vases showed war-chariots or racing-chariots (Pl. XVIII, Fig. 146).

The Greek war-chariot may be studied on a practically endless series of vases. The few reproduced here in Figs. 147–152 and Pls. XIX, XX and XXI give an idea of its form and structure.

114

The above-mentioned examples confirm that technologically the Greek chariot reached a high standard. Its body was extremely light; the frame was made of bent rods with their spaces filled in with woven thongs or wicker-work. The wheels were comparatively low so that the centre of gravity could be, if possible, at a deep point to prevent easy capsizing; they were made partly or completely of metal and rotated round a fixed axle. At first four spokes were used, but later their number was increased to six, seven or eight. The pole started from the carriage-body and stretched upwards; in some cases a second pole starting from the upper edge of the dashboard supported the lower pole, just as we have seen with the Assyrian carriage. Originally, the chariot was pulled by a pair, but later four horses were used. At the beginning of the sixth century B.C., the way of harnessing was changed: the outside horses of the *quadriga* were harnessed to the vehicle

151 Detail of an amphora by the Rycroft Painter
152 Detail of a crater by Polygnotos

152

115

153

154

with separate straps. This innovation remained in use for half a century, until it was discovered that it had no practical advantage at all, since the outside horses did not partake in the traction of the vehicle anyway.

Various other objects also contribute to our knowledge on the subject. From these we present two terra-cotta models (Figs. 153 and 154) and the picture on a bronze *crater* (Fig. 155).

Were the Greeks good technologists? In the 1920s Oswald Spengler was responsible for the erroneous idea that the man of the classical age must have been antagonistic to technology, and it was widely believed that the Greeks were a 'non-technical' people. As we have seen, the Greek war-chariot alone is enough to disprove this false notion, but the 127 columns of the Temple of Artemis at Ephesus, for example, supply further evidence in support of the Greeks' technical aptitude. No 'non-technical' people could have transported and set up such monumental columns. Vitruvius tells us about the high technical efficiency with which Chersiphron, one of the engineers partaking in the building of the Temple, had solved the problem: since owing to their heavy weight the marble columns could not be transported on wheels, Chersiphron had the columns rolled to the building site in cylindrical sheaves.

The cross-bar type of wheel. A further proof of the Greeks' efficiency in solving their technical problems is that, in addition to the spoked wheel which had to be wrought in the hands of specialized craftsmen, they produced—probably domestically— also simpler, cross-bar ('H'-type) wheels. It is evident that, while the high-born and rich upper social classes used the spoked wheel, the less wealthy had to content themselves with the cheaper

155

153 Terra-cotta horse-cart with amphorae
154 Terra-cotta funeral wagon
155 Warrior and war-chariot on the crater from Vix
156 Greek wedding procession
157 Lekythos with wedding procession by the Amasis Painter

cross-bar type. In his *Works and Days*, Hesiod gives precise instructions how to make a cart and cross-bar wheels, which also proves that the latter were widely used among the people.

116

The artists of the Greek vases, reliefs and other representations found the spectacular and decorative spoke-wheeled war-chariot a more profitable and popular subject than the cart or the wagon and seldom used their brush or chisel for the representation of such simple, rustic vehicles, unless it was to include them in some special scene.

156

157

117

159

158

Wedding, harvest, vintage and funeral scenes. Examples of the above may be seen in Figs. 156–159, showing a wedding procession, farm-workers and a funeral, respectively. It is interesting to note that in all these pictures the two-wheeled carts have the same cross-bar type of wheels. The uniform character of the illustrated vehicles proves that they represent the type generally used for domestic and agricultural jobs; only in exceptional cases were they turned to any other use.

The cross-bar type of wheel occurs even in our days, especially in China. In the Mongolian People's Republic (Ulyastay, Djabhan aymak) the cart-wheels are fitted with a strip of rubber tyre, of a type used everywhere today (Fig. 160) instead of the old type of rim, but this is about the only difference.

Pleasure-driving. The Greeks regarded driving as a mark of enervation and arrogance. Consequently, pleasure-driving was rather an exceptional sight. People usually rode asses or mules, and even women were discouraged from going out for drives.

Chariot racing is probably as old as the well-running chariot itself. 'Organized' and 'regular' chariot races began, however, probably with the Olympic games only, that is, in 776 B.C.; at least, this was the year in which the Greeks started to record the winners' names. The fact that the first chariot races coincided with the introduction of the Olympic games appears from the legendary description of the origin of the races. At the beginning they were organized in the open air; the racing-field was surrounded by a shallow ditch or a picket-fence; the two ends of the track were marked by a heap of stones or a wooden post. Later hippodromes were built for this purpose, usually in the midst of olive-groves. The hippodrome courses, 403 yards (370 metres) long, were not elliptical or rounded as the present-day race courses but straight, with a 'hair-pin bend' at each end, marked by poles. Passing there and back counted as one full length; this had to be covered six or twelve times in a race.

158 Detail of a black-figured vase
159 Funeral scene
160 Cart with cross-bar type wheels

118

The racing-chariots had low wheels to ensure a deep centre of gravity, lest the vehicle should tip over easily. The body was only large enough to hold a driver in standing position; it was made of metal, covered with bark-matting and padded at the front to permit the driver to lean against the dashboard with his knees.

Chariot racing soon developed from a competition between drivers into a passionate pastime for the spectators, the 'fans'. Parties and factions were formed. The increasing sway of the craze for races appears from the *Clouds* by Aristophanes, which contains many references to the chariot. Right at its beginning, Strepsiades, a citizen of Athens, complains about his son's passion for the races. "He rides, he drives, he dreams of horses..." says the anxious father. We also learn from Aristophanes something about prices, for Strepsiades owes twelve ounces for a race-horse, and three for a light carriage and two wheels, which means that a race-horse must have cost four times as much as a chariot. People of rank kept racing-stables; we know, for instance, that in 416 B.C. Alcibiades took part in the Olympic races with nine chariots, which carried off the first, second and fourth prizes.

The travelling-carriage was known also in Greece. Plutarch describes how, when on their way to Delphi, the Peloponnesian

160

ambassadors slept with their wives and children in a travelling-carriage at Megara and were pushed into a nearby lake, carriage and all, by some Megaran drunkards. The Greeks called the covered carriage *harmamaxa;* it was a vehicle chiefly for the use of women and old people.

The roads. Communication was naturally hindered by the lack of good roads. Four-wheeled wagons were rarely used because the Greek terrain and the condition of the roads suited the two-wheeled carts better. According to Pausanias, many of the Greek roads were "steep and tiring even for the pedestrians", and many were impassable by carriage because of their narrowness.

Stone rut-roads. Similarly to the Maltese, the Greeks also cut tracks into the rocks, mainly on roads leading to the temples. The carts loaded with the statues of gods and sacrificial offerings were pushed in these two inches deep ruts. In some places, however, similar ruts were cut also for secular purposes, especially in the mountain regions where it was necessary to make the

161

rolling of the vehicles safer. Confined to the tracks, naturally, it was difficult for carts to pass one another, and this gave rise to many a bitter dispute. The fatal quarrel between Oedipus and Laios which, as we know, ended in Oedipus' killing his father probably also started with a dispute over shunting.

The diffusion of Greek culture. During the centuries preceding our era, Greek culture spread also to the Middle East and Egypt, carrying along with its many products the actual carriage and its various forms of representation. The convergence and amalgamation of the different styles gave birth to new variants of a mixed character. This may be well studied on the relief found near Brussa (Fig. 161). The contrast between the details of the relief is striking: the driver and the horses are definitely Grecian in style; the former, instead of standing erect, assumes a supple bearing, while the saddled horse (the one on the left) tosses its head in a way that departs widely from the accepted rules of eastern art. Against this, the wheels bear witness to eastern influence: they have eight spokes instead of four.

The chariot in Greek mythology. Naturally, the Greeks also believed the chariot to be of supernatural origin and readily used it as a mythical element. Thus according to the Greek myth, Erechtheus was the first who dared harness a horse to a carriage. As a reward for this feat Zeus made him driver of the stars. Eos, the rosy-fingered goddess of dawn, clad in a saffron-coloured mantle, emerges from the ocean in a chariot. The name of Phaethon, son of Helios, is also closely linked with a celestial vehicle: according to the myths, he begged his father to allow him to drive the sun-chariot only for a single day. Old Helios was reluctant to consent, and—as it appears from the rest of the story—his anxiety was well founded, for the horses bolted with the sun-chariot and rode so near the earth that the forests caught fire, the rivers dried out, and destruction threatened the whole terrestrial world. Zeus then hurled thunderbolts at Phaethon to save the earth. The most frequently represented myth relating to the chariot is perhaps that of the race between Pelops and Oenomaos or the preliminaries leading up to this event. Scenes of these appear on the Olympian Zeus Temple and on numerous vases. According to Pausanias, it took place as follows. Oenomaos, king of Elias, would give his daughter, Hippodamia, in marriage only to the suitor who first beat him in a chariot race, but any gallant who failed was to pay with his life. However, Hippodamia fell passionately in love with one of the young men, named Pelops. To save his life, she sacrificed that of her father. She hired Oenomaos' driver, Myrtilos, to replace the iron nails in the King's chariot by black waxen ones. During

162

the race the wheels came off, the chariot turned over, and the King, thrown to the ground, was stabbed to death by Pelops.

Now let us leave the Greeks at this stage and examine the rôle the carriage played in other parts of Europe in the same period.

Western and Central Europe in the Bronze and Iron Ages. In the south-east and south Mediterranean territories agriculture and stock-breeding quickened the pace of evolution, compared to other parts of Europe where progress was slower and showed marked differences in the various regions. While Greek civilization was already flourishing, the tribes and peoples of Western and Central Europe had not even reached the first stage of civilized society, that is, the organized state; while in the north the Bronze Age still prevailed.

The huge stone chest found in 1748 at Kivik (Scania, south-west Sweden), measuring 13 feet 7 inches (4 metres and 14 centimetres) in length, 35 inches (90 centimetres) in width and 47 inches (one metre and 20 centimetres) in height, dates from the northern Bronze Age. In all probability, it was the tomb of a chieftain. Slab VII of the chest (Fig. 162) is of particular interest to us. It shows the roughly sketched but still clearly recognizable outlines of a racing-chariot, with two four-spoked wheels. Although the driver looks as if he were floating in the air, actually he is in a standing position and urging his horses forward. The reins do not pass through a ring but lead direct to the horses' mouths, as seen on the Mycenaean sepulchral stelae. All experts agree that the tomb dates from the Bronze Age, but opinions differ as to whether it should be assigned to period I, II or III of that age. It is also unanimously believed that the slabs of the tomb represent ritual scenes, which implies that the vehicle in question must have been a holy or processional chariot. First it was driven round in the ceremony, after which it served for racing or even fighting. The scene on the Villfara stone (Fig. 163) —a find from the same place and age—also includes a chariot.

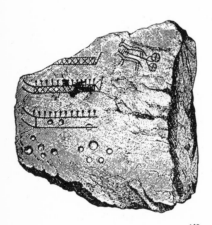

163

Stonehenge. This famous British Bronze Age monument near Amesbury (Wiltshire) is a circle of megaliths which once served as a ritual centre and burial place. It was probably built in several stages from the beginning to the end of the Bronze Age. Stuart Piggott assigns part of the structure to the middle of the second millennium. His dating is based on radiocarbon methods, and some arms and tool designs found engraved in the stones. Here was also a race course, 3,030 yards (2,700 metres) long, near the monument, specially built for chariot races—an item of the funeral games apparently.

162 Horse-drawn chariot on slab of a stone chest in a tomb
163 Horse-drawn chariot on a stone
164 Cultic chariot of Dupliaya

122

Ritual chariots. From the Bronze Age onwards, the archaeological finds include numerous wheeled sun symbols, sacrificial scenes and cauldrons, related evidently to some religious cult or after-life conception.

The only Central European Bronze Age finds of importance are the works of art of the Danubian Versec culture, which happen to include chariots used for cult purposes. Two such vehicles have been recovered at Dupliaya in the Voivodina region (Yugoslavia); the one is a two-wheeled chariot, the other (Fig. 164)

164

has two wheels at the back and a third wheel in the front between shafts. The latter work is assigned to about 1400 B.C. The German scholar E. Sprockhoff traced it to the classic Greeks, and his dating is, indeed, supported by a *paian* (chorus) of Alkaios, fragments of which have come down to us. According to these, Zeus wanted to send the newborn Apollo to Delphi in a swan-drawn chariot to proclaim justice and law to the Greeks. The Dupliaya find is supposed to be the earthly equivalent of the mythical carriage.

The Trundholm chariot. This famous Bronze Age discovery (Pl. XXII), dating from about 1300–1200 B.C., was uprooted from the earth at the bottom of a bog near Nykjbing by a plough in September 1902. Although it fell to pieces, its reconstruction did not present any difficulties. The gold disk weighing three and a half pounds (1.55 kilos) is probably a sun symbol. There is no doubt about its having some magic or religious implication, nor about its representing a celestial body, but whether it is the sun

123

or the moon is still an open question, widely discussed among experts. The solution of the problem depends on whether in ancient Europe time was reckoned according to the solar or lunar course. Many investigators maintain that a lunar calendar was used. From our point of view it is, however, of little import whether the disk represents the sun or the moon or—as some other scholars believe—the image of some deity. The fact remains that it served for ritual purposes and, according to the position of other broken objects found in the bog, had been thrown into the water—the Trundholm bog was still a lake at that time—as part of some ceremony. The horse and the carriage were mounted on six four-spoked wheels.

Skallerup, Peckatel and Milavec. These three queer names denote find-spots situated (from north to south) in Denmark (Sjaelland), Germany (Mecklenburg) and Czechoslovakia, respectively. In each of them wheeled cauldrons dating from the Bronze Age have come to light. Regarding the Skallerup relic presented in Fig. 165, some archaeologists believe that it originated in some part of Central Europe, from where it was imported by the Danes. The Peckatel find which—similarly to the Skallerup one—has been recovered from a tomb is a simple bronze cauldron on four wheels (Fig. 166). The Milavec carriage resembles the latter. The wheeled cauldrons were probably used to contain the ashes of cremated chieftains.

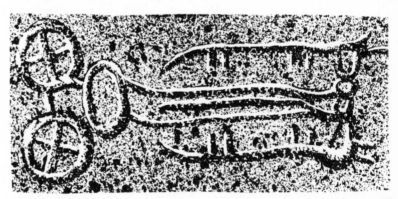

The Scandinavian rock drawings. These extremely interesting remains of the northern Bronze and Iron Ages form a practically inexhaustible archive of the prehistory of the Scandinavian peninsula. They represent a wide range of subjects, among which the carriage occurs frequently (Figs. 167–170). Most of the representations are engraved on polished slabs of solitary rocks.

The above-mentioned rock drawings confirm that the two-wheeled chariot and four-wheeled wagon were known in the north of Europe in the Bronze Age. Certain structural features of the

165 Cauldron on wheels
166 Bronze cauldron on wheels
167 Wagon from a rock drawing at Rished
168 Wagon from a rock drawing at Langön
169 Rock drawing resembling a cultic carriage
170 Rock drawing with representation of carriages and drivers

124

wagons represented have survived until today and can still be seen on the four-wheeled vehicles used in rural Sweden and in the south-western corner of Finland.

It is practically impossible to tell which of these rock drawings belong to the Bronze Age and which to the Iron Age; we are therefore presenting them together, even if this means striding ahead in history into the Iron Age.

168

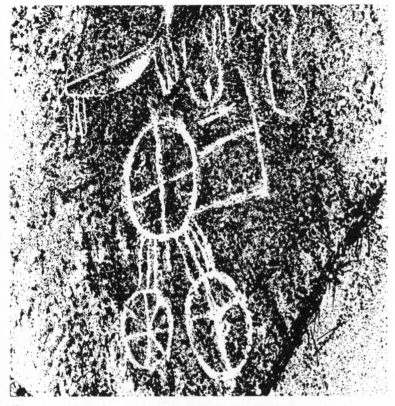

169

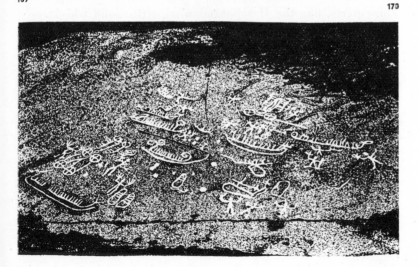

170

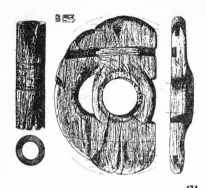

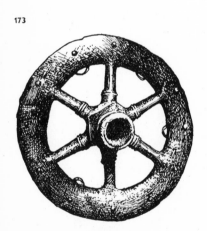

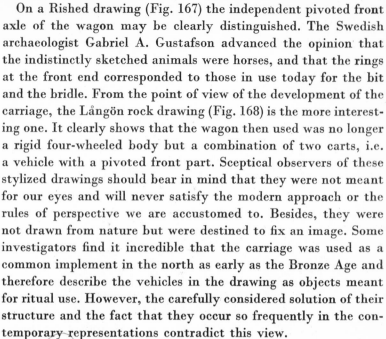

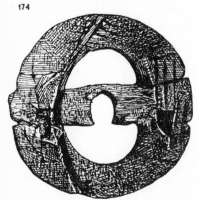

On a Rished drawing (Fig. 167) the independent pivoted front axle of the wagon may be clearly distinguished. The Swedish archaeologist Gabriel A. Gustafson advanced the opinion that the indistinctly sketched animals were horses, and that the rings at the front end corresponded to those in use today for the bit and the bridle. From the point of view of the development of the carriage, the Långön rock drawing (Fig. 168) is the more interesting one. It clearly shows that the wagon then used was no longer a rigid four-wheeled body but a combination of two carts, i.e. a vehicle with a pivoted front part. Sceptical observers of these stylized drawings should bear in mind that they were not meant for our eyes and will never satisfy the modern approach or the rules of perspective we are accustomed to. Besides, they were not drawn from nature but were destined to fix an image. Some investigators find it incredible that the carriage was used as a common implement in the north as early as the Bronze Age and therefore describe the vehicles in the drawing as objects meant for ritual use. However, the carefully considered solution of their structure and the fact that they occur so frequently in the contemporary representations contradict this view.

Wheels. Bronze Age wheels may be studied not only on rock drawings but also on actual finds. Most of them have been recovered from the swamps and bogs of Scandinavia (Figs. 171–172). In France quarrymen working on a high hill in La Côte-Saint-André (*Dép.* Isère) found four spoked wheels of bronze. Their casting bears witness to excellent workmanship; their diameter is $20^1/_3$ inches (52 centimetres); the length of the hub measures $13^2/_3$ inches (35 centimetres) (Fig. 173).

Of the two Italian wheels found among the remains of lake dwellings near Mercurago (Lago Maggiore), one is generally believed to be a Bronze Age wheel (Fig. 174). It is composed of three parts, like the Mesopotamian tripartite solid wheels, with the difference, however, that the two outer parts are bent to a semicircle, and the axle-hole is bored into the middle part forming the diameter of the wheel. There is thus a semicircular space between each of the two outer curved parts and the straight middle part.

The other wheel (Fig. 175), as we already mentioned before, dates from a later period: it has six spokes which are not radially arranged as usual but resemble the H-type design.

According to H. Mötefindt, the above described wheels represent the 'missing link' between the solid wheel and the spoked wheel. The trouble is, however, that they are, beyond doubt, more recent than the perfect spoked wheels found in Mycenae and Knossos, not to mention the still older Asian wheels. Gordon V. Childe is therefore right in stating that the famous Mercurago wheels which have given rise to such copious use of printer's ink are only the products of a wheelwright who had seen a spoked wheel without being initiated into the mysteries of its construction.

Many features of the Bronze Age wheel persisted in the Iron Age, even in the La Tène period. Thus the hub remained equally long on both sides, compared to the plane of the spokes. As the physical laws of camber were unknown, the wheels suffered lateral thrust on the uneven roads, which naturally shortened the life of the spokes.

175

The Hallstatt period. Carriages buried with the dead during the early Iron Age, known as the Hallstatt period, have been recovered in large quantities in many parts of Europe, from northern Spain to France, the Rhineland and Switzerland, and from southern Germany to Czechoslovakia, Hungary and Rumania. The peoples then inhabiting these areas (Celts and Illyrs) were liberal in filling the graves with various objects, including in many cases complete carriages. The latter were not hearses or funeral wagons but ordinary conveyances, interred together with the jewellery and arms of the dead personage for his use in the next world.

In France Hallstatt-period *tumuli* containing carriages have been found in particularly large numbers in the *départements* of Champagne, Marne and Aisne. The richest carriage grave of the so-called Marne culture is the famous La George-Meillet *tumulus*. In this the remains of the corpse were found lying between the wheels, with a sword and battle-axe on his left, and a spear and a bundle of rods on his right.

The so-called eastern group of find spots which is closely related to the Rhineland and South Germany, and which, together with these regions, forms an archaeological province extending from Central France to Czechoslovakia has many sites abounding in remains of carriages. The vehicles found in the graves are four-wheeled; the spokes are of wood, but they are covered with bronze or wrought iron.

Strettweg. Among the ritual carriages of the Hallstatt period, the Strettweg (near Judenburg, Steiermark, Austria) carriage is the most famous one (Fig. 176). This is not surprising if one considers that on the vehicle is represented a whole sacrificial scene. In the middle a goddess is seen, raising high a sacrificial vessel; she is surrounded by four lancemen and two mounted figures. The carriage is probably the product of a Central Italian workshop; it dates from the seventh century, but was buried only in the fifth century B.C. A similar ritual carriage, made of lead, was recovered from a Hallstatt-period graveyard at Frög

171 Wheel from the Dystrup Bog
172 Wheel, found at Lilla Mellösa
173 Wheel of a processional carriage
174 Wooden three-piece wheel from the peat-bog at Mercurago
175 Wooden wheel made of several pieces from the peat-bog at Mercurago

127

(near Rosegg) in 1882, where it lay beside a human skeleton (Fig. 177).

Kánya. The carriage-urn excavated at Kánya (County of Somogy, Hungary, Fig. 178) also belongs to the ritual carriage category in a wider sense of the word. It is a sepulchral urn on wheels, which contained the ashes of a cremated body; the top of the vessel was covered with a plate. According to József Csalog, the Hungarian archaeologist who first reviewed the find, the idea the early Iron Age man had in mind was that the dead personage passed into the next world in a carriage.

In this connection Csalog refers to the graphite-incised figured urn with incised ritual scene found at Sopron (Fig. 179). The scene represents a funeral service or procession and the sacrifice to be offered, or perhaps a journey into the next world.

176

128

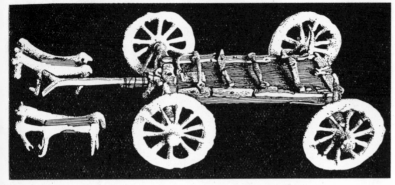

177

The so-called Pomeranian face-urns—a characteristic type of sepulchral vessels, moulded in the shape of a human face—are closely related to the Scandinavian rock drawings and to the incised scenes on the Sopron urn. They come from the territory between the Lower Vistula and the Lower Oder. Some of the primitive incised drawings figuring on them also represent carriages (Pls. XXIII and XXIV). The face-urns prove beyond doubt that rationally designed wagons with spoked wheels and a pair of shafts were already in use in these regions between 800 and 500 B.C.

178

Regarding the Hallstatt war-chariot some idea may be gathered from the upper row of the decoration on the Kuffarn bronze *situla* (Fig. 180).

179

The La Tène carriages. In the La Tène period of the Iron Age—which followed the Hallstatt culture and represents an epoch associated with the Celts—the carriage burials became more frequent. A chieftain's grave excavated at Somme-Bionne revealed two wheels buried in separate holes (Fig. 181); the pole of the same vehicle was led from the main pit into a smaller one through a channel 27$^1/_3$ inches (70 centimetres) long; the harness was found in the same place as the pole. The skeleton lay between

129

180

181

the wheels; originally the body must have rested in the funeral cart. The wheel gauge measured $54^2/_3$ inches (1 metre and 40 centimetres). In contrast to the Hallstatt-period carriage structures, the La Tène vehicles are all two-wheeled; the carriage-body is closed at the front and open at the back.

The origin of the Celts—the carriers of the La Tène culture—is lost in the mists of time. Their home was in the Upper Marne and Upper Rhine regions. From our point of view they represent an important ethnic group, for they were the most skilful cartwrights of ancient times. Migrating to Gaul, the Iberian peninsula and the British Isles, and later to Northern Italy, South and Central Germany, Czechoslovakia, Hungary and the Balkan peninsula, they spread their civilization throughout Europe. The cartwright technique of the antique world owes a great deal to the Celts. The Romans took over the Celtic carriage types, including their names, for example the *carpentum* (a two-wheeled state-carriage) and the *raeda* (their most common travelling-vehicle).

The Bell carriage. It is impossible to dwell in detail on the wide range of Celtic vehicles which have come to light, but as an interesting example we present the Bell carriage (German Federal Republic) (Fig. 182) whose remains confirm beyond doubt that the front axle turned on a pivot.

The Dejbjaerg wagon. In 1881 and 1883 some mysterious bits of wood, bronze and iron were found in the swamps of Dejbjaerg,

130

near Ringkjbing (Denmark). It was only later that they were identified as the parts of two wagons. One was successfully reconstructed (Fig. 183), although there is still some doubt regarding the proper placing of some of the components. Only the wheels and the axles are indisputably authentic; the assembling of the four sides of the carriage-body and the fixing of the latter to the axles has given rise to some controversy among the experts. One of the disputed points is whether the front axle of the vehicle could be swung sideways or not. Some analogies bear evidence to the affirmative. This theory was accepted also by

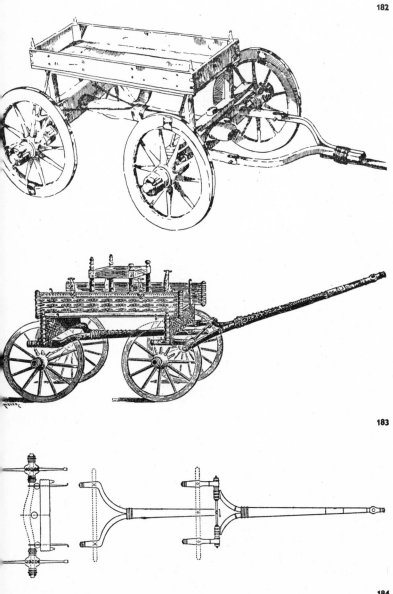

182

183

184

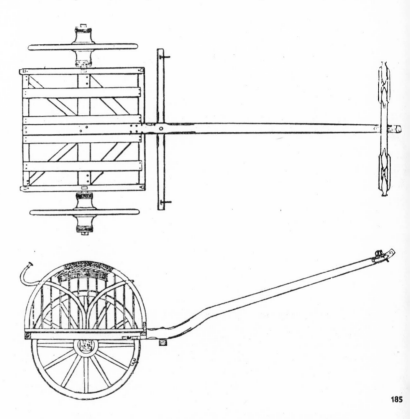

185 Reconstruction of the Celtic chariot found at Llynn Cerrig

O. Klindt-Jensen whose drawing of the components of this carriage is shown in Fig. 184. The hub is provided with bronze lining both inside and outside; the wheel has thirteen spokes, this being perhaps regarded as a lucky number.

War-chariots. Between the fifth and third centuries B.C. only the western Celts continued to use the chariot for military purposes. The Celtic war-chariot is well known to us both from the tombs of chieftains and from other reconstructed archaeological relics (Fig. 185). They were built chiefly of wood, leather and

185

wicker-work. Not a single Celtic chariot axle has survived, but some wheels have been recovered intact. They had ten to fourteen lathe-turned spokes of hornbeam or pine wood. The hub which was made of elm or pine protruded fairly prominently; in some cases its length reached even twelve to fifteen inches (30 to 38 centimetres). The felloe was bent of a single piece of ash wood and was fitted with an iron tyre.

In Britain the Celtic chariot persisted longer than elsewhere; numerous archaeological finds and literary sources confirm this assumption. The most important finds come from Celtic burial places, called 'Danish Graves'. (The name itself has of course no ethnic implication at all.) Some of the richest La Tène horse

132

furniture and carriage elements were recovered near Stanwick in Yorkshire. A further relic which was found at Glastonbury, Somerset, is a very interesting lathe-turned hub with twelve spokes. In the years 1815–1817, the Rev. E. W. Stillingfleet excavated three graves between the Arras and Hessleskew farms in Yorkshire, about three miles from Weighton. In the romantic style of the age they were named the King's Grave, the Queen's Grave and the Charioteer's Grave. The first contained the remains of an old man lying in a chariot whose iron and oak components (tyre and hub) survive. The Queen's Grave did not contain any vehicle, but in the third grave the skeleton lay on a shield in a carriage. In 1877 Canon Greenwell opened up a further carriage grave; in this two wheels lay next to each other on one side of the skeleton.

The historians' view on the Celtic war-chariot. The chariots and the military tactics of the Celts of Britain have been described in full detail by Strabo and Diodoros; their reports are, however, probably based on earlier patterns, left by still more ancient historians and applying to battles fought elsewhere and between other enemies. This cannot be said of the records of Julius Caesar, for they are based on his personal experience. In his *De bello Gallico* he tells us that when the Seventh Roman Legion left their camp in Britain in 55 B.C., they were attacked by the British cavalry and chariotry. Caesar describes the event as follows: —

> This is how the chariotry fights: First they career all round the enemy, throwing missile weapons; generally, they scare the horses and create confusion among the enemy troops by the mere din of their wheels. Once they penetrate the lines of the cavalry, they jump off their chariots and continue to fight on foot. Meanwhile the drivers gradually retire from the battle scene and take up a position that may be reached by the warriors without difficulty, should heavy odds force them to retreat. Thus they combine the speed of the cavalry with the perseverance of the infantry. With daily training and inuring they have acquired such skill that even driving at full gallop they can stop their horses short on unexpected steep slopes; they are able to use their brakes and turn round instantaneously; they can run forward on the pole, stand on the yoke and thence jump back into the carriage.

It appears from the above description that tactically the war-chariot was used only for approaching the enemy at a high speed and for creating a psychological effect conducive to the success of the attack.

Tacitus tells us that the Britons took their wives along to the battle that the latter might witness their victory; the women were seated in wagons at the edge of the battle-field.

The Germans migrated from their North European settlements to the south, as far as the Rhine, between the sixth and first centuries B.C. It is held that they easily turned their backs on the dwelling-places they had lost interest in, or which were no longer of any special value, and often went off to seek new homes elsewhere. On such occasions they travelled with their families and chattels by four-wheeled wagons. Our knowledge of the Germans conforms more or less with the information Tacitus gives us in his writings about this race; in fact, generally Tacitus is quoted whenever the customs and implements of early German tribes are discussed. It is from this ancient literary source of German prehistory that we know that the Germans harnessed snow-white horses to their ritual wagons, and that the same horses were never used for any work benefitting man. According to Tacitus, the Germans worshipped the Earth Goddess, Nerthus.

> In an island of the ocean is a holy grove and in it a consecrated chariot, covered with carpets; a single priest is permitted to touch it; he interprets the presence of the goddess in her shrine and follows with deep reverence as she rides away, drawn by oxen.

Carriages of indisputably German origin are very scarce. The few vehicles which may have been used by the Germans are similar to the Celtic type. This is only natural, considering that the Germans were behind the Celts in civilization, and most implements requiring a higher technical skill or knowledge were taken over by them from the Celts.

The Goths left the shores of the Baltic to migrate to those of the Black Sea in the third century. Christianity began to spread among them a century later, but Athanaric, the king of the Western Goths, condemned the new creed. Sozomenos tells us that, to trace the secret Christians, he gave orders for an idol— probably a deity of their ancient religion—to be placed in a carriage and taken to the tents of the suspected converts. Those who did not receive it with due reverence gave away their Christian belief. The carrying round of ritual pictures by vehicles appears to be based on ancient customs. In his writings about converted Goths, St. Ambrose states that "The carriage which was once their home now serves as their temple." The wheeled vehicle must have played at least as important a part in the life of the Goths as it did in that of the nomads of the steppes; they used it not only as a dwelling and a temple but also as a fortification: when later the Roman emperor Gallienus attacked the Goths, it was their wagon camp which saved them from perishing. The army of the Goths owed their escape to a 'carriage fortification' formed of covered wagons also in their war against Emperor Claudius and in the Adrianople battle in 378 A.D.

Between the Bronze Age and the end of the La Tène period, the carriage was modernized by numerous innovations which greatly increased its use. One of the major improvements introduced was the application of the pivoted front axle.

In connection with the 'family-tree' of the carriage, we have stated in Chapter I that the wagon with a pivoted front part was of a different origin than the four-wheeled box-wagon with fixed axles (like the one on the 'standard' of Ur). While the latter developed from the sledge, the wagon with the pivoted front axle was a combination of two carts. The Långön rock drawing (Fig. 168)

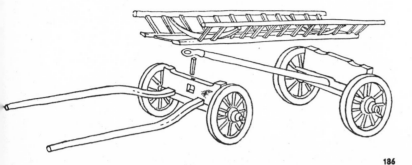

186

clearly illustrates this evolution, and—taking that the reconstruction is correct—the Dejbjaerg carriage also shows a primitive pivoted front axle. For easier comprehension we present the Italian (Sandrio) wagon (Fig. 186) which is a yet more modern example illustrating the above-mentioned development. However, the Celts knew nothing about the technical advantages of camber, i.e. that if the wheel is not fixed at a right angle to the axle but has a certain downward-inward inclination, with the pin strictly in horizontal position, it has a certain latitude to wobble and is less exposed to lateral pressure. The camber of spokes was a still later invention.

Chapter VI

The Etruscans — The Etruscan carriage and war-chariot — The Romans — The *plaustrum* — The *carpentum* — The *pilentum* — The use of carriages by women... and by men — The Roman roads — How the Romans travelled — The *raeda* and the *carruca dormitoria* — The *cisium* — Illustrious travellers — The *cisiarii* — The Roman post — Notes from the history of the *cursus publicus* — The posting-system in the East-Roman Empire — The Theodosian Code — The load-carrying capacity of the carriages — Other types of Roman carriages — Street traffic — Funeral processions — Triumphal processions — Chariot races — The *tensa* — The circus chariot races and the drivers — Technical innovations to the Roman carriage — Thracian carriages — Pannonian carriages — The Adamklissi victory memorial

The Etruscans. Before examining the history of the Roman wheeled vehicles, we have to go back to their origin and consider in the first place the rôle of the Etruscans. Regarding the widely discussed provenance of this people, let us confine ourselves to stating that they immigrated probably from Asia Minor and came into contact with flourishing Greek colonies in Italy.

Thus the Italian–Etruscan civilization developed mainly under Greek influence. This is manifest also in the Etruscan carriages and harnessing. Yet there are certain types of vehicles of Etruscan origin which have no Greek analogy, as, for instance, the official carriage of the Etruscan magistrate (Pl. XXV).

The wagon-burial, while unknown to the Greeks, was a widespread custom with the Etruscans. The earliest Etruscan relics

187 Bronze Etruscan chariot
188 The last journey

187

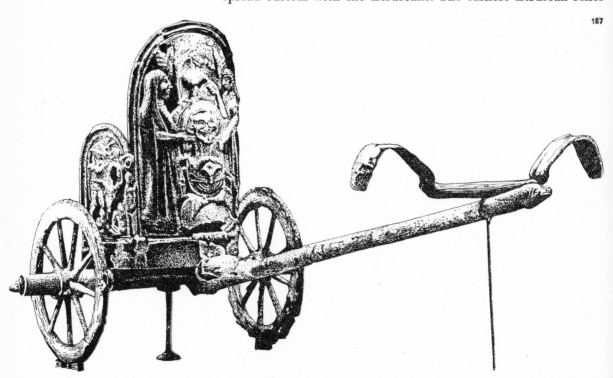

136

188

of such burials were found in Vetulonia; other wagons have been excavated from a grave at Marsiliana; but the best example of the richness of Etruscan graves is the Tomba Regolini-Galassi discovered at Caere (now Cerveteri) in 1836. The fabulous treasures piled up in this grave could have been accumulated only by a wealthy and powerful man. Apparently he did not wish to part from his treasures even after death, so he had all his belongings, including wife and carriage, buried in his grave.

The Etruscan war-chariot followed the Greek example in every respect but may be regarded at the same time as the archetype and model of the Roman war-chariot. The characteristic Etruscan racing-chariot, the *triga* (Pl. XXVI), is represented on a series of reliefs and vases. The remarkable and important bronze chariot recovered at Monteleone di Spoleto is now a carefully guarded treasure of the New York Metropolitan Museum (Fig. 187). Its perfection bears witness to the high technical skill and artistic sense of its maker. The two wheels with typical protruding hubs are of excellent workmanship, but the three bronze reliefs decorating the carriage are apt to rouse even greater admiration. The one on the left side of the vehicle represents a chariot scene.

Journeys into the other world. On the burial stelae—which are Bolognese specialities—the dead proceed towards their destination in the next world on various types of *bigas* (Pl. XXVII). The relief of a sarcophagus found at Vulci also represents such a last journey. The couple is seated on a cross-bar type carriage whose bottom is raised high above the shaft (Fig. 188).

The wagon and cart appear less frequently on the Etruscan products of art than the chariot or the carriage. As a rule, the

137

former are represented with solid wheels or cross-bar wheels; the latter, with spoked wheels. The original of the small bronze cart drawn by a pair of cows (Fig. 189) very likely also ran on cross-bar wheels, and only technical difficulties have forced the maker of its small model to indicate the bars by two protuberant lines only.

The Etruscan finds include a wide range of various cult and practical objects placed on wheels. Thus, for instance, the lower part of the heating-pan with a figure, shown in Pl. XXVIII, also forms a perfect four-wheeled vehicle.

The Etruscan culture preserved its individual character even after the whole of Etruria had come under Roman suzerainty in the third century B.C. The cultural impact of the Etruscan people penetrated into practically every field of Roman life; the Romans adopted their carriage types and carriage-building methods as well as their road-constructing techniques and incorporated them into their own civilization.

The Romans. The above process was the more natural as the Romans themselves were no great masters in the art of carriage-building. On the other hand, they well knew how to turn to their own advantage the results achieved by the conquered and subjugated peoples in various fields of culture and civilization. They took over numerous practical improvements from the Etruscans, just as from the Celts and other nations, and although the Celts may have had an especially large share in the development of the Roman carriage, the first traces of its appearance are associated with the Etruscans. Tradition has it that Tarquinius Priscus who was to be the fifth king of Rome of Etruscan origin was travelling in a wagon from his native village, Tarquinia, to Rome, when an eagle snatched his cap from his head, prophesying thereby that Tarquinius Priscus would become king. According to some other legend, a *quadriga* made by Etruscan artists at the behest of Tarquinius Priscus symbolized the eternal existence of the empire.

The 'plaustrum'. The earliest and simplest Roman vehicle was the *plaustrum* (Fig. 190) which consisted of a mere 'platform on wheels'. Its solid wheels did not rotate round the axis but were firmly attached to the latter; they produced a terrific creaking noise, and the vehicle was often referred to by the attribute 'strident'. It was used primarily in agriculture. In a very practical book on this subject *(De agricultura)* Marcus Portius Cato determined the precise number of *plaustra* required for the cultivation and maintenance of vineyards and olive groves. The *plaustrum* was the most versatile carting-vehicle; it was used as such also in town, but sometimes it served for special purposes. The *sella curulis* was originally no more than a chair placed on a *plaustrum*. Roman peasant kings travelled by, and dealt justice from, vehicles of this kind.

190

Other types of Roman vehicles. The vast territory of the Roman Empire was inhabited by a great variety of peoples, which accounts for the large number of different types of vehicles known to the Romans. In addition to these circumstances, frequent overlapping in the names for the diverse vehicles renders the picture even more confused. In the course of time the same names were applied to vehicles of different form and structure, and even one and the same type of vehicle often had several different names. The Romans used the wheeled vehicle principally for carting (i.e. for carrying in the crop, supplying the urban population with food and transporting building materials). The simplest type of cart—a slightly improved version of the *plaustrum*—consisted of a pair of spoked wheels and a plain superstructure. This type of vehicle figures on a large number of representations. In a mosaic picture found at Ostia, the cart carries a passenger (Fig. 191), while an only slightly different cart—with a canopy on top—(Pl. XXIX) appears to have been used as a family carriage: this one was shown on one side of a child's sarcophagus. In Rome itself only the Vestal priestesses, triumphators, high officials, priests officiating at festive ceremonies or travellers just arriving in town were permitted the use of horse-drawn carts or carriages. Similar rules may have prevailed in the *municipia* and colonies; they were strictly observed, and even minute offences

191

were carefully watched. Thus when Marcus Furius Camillus entered Rome after the Veii conquest (396 B.C.) in a carriage drawn by white horses, he was reproached with trying to outdo the horses of Jupiter and Sol. Permission for the personal use of a carriage was considered as a special favour and a great privilege. It is said that the women of Rome were granted the use of the *carpentum* within the city walls on festive occasions in recognition of their generous attitude after the occupation of Veii when they offered to part with their gold jewellery. The prostitutes and women of easy virtue did not share in this honour.

The 'carpentum' was usually a two-wheeled, pair-drawn carriage (Fig. 192). It was the vehicle of the clergy and was used also for transferring devotional objects to the Capitol; four-wheeled vehicles were used only by the emperor, the nobility and the higher magistrates. Their carriages were often covered with a roof supported by statues of pillars at the four corners. The inside of the carriage was generally covered with some expensive fabric; its seat was sometimes suspended on straps. The newly wedded bride was taken home by her husband in a *carpentum*. Wrapped in her bridal veil, she sat in the body of the carriage with the bridegroom on her right and the 'best man' on her left. The procession was headed by the friends of the bridegroom, carrying flaming torches. When they arrived at the house of the young husband, they burned the shaft of the carriage, lest the wife should use it to return to the paternal home. The funeral cart was called *carpentum mortuarium*; it was a two-wheeled vehicle, as seen in Pl. XXX.

The 'pilentum' was originally a sacral vehicle, used for the transport of divine statues and other objects regarded as sacred. A fine specimen of this type is the goddess Cybele's four-wheeled processional cart, now preserved in New York (Pl. XXXI). It is

192

191 A plaustrum mosaic from the baths at Ostia
192 Terra-cotta sculpture of a covered carpentum

140

actually an improved version of the *plaustrum*. Later the same type of vehicle was used by the Vestal virgins and by old ladies in festive processions. The *pilentum* is mentioned also in Virgil's *Aeneid:* in a scene represented on Aeneas' shield, upholstered *pilenta* traverse the city.

The use of carriages by women . . . Women's rights to travel by carriage were, however, further restricted during the second Punic war (218–201 B.C.) and were completely abolished under Caesar. Though a few female members of the imperial household were still allowed to use the *carpentum*, this privilege required the consent of the Senate. It was granted to Livia, the wife of Emperor Augustus; Messalina, the ill-famed third wife of Claudius, was also allowed to ride in a *carpentum* in the triumphal procession held by the Emperor on his return from his conquests in Britain. (The time soon came, however, when Messalina was content with a wheel-barrow, for when the conspiracy against Claudius was discovered, she fled in the direction of Ostia first on foot and later hidden in a wheel-barrow used for carting away garden rubbish.) Claudius' next wife, Agrippina, also contrived to obtain a permit for the use of the *carpentum*. However, travelling by wheeled vehicle soon became a general habit, so much so that by the fourth century it was unthinkable that the dowry of a well-to-do bride—not to mention ladies of high birth—should not include a gilded wagon. This appears from the writings of the Church Father St. Jerome (340/50–420); according to him "The marrying woman needs a good many things: expensive clothes, gold and precious stones, costly paraphernalia, servants and all sorts of utensils, a sedan chair and a gilded wagon."

. . . and by men. Sometimes men also travelled by wheeled vehicle in the streets of Rome. The Senate granted this facility in exceptional cases. We learn, for instance, from Pliny the Elder that *pontifex maximus* Lucius Caecilius Metellus enjoyed the privilege because in 241 B.C. he had lost his sight rescuing the *palladium*, the statue of Minerva or Pallas Athene, from the burning Temple of Vesta. "The people of Rome have granted him a right no other man has enjoyed since the foundation of Rome: he was permitted to be driven to the Curia in a chariot each time he went to the Senate. A high distinction and an august privilege, but it cost him his eyesight."

Later, the use of the chariot by men became apparently quite commonplace, and—if the literary information available is worthy of credit—those entitled to it exercised their rights just as conscientiously as they watched that no unauthorized person should get into a vehicle. When Emperor Trajan left his palace to go to the Senate on foot, the panegyrist, quite beside himself, went into raptures over so much manliness. Seneca was not ashamed to confess that, since his feet had never been in contact with snow, he did not know what it felt like. On the fragment of a sarcophagus representing a Roman street scene (Pl. XXXII), a couple are seen driving in a carriage in the bustling traffic of the city with a perfectly matter-of-fact air.

The Roman roads. Naturally, the technical improvement of the wheeled vehicle and the development of a bustling traffic required suitable roads. Road-construction was slow to start in Rome. Though the twelve-tabled law already contained certain provisions concerning the building and maintenance of roads, it did not define these activities as incumbent on the State; instead, it stressed the obligation of landowners to provide for the upkeep of the roads adjoining their estates. The Romans owed their fundamental knowledge of road-construction—like so many other features of civilization—to the Etruscan people, but in this field, too, they filled the adopted principles with regenerative force. The carefully designed and organized road network, with Rome in the centre of the 'cobweb', was the work of Roman statesmen and chieftains.

The 'queen of the roads'. In the military-minded Roman Empire, road-construction served strategic purposes in the first place. Most of the ancient journeys known to us from literature took place through the Appian Way (Via Appia), the 'queen of the roads', built in 312 B.C. to connect Rome with Puteoli and Brundisium, the two most important ancient ports of Italy. It was along this road—so Lucretius tells us—that the rich, bored with the city, travelled at full speed to their summer residences in the Albanus mountains; along it dressy ladies, accompanied by a host of cavaliers, showed off their elegance, according to Cicero; Cynthia, mistress of Propertius, also took this road, deceiving her lover, whom she told that she was going to Lanuvium to offer a sacrifice to Juno; in reality she had a rival of Propertius with her in her silk-curtained carriage, around which (the poet seems to have had precise information on the affair) two dogs from Molossus gamboled and frolicked.

A Roman *Itinerarium* indicates the following distances, as measured along the Appian Way: Rome–Capua 136 *millia*, Capua–Beneventum 33 *millia*, Beneventum–Tarentum 157 *millia* and Tarentum–Brundisium 44 *millia*, which amounts to about 342 miles (547 kilometres) in all. According to Ovidius, this distance could be comfortably covered by a carriage in somewhat less than ten days. $33^3/_5$ miles (54 kilometres) a day is certainly not a high average; consequently, people wishing to travel fast went on horseback rather than by wheeled vehicle.

142

How the Romans travelled. Two-wheeled carts and four-wheeled wagons were equally in use; the choice between the two was evidently determined by the nature of the transport and by the condition of the roads used. For short journeys, especially in mountainous regions, the cart was given preference, but for the transportation of heavy loads, for journeys on flat land, on ceremonial occasions and for longer trips, the four-wheeled wagon was harnessed. From the numerous literary data available on the subject, we can gather a fairly exact picture of how a Roman of rank and position travelled. The travelling-wagon was drawn by mules or small but fast Gallic horses. The draught-animals were generally covered with purple or embroidered cloth; the gilded harness and bit glittered from afar; the wagon itself was mounted with gold and silver (Pl. XXXIII), so that its price equalled the value of a village estate. The curtains were of silk or some other expensive cloth.

For the wealthy and high-born Roman citizen it was nothing out of the ordinary to go on a journey; in fact, all one needed for travelling was money and servants. Pliny, for instance, had travelled a great deal. If he wanted to visit his Italian estates or go to Bithynia in Asia Minor, he just had to give orders for harnessing. He read and dictated in his carriage, which his friends may have found an affectation, for in one of his letters he is quite apologetic about it.

They not only read but also ate while travelling. In a letter quoted by Suetonius, Augustus Octavius wrote: "I ate a little bread and some dates in my carriage." Further, we know from Suetonius that Claudius who was addicted to dicing indulged in gambling also under way; the board for the game was fitted to his carriage to prevent his game from being disturbed. The equipment of a travelling-carriage often included other objects for the convenience of its occupants, such as a travelling sun-dial or a distance-measuring device.

The 'essedum' was a vehicle of Celtic origin, known both in Britain and Gaul, and used by the Romans as early as in the first century A.D. The term *essedum* was used for a great variety of vehicles: sometimes it was applied to two-wheeled war-chariots, sometimes—as in the example quoted above—to travelling-carriages, and occasionally also to farm-carts.

The 'raeda' and the 'carruca dormitoria'. It was not unusual for the Roman traveller to sleep in his carriage. The *raeda*—the frequently used travelling-vehicle—was, for instance, suitable for this purpose without requiring any special preparation. The *carruca dormitoria*, another type of travelling-carriage, was—as its very name denotes—a 'sleeper'.

Since both the *raeda* and the *carruca* were used also as ceremonial carriages, they were decorated sometimes with bronze
and ivory reliefs or, later, even with gold and silver *repoussé*
work. However, people were not allowed to decorate their vehicles with gold or silver at their own discretion. Precise laws
regulated and, in certain cases, prohibited its application. It was
Alexander Severus (222–235 A.D.) who permitted the Roman
senators to travel in silvered *carrucas* or *raedas*, but it was only
under Emperor Aurelian (270–275 A.D.) that private individuals,
who formerly could use copper-mounted vehicles at the best,
were also allowed to keep silver-mounted carriages.

193

The 'cisium' (Fig. 193) is also often mentioned among the Roman travelling-vehicles. It differed from the *raeda* in as much as it
ran on two wheels, instead of four.

Illustrious travellers. Horace wrote that he considered himself
lucky that he had not had to take upon himself the superfluous
and uncomfortable burdens of the haughty and wealthy, for if
he had been one of them, he would have had to keep a large
number of stable boys, horses and carriages; as it was, he was
content to trot to Tarentum on mule-back; thus people could not
even call him miserly, as Tullius Cicero had bluffly called Maece-
nas because the latter took only five servants along on one of his
journeys to Tibur.

Seneca mentions as an odd idea that once he and his friend
Maximus went to the country accompanied by a single servant
only, and that they themselves also travelled in a peasant cart;

144

however, the two happy days of the journey had taught him how many superfluous things people took along when travelling. Against this, we learn that when a certain Milo—not even a personage of renown—travelled with his wife to Lanuvium, he was accompanied by a host of slaves and servants, and the baggage included his private chapel.

Horace—in the fifth satire—gives us the realistic description of a journey around 30 B.C. Part of the way Horace travelled by boat, which indicates that this conveyance must have been more comfortable than the jolting wagon. The satiric letter acquaints us with the vicissitudes the traveller was exposed to on a fifteen-days journey.

The emperors, naturally, travelled with even greater pomp. While Caesar travelled a great deal and was content with little comfort, Caligula requisitioned every private carriage and common vehicle whenever it was getting too hot for him in Rome, and he had to flee to Lyon through the Alps. Nero's train, it is said, never consisted of less than a thousand vehicles; the hoofs of his mules were silver-shoed, his drivers' costumes were made of purple cloth from Canusium. Heliogabalus was content with a train of sixty vehicles, but the Emperor's own carriage was adorned with gems and precious stones. And let us quote here a little incident from the life of Vespasian (recorded for posterity by Suetonius). According to this historian, the Emperor's driver aroused the suspicion of his august master by getting the mules shoed while under way. Vespasian thought that it was but a trick which his man employed to enable a petitioner to get close to his carriage. He teased the driver, asking him how much he earned on the shoeing and insisted on a share of the money.

Technical curiosities. Finally, here are two technical curiosities to add to this chapter on the fancies of emperors: When Emperor Commodus was murdered in 192 A.D., his successor, Pertinax, found that various curious carriages were part of his inheritance, among them a vehicle which measured the distance it covered: a clever device dropped a pebble into a metal cup after each mile, thus indicating the distance by sound, as the typewriter indicates the end of each line by the ringing of a bell. The other carriage was the ancestor of the motor-car, except that the slaves hidden in its structure drove the vehicle with their hands and feet.

The 'cisiarii'. Naturally, the simpler citizens—not to mention people without civic rights—had no carriages of their own. They had to make do with horse or mule-riding, or walk. But if a middle-class citizen—a lower official or tradesman—had money enough, he could hire a vehicle from a *cisiarius*. The *cisiarii* took

145

up their station at the towngates, not only in Rome but also in other large towns. The Latin name for the hired carriage was sometimes *cisium* and sometimes *raeda meritoria*. It was used by Julius Caesar himself who, as Suetonius writes, "covered great distances with incredible speed, making a hundred miles a day in hired carriage and with little baggage." And since he did the Rome–Rhone journey—about 800 *millia* (750 miles or 1,200 kilometres)—in less than eight days, the handsome daily average of a hundred miles must have been covered by him either in as many hours less than twenty-four as he had devoted to sleep (which would have been a fantastic performance under the then prevailing travelling conditions), or he must have slept in his carriage.

The Roman post may be best compared to the communication facilities of the seventeenth to nineteenth centuries. It was a punctually functioning organization, operating with relay horses and rest-houses at intervals of a day's distance. The Latin name for the mail-coach was *cursus publicus*, but the term *publicus* should not deceive the reader: it did not mean that it was for general use by the public but only that it belonged to the State; in fact, the post system was restricted to the use of the government, and even government officials could avail themselves of this facility only with special permission. The regulations were rigorously observed, so that when as a civil servant, Pertinax (later emperor) took the postal coach without the permission of the Syrian proconsul, he was strictly punished: he had to go long miles on foot.

It was regrettable that the postal service could not develop into an established public service, but the ever suspicious Roman despots, scenting conspiracy in every nook, excluded the ordinary mortal from the blessings of this facility. In the circumstances, the *cursus publicus* became the 'State security' organ of the Empire: it functioned as a monstrous spy and intelligence service, and was available only to reliable individuals.

As despatch-riding does not belong to our subject-matter, let us begin the story of the Roman post with Emperor Hadrian who is said to have been the founder of the mail-coach service. The fact that he himself was extremely fond of travelling and was on the move in his empire for not less than twelve years confirms this assertion. According to Suetonius, Emperor Augustus, too, had a share in the development of the Roman postal network. Wanting to be informed as fast as possible on everything that took place in the provinces, he first established a post-runner relay service; later he had the runners replaced by mail-coaches communicating directly between the provinces and Rome. Evidently, the latter system proved more efficient, as the couriers bringing the news in the mail-coach could, if circumstances so demanded, report also in person on the local events.

The posting system in the eastern Empire attained the same high standards as in the west; however, matters reached a point where anyone backed by the slightest influence or friendly connection could avail himself of the *cursus publicus*, maintained at high costs by the State. Under Constantinus II (353–361 A.D.) even Christian bishops travelled by mail-coach. Ammianus Marcellinus actually reproached Constantinus—after his death, to be sure!—for taking sides now with the Orthodox Church, now with the Arians, but permitting at the same time various bishops to run about in gangs to their synods, using the public post-horses for this purpose.

The Theodosian Code, issued by the Eastern Emperor Theodosius in 438 A.D., brought the *cursus publicus* under new regulations. Valentinian III extended its effect to the Western Empire, and in 506 it was adopted also by Alaric II, king of the Visigoths. The Code specified the various types of vehicles used by the post which had grown into a widely ramifying organization by that time; it also set out the maximum load for each type of vehicle.

The load-carrying restrictions. The Theodosian Code fixed the upper limit of the loads as follows:

birota	200 Roman *librae*	66 kilos	145 lbs.
vereda	300 Roman *librae*	99 kilos	228 lbs.
currus	600 Roman *librae*	198 kilos	436 lbs.
raeda, carpentum or *vehiculum*	1,000 Roman *librae*	330 kilos	726 lbs.
angaria, clabulare	1,500 Roman *librae*	495 kilos	1,089 lbs.

Moderate figures, indeed! Even the highest limit did not exceed five quintals—a load that can scarcely be regarded as inordinately high. Still, the Code was stringent; it punished not only the loading of excess weight but also the construction of any vehicle whose carrying capacity exceeded the limits specified for the respective category. The punishments were of Draconian severity: exile for free citizens, and mine servitude for the slaves.

In addition to the *raeda* and the *carpentum* discussed above, the light *birota*, the *vereda* and—for heavier loads—the *currus* also appeared among the vehicles listed. (It should be noted that the term *currus* was applied to a wide range of vehicles, but first of all to the racing-*biga*, *triga* and *quadriga*; carriages used in triumphal processions were also called *currus*, but the full name for them was *currus triumphalis*.) The *raeda* and the *currus*, as vehicles of medium capacity, were used for the transport of lighter loads of great value, e.g. precious metals. For travelling by

147

easy stages and for the conveyance of the sick and wounded of the legions, the Romans had the *angaria* and the *clabula* or *clabulare;* the latter was a large open wagon with latticed sides, suitable both for passenger and goods transport. It was used for the transportation of soldiers and army goods; officials of a lower rank were entitled to this means of communication alone, within the frames of the *cursus publicus.*

The provisions of the Theodosian Code covered other fields as well. They obliged the civil and military dignitaries to keep carriages equal to their rank and position. They also specified the number and kind of draught-animals to be harnessed to the various types of vehicles. Regarding the *raeda*, the Code stipulated, for instance, that it must be drawn by eight mules in summer and ten in winter *(octo mulae iungantur ad raedam aestivo videlicet tempore hiemali decem)*. Every *raeda* was to be escorted by two mounted guards *(duo palatini prosecutores)*—a regulation that does not cast a very favourable light on the public-security conditions of the period.

Why were the loading-limits fixed at such a low level? In our opinion the strict regulations concerning loading-weights were introduced, above all, with a view to sparing the roads, and not on account of the capacity of the vehicles or for reasons of draught-animal protection. The admirable roads constructed by the Romans had one great shortcoming: they were rigid, and the unsprung vehicles overturned and rapidly destroyed their un-yielding surface. (The Romans built their roads by the same method as the flooring of their houses, for instance.) The repairing of such road structures was no simple matter either; consequently, the Romans prevented their undue wear by prohibiting the use of too heavy vehicles.

The primitive method of harnessing, exploiting only a fraction of the physical power of the draught-animal, may have been another reason for the regulation of the loading-weights. In his study on harnessing, Lefebvre des Noëttes even suspects some misunderstanding about the number of draught-animals specified in the Code. According to him, the word *iungere* has been interpreted erroneously: it does not mean 'to harness' in this case but only to 'tie before', 'fasten to' or 'attach to'. In his opinion only a pair was harnessed, and the rest of the animals were 'trace animals' which did no actual pulling.

Street traffic. While the highways carried a bustling traffic, communication in the streets, especially in those of Rome, was limited by numerous regulations and prohibitions. As mentioned already, the use of horse-drawn vehicles was reserved for the privileged. Julius Caesar confirmed the earlier regulations according to which only individuals belonging to the specified categories could drive through the streets of Rome between sunrise and sunset; *plaustra* carrying building materials were, however, also exempted from the restrictions. We do not know the authentic reason for these regulations, but it is supposed that the vehicles must have made an infernal noise in the streets and probably caused various other inconveniences, too. The din of the solid wheels and springless spoked metal wheels must have been deafening on the bumpy roads; the splashing mud or clouds of dust raised by the vehicles—not to mention the danger of getting run over—probably greatly annoyed those going about on foot.

From the street scenes in Horace's *Epistles* it appears that, in addition to the carting of building materials, funeral processions were also exempted from the strict prohibitions concerning daytime traffic. In his description "excited contractors bustle about with their mules and porters, huge cranes lift now stones, now beams; doleful funeral processions wind their way among the carts; here an angry dog, there a grouting, muddy pig..." complete the picture. At the beginning the prohibitions affected only Rome. (This may have been the reason of Seneca's complaint that the perpetual rumble of carriages left one no peace at all in the town of Baiae.) In the centuries that followed, the restrictions were extended to the whole of Italy; Claudius issued orders according to which travellers were allowed to pass through the city only on foot or in sedan-chairs or litters.

The funeral processions were simple or sumptuous, according to the social position of the deceased. In case of a plain funeral, the body was placed on a *plaustrum;* only a magistrate or his wife could go on their last journey in a *carpentum* or *currus.* The funeral ceremony of distinguished personages included a procession of the ancestors: actors engaged for the occasion wore the wax masks of the dead man's forefathers of rank, as if to represent them in this manner among the mourners.

The triumphal march was the highest military distinction in ancient Rome. On such occasions the victorious commander rode standing in a *currus triumphalis;* his cheeks were rouged, and he held a laurel branch and an ivory sceptre in his hand. If the triumphal cart was made of ivory—which was often the case—it was called a *currus eburneus;* otherwise it was known as *currus albus.* According to Livy, the first to enter Rome standing in a triumphal car drawn by four white horses was Marcus Furius Camillus (365 B.C.). The Romans then disapproved of this display which they regarded as indecent and presuming, but later it ceased to rouse indignation, even when Julius Caesar held five triumphal processions—each with different pomp and ceremony—to celebrate his victories at various battle-fields.

In the imperial period it became a custom that only emperors could hold triumphal processions (Pl. XXXIV); they claimed

149

this right (with the exclusion of the chieftains) on the ground that they were the highest war lords. Other customs also underwent changes: the number of horses was increased sometimes from four to six—if the representations which have come down to us are correct. On some occasions the triumphal cart was drawn by elephants; this was permitted by the Senate if the scene of the victory was Africa or Asia. Thus in 233 A.D., Emperor Alexander Severus' triumphal cart was also drawn by elephants, following his victory over Artaxerxes.

Though the triumphal carts were upholstered, elderly victors suffered greatly from the jolting of the vehicle, for they had to stand just above the axle throughout the long triumphal march, without as much as a minute's rest. It is said that on one occasion Vespasian found the slow and long procession so exhausting that he broke out exclaiming: "It serves me right for wanting a triumphal march, an old man like me!"

In the Eastern Empire the emperors lived in an even greater style than in the West. The patriarch Johannes Chrysostomos describes the triumphal cart of Emperor Arcadius (395–408 A.D.) as follows: —

> The vehicle, made of pure gold, compels admiration, and this not without reason. The spectators marvel at the purple curtains and white carpets, the precious stones and gold foils which sparkle and glitter when the vehicle is in motion, radiating a dazzling light.

Chariot races. Originally the Roman circus games consisted only of chariot and horse races; gladiator fights were introduced only later; eventually, galley fights were also added to the circus programmes. Chariot racing—which the Romans adopted from the southern Italian Greeks—represented the main entertainment of the citizens of Rome towards the end of the republic and under the imperial rule.

The races were preceded by festive ceremonials. The magistrate organizing the games led a procession carrying the statues of the gods. They advanced to the sound of flutes and trumpets and were acclaimed by the public who rose from their seats to applaud. The statues of the gods, carried on a ceremonial vehicle, the *tensa* (Fig. 194), were called upon in a loud voice (the way Italians now invoke the name of their individual patron saint on the occasion of festive processions), and if the *tensa* happened to tilt, just at the moment the Roman circus spectator cried out the name of his favourite god, the 'miracle' was complete: the god had signalled his support.

The 'tensa' was always regarded as the vehicle of the gods, whether it was used in processions before circus games or on other occasions. At the beginning it carried only the divine statues, but later also those of the deified emperors. The vehicle

194

194 Medal of Emperor Tiberius, with the representation of a tensa
195 Model of a Roman racing-chariot
196 Detail of the relief on the Marcus Aurelius column in Rome
197 A boy on a carriage with shafts
198 Wagon carrying wine, drawn by three mules

150

was built of wood and was ornamented with gold, silver and ivory, according to the fancy and discretion of its designer. The *tensa* was usually drawn by white horses, mules or oxen, sometimes by elephants or even by men. The reins were held by the *tensarius* who did not sit in the vehicle but walked beside it.

According to the holy precepts, he was not to touch the reins with his left hand once the *tensa* started going; a still stricter rule prohibited the *tensa* from stopping even for a second until it had reached the place of honour allocated to the statues. If any mishap—like the breaking of a wheel or axle, the fall of an

animal or its getting entangled in the traces—caused the vehicle to stop, the whole procession had to be started all over again.

The circus chariot races (Pl. XXXV). The vehicles used were similar to the earlier Greek war-chariots (Fig. 195). A ruthless and unsparing fight began after the starting signal. Running athwart each other's course or touching were not forbidden; on the contrary, fouling the other's shaft was the very trial of a competitor's skill and courage. Not infrequently the drivers attacked each other with the whip. Many accidents occurred at the bends, for if the competitor drove too near the *meta*, the turning-post of stone in the middle of the circus, his chariot could easily overturn. If a vehicle crashed, the next ones coming up ran over its unfortunate driver, or his own horses dragged him along, unless he succeeded in cutting the reins in time. (The reins were tied round his waist, and he carried a knife in his belt for such emergencies.) It even occurred that a fallen driver shoved one of his fellow-competitors off an oncoming chariot, seized the reins and won the race with the other's vehicle. The many accidents and the excitement elicited by the dangers of the competition were the very attraction of the chariot races.

The drivers. Thus the races enjoyed great popularity, and every class of the population was carried away by passionate enthusiasm. The emperors were just as infatuated with their favourite charioteers or with the faction, under whose colours they competed, as the simplest Roman proletarian. Although the drivers could climb only the lower rungs of the social ladder, they often acquired fabulous wealth, for the victors won important sums of money, besides the palm. The famous *auriga* Cocles, for instance, who around 150 A.D. won 4,500 victories retired with a fortune of 35 million *sestertii*. The portrait of Scorpus, a similarly wealthy charioteer, has come down to us on a slab. Martial drafted his epitaph as follows: —

199

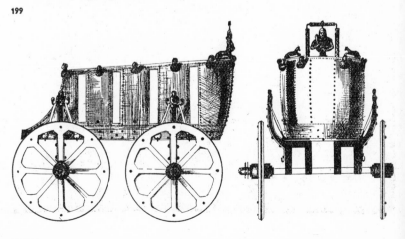

152

I am Scorpus, the pride of the noisy circus. But alas! short was the time Rome could applaud me: when I reached thrice nine years, I was carried off by a jealous Fate who, counting my victories, believed that I was old.

Technical innovations to the Roman carriage. As mentioned, the Romans themselves did little to improve the wheeled vehicle. 'Innovations' like the harnessing of horses before Nero's chariot can only be regarded but as the idea of a raving lunatic, lacking any practical significance. Anyhow, we know from Suetonius that Nero suffered for his swagger, for he tumbled out of his ten-horse carriage.

The highly developed military machinery of the Roman Empire afforded the wheeled vehicle a wide field of application. The best historic sources illustrating its various uses are the reliefs on the columns set up to honour Marcus Aurelius and Trajan. They show whole trains of vehicles (Fig. 196).

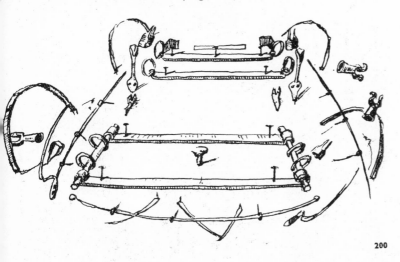

200

Numerous carriages have been found also in the Roman provinces, including items of unique technical importance. The pair of shafts was, for instance, used in Gaul; the carriages recovered in former Gallic territory represent the first traces of the pair of shafts in Europe (Fig. 197), although they had been known in China centuries earlier. The Vaison-la-Romaine travelling-wagon (Pl. XXXVI) is also a Gallic vehicle. The Gallo–Roman relief showing a massive wagon, a *plaustrum maior* (Fig. 198), is also of Gallic origin. In the relief it carries a barrel of approximately 88 gallons (400 litres) capacity. It is an interesting feature that the wagon is drawn by three mules and not by two or four as is usual.

Remains of actual carriages found on the territory of the Roman Empire included suspended carriage-bodies which were used also in the various provinces; those of Thracian origin are of special interest.

153

201

154

The Thracian carriages. The Thracians who inhabited the territory of present-day Bulgaria adopted the Hellenic civilization and took over the war-chariot from the Greeks, but the suspended carriage-bodies excavated by the Bulgarian archaeologist Ivan Venedikov during the past couple of decades date from the period of Roman rule in Thrace. According to Venedikov, the use of this type of vehicle started in Italy and spread to every Roman province. The reconstruction of a suspended carriage may be studied on Fig. 199. Another similar vehicle is shown in pieces, as discovered by the excavators, in Fig. 200.

Venedikov's finds threw new light upon the role of the hooks which—on the basis of Roman carriages recovered in Hungary and the Rhineland—past archaeologists had regarded as mere decorative elements. They believed that the material and load-bearing capacity of the hooks were not suitable for supporting the weight of a carriage-body. However, on the strength of the Thracian carriages it is now supposed that the hooks fixed at the ends of the suspension rods resting on the back wheels were adapted for this purpose.

The Pannonian carriages. In addition to the remains of Roman carriages, the territory of Pannonia (present-day western Hungary) yielded a large number of other actual carriages, as wagon-burial was a widespread custom both among the inhabitants of Illyrian ethnic origin and among the high-born Celts of the Eravisc and Azal tribes. No relics of Celtic wagon-burials have been found so far in Yugoslavia, Rumania or Bulgaria, probably because the Celtic invasion reached these areas only after these funeral rites had been replaced by cremation.

A very interesting carriage representation, however, has come down to us with the Adamklissi victory memorial (second century A.D.), found at Dobruja (Rumania); the illustrated vehicles are similar in structure to that presented in Fig. 201.

With this we close the story of the ancient carriage; its further development during the Middle Ages is the subject of the following chapters.

201 A metope of the Adamklissi memorial

Chapter VII

The deterioration of the European road-system and the collapse of the mail-coach service after the fall of the Roman Empire — Byzantium — Western Europe — The Merovingians — The Carolingians — The inhabitants of the British Isles — Travelling in the early Middle Ages — The *carruca nutans* — Attempts at the technical improvement of the carriage — Modern harnessing — The carriage with shafts — The modern breast-band — The horse-collar — The pivoted front axle — The perch — The carriage in the early Middle Ages — The wheelwright — Goods transport — The ritual rôle of the wheeled vehicle in the early Middle Ages — The Oseberg carriage — The migration period — The Hungarians

After the fall of the Roman Empire, technology in general, and especially the road-system, showed signs of deterioration throughout Europe. This is the more surprising as in some other fields human intellect and perseverance continued to advance culture and civilization. The reasons for this should be sought for in the economic transformation that followed the breaking up of the Roman Empire and in the fact that the goods traffic adjusted itself to the newly developing centres of goods-producing Europe. Last but not least, the road-system had depended largely on the central administration of the Empire: only its military rigour was able to impose upon the subjects the acceptance of a higher State ideal which, in the case of the road-system, benefited the highest ruling class only, but was disadvantageous to the people.

In Europe the splendid road network of the Romans grew sadly neglected. With lack of material means and trained road-building technicians, the deteriorated stone pavements were left unrepaired; their upkeep was confined to filling up the pot-holes on the surface with earth, as a result of which the 'repaired' sections became a sea of mud in rainy weather, while in summer clouds of dust drifted above them. Mud, dust and pot-holes did not, however, prevent the primitive wagons and carts from continuing—if in lesser numbers—to transport the wheat and timber required by the population, and the poorer classes used these carting-vehicles also for travelling.

The collapse of the mail-coach service. As mentioned in the preceding chapter, the maintenance of the *cursus publicus*—this amazing institution—required formidable amounts of money. It also meant a heavy burden to and required great sacrifices from the road-side agricultural population who—according to the prevailing regulations—were obliged to provide for the passengers of the *cursus publicus*, to offer them sleeping accommodation and food, and help also with the upkeep of the roads. No wonder, therefore, that the people were not enthusiastic about an institution which for them meant disadvantages only, without any benefit. Nor is it surprising that, when the Roman Empire collapsed, the *cursus publicus* was buried under its ruins. With the fall of the central power, the directive force which had provided also for the necessary funds ceased to exist. Moreover, there was no state power to enforce the discipline which had prevailed before, and which was indispensable for the maintenance of the organization.

The oppressed simple folk—who had for centuries regarded the postal service with jealousy and even hatred as an organization that served the interests of the privileged—now stood indifferently by and found even a certain satisfaction or malicious glee in the cessation of the *cursus publicus*. As soon as the foundations of the organs of power crumbled into dust under the blows of history's sledge-hammer, the institutions built on them disappeared as well.

In the early Middle Ages there was no cohesive force to replace the organizing and co-ordinating power of the collapsed Roman Empire, but the traditions of the Eastern Empire lived on in Byzantium.

Byzantium did not deny the legacy she owed to the ancient world; apart from certain changes in form, actually the types of the earlier Roman wheeled vehicles persisted. Representations of these have come down to us in legal descriptions, on ivory carvings and on textiles (Fig. 202 and Pl. XXXVII).

202

The sources indicate that, in the field of carriage-building, Byzantium was influenced exclusively by Roman traditions. Neither the *biga*—the war-chariot and racing-chariot—nor the *tensa*-type carriages show any innovation. The ancient method of harnessing did not undergo any change either.

In Western Europe, from the beginning of the modern age until the formation of the Frankish Empire, there was an interruption in road construction.

202 War-chariots

157

Though, according to tradition, the Merovingian dynasty (481–751 A.D.) travelled by ox-drawn wagons, these vehicles did not require engineered roads; ordinary earth tracks answered their purposes. The names for the different types of wagons, known to us from contemporary poetry, are rather confusing, owing to their erratic use. It is presumed that in many cases the choice of the name was determined by the word or rhyme which fitted best into the author's poem. According to Einhard *(Vita Caroli Magni)*, King Chilperic (561–584 A.D.) used an ox-drawn *carpentum* on his journeys, which the driver steered in peasant-fashion. In another document we read that the *rois fainéants* (i.e. the last kings of the Merovingian dynasty, from Thierry III to Chilperic) travelled by ox-drawn chariots, while in still other sources the term *basterne* is used to denote the wagon of the Merovingian rulers. To make the confusion complete, certain linguists doubt that the word *basterne* meant a wheeled vehicle at all, and there are, indeed, serious arguments in favour of the supposition that the term actually applied to a sedan-chair *(litière)*. However, no matter where the truth lies, we may well assume that the use of the *carpentum*, chariot or *basterne* played a certain part in the criticism scourging the softness and enervation of the Merovingians.

The bas-relief from Vienne (France, *Dép*. Isère), showing the transportation of a relic on a *cisium* (Fig. 203), dates from the time of the Merovingians. The *Pentateuch* miniature from Tours recalls the same period, although the carriage-body appearing therein is of a new form (Fig. 204).

In the Carolingian period (751–987 A.D.), Charlemagne decided to reconstruct the deteriorated old Roman road network, but, although he promised the princes, bishops and abbots various favours to secure their co-operation, he did not succeed in building anything comparable to the earlier Roman road-

203

203 **Transportation of a relic**
204 **Miniature from the Pentateuch of Tours**
205 **Cart on the base of a cross**

204

system. According to the chroniclers, Charlemagne travelled on
a wagon drawn by two pairs of oxen to demonstrate his power
and sovereign rights; however, this may not have been his only
reason for doing so: we understand from the chanson of Gui de
Bourgogne that he was anxious to conceal his physical weakness
and inability to ride a horse any more.

> *Ne voil que l'an me tiegne a coart n'a lanier,*
> *Que je encor ne puisse monter sor mon destrier.*

(I do not want to seem a coward or sickly that I can no more
mount my horse.)

Similarly, when the angel calls upon him to hasten to the
assistance of Anseis, the King feels too weak for riding and has a
carriage built for the journey.

> *Ne m'a mestier palefrois ne ronchis*
> *A moi porter, trop sui vieus et aflis.*
> *Or ferai faire un car.*

(I no more need a steed or a stallion to carry me, I am too old
and weak. Therefore I shall have a carriage made.)

The inhabitants of the British Isles also neglected the upkeep
of the Roman road-system; the old roads became again 'green
ways'. However, they still used the Dover–Cornwall road, and
the Icknield way through Wiltshire and Berkshire to Norfolk,
etc., which had been used by the Romans before them.

The relief on the base of a cross in Ireland (Fig. 205) shows a
conventional Celtic cart; only the way of harnessing presents
some novel features.

The roads in Europe outside the territory of the former Roman
Empire were even worse than the neglected highways of the
Roman road-system. Though wagons and carts were used, the

205

159

peoples inhabiting these parts were content with rough-and-ready earth roads or cart tracks.

Travelling on the primitive, jolting vehicle under the then prevailing road conditions was an enterprise in itself, but the threat of robber knights and waylayers rendered it even more risky and adventurous. The high and often arbitrarily assessed tolls further discouraged people from undertaking longer journeys.

The wheeled vehicle was used for travelling by the poor country folk only. Knights and noblemen travelled on horseback, and even young ladies preferred this means of communication. Travelling by a wagon was regarded as a sign of weakness, helplessness, senility or enervation, although it needed some determination; even priests and monks rode mules.

People with enough strength to mount and hang on to a horse or mule chose this latter way of travelling rather than be jarred to the bone in a rickety box. Naturally, other factors also played a part in the traveller's choice between horse-riding and the carriage; thus physical defects or diseases prevented some people from riding. Pious and old ladies also used the carriage—perhaps out of decency or prudishness; we know, for instance, that in 566 A.D. Princess Gelasswintha travelled from Toledo to Rouen by wheeled vehicle, and—according to the *Elsässer Chronik*—even St. Odile, the patron of Alsace, used a carriage when visiting her father, King Adalric, in Hohenburg.

The 'carruca nutans' —or swinging carriage. To reduce the discomfort caused by jolting, the earlier Roman innovation, the suspension of the carriage-body, was revived (Fig. 206). The suspended box had been known also to the Slav tribes of South-Eastern Europe. Ibrahim ibn Jáqub recorded that the Slav kings travelled on broad, high wagons with four pillars at the corners on which the carriage-body was suspended by means of chains.

This innovation did not become very widespread for the simple reason that it did not ensure more comfort than the ordinary wagon. Swinging may have reduced the jolting to some extent, but as they could not control the swinging motion, the conveyance proved undesirable for longer journeys: it was all right to swing about for a while, but it soon became nauseating and the traveller found that it was more than he had bargained for.

Attempts at technical improvements. The sculptural and graphic representations which have come down to us from the first six centuries following the fall of the Western Empire reveal no important deviation from earlier models in the structure of the carriage or in the way of harnessing. But when slavery was

206

206 Carruca nutans, carriage with suspended body

160

replaced by subsistence farming, under the feudal economic system, a new situation arose: the villein—who surrendered the feudal landlord only part of the crop he produced on the land allocated to him—found it in his own interest to improve his methods and implements of agricultural production; his efforts in this direction resulted in the modernization of the cart and wagon, in the improvement of the system of harnessing and in a better exploitation of the horse's traction-power. We must underline that the latter statement refers specifically to the horses, as no way had been found to increase the utilization of the power of draught-oxen, either in the Middle Ages or up to today: the yoke has remained unchanged in the past five thousand years.

Modern harnessing. In the case of the horse the situation was different. As already mentioned, the earlier method of harnessing did not permit the utilization of the horse's power to the best advantage: the old type of collar greatly hindered the animal in pulling. Endeavours to improve the implements of labour resulted in relieving the horse from the torturing, choking pressure and power-reducing effects of the obsolete harness. It was achieved by the introduction of three different innovations: the shafts, the modern breast-band and the horse-collar.

The shafts had been known in China centuries before they came into use in Europe. There is just a single Roman monument, the relief of Trier (Fig. 197), in which the shafts appear, but until analogies are known to us, we have to consider it as a unique specimen and uncommon exception. Maybe it was used on toy vehicles for children, but it does not occur regularly before the Middle Ages.

There is probably no direct or indirect connection between the Chinese and European shafts. Here again we are faced with an example of human ingenuity which, directed towards the same objective, produces similar results in different, often quite independent parts of the world. However, the Trier example shows that man sometimes fails to realize the significance of an innovation.

A new type of breast-band—the second solution to the problem—appeared in Western Europe in the Merovingian period. The Stuttgart Psalter from the ninth century contains an illustration (Fig. 207); in this the artist—whether consciously or not—represents his actual surroundings in detail. According to Haudricourt's linguistic argumentation, the various terms for 'breast-band' used in the different Slav languages and deriving from the Old High German word *shilo* (*Siele* in modern German) prove that the adoption of the German name must have taken place before the separation of the various Slav peoples, i.e. before

161

the sixth century. According to this, the modern breast-band (or at least the term for it) had been known in Europe east of the Rhineland and north of the Carpathian Mountains as early as in the sixth century.

The term *Kummet*, the equivalent of horse-collar, was, on the other hand, adopted in the Slav languages from the German in the eighth-ninth centuries, i.e. after their separation. Linguistic evidence to this effect is corroborated by practical examples. Figs. 208 and 209 give a clear picture of the results achieved through the use of the hames: in these representations the horses no longer strain their neck by holding it back, cramped, in an unnatural position; instead they lean against the hames with all their weight.

The pivoted front axle also belongs to the important improvements introduced in the Middle Ages, although the closer date of its appearance is difficult to determine. Contemporary representations reveal but little in this connection; the pivoted front being hidden under the carriage-body, its structure is hardly visible on the miniatures and paintings. An indirect indication of its existence, however, is that on some representations the front wheels of the wagons are smaller than the back wheels; this is always so with wagons provided with a pivoted front axle because a pivot is wedged between the so-called bolster (above the front axle) and the body. There are numerous indications that the structure had been used already by the Celts, so that it may be regarded as one of the many rediscovered innovations.

The perch is the pole connecting the front and rear axles under the body of a four-wheeled vehicle. If the wagon with a pivoted

207

front part is of the type developed by the joining of two carts, the perch corresponds to the pole of the back cart. The perch became an essential part of the more modern vehicle. We know of various types of wagons distinguished by their perch, whose area of diffusion is geographically definable. The European wagon, for instance, differs from the Asian precisely on account of its perch which, however, does not imply that the wagon without a perch is quite unknown in Europe. It occurs here, too, but is used for specific purposes only, such as the transportation of stone, dung, etc.

208

The carriage in the early Middle Ages. Summing up the foregoing, we may state that there were three main types of wheeled vehicles in use in the early Middle Ages: (a) the wagon (the French *chariot*, a four-wheeled vehicle with a single pole or with a pair of shafts *[brancard]*); (b) the single-pole cart *(char)*; (c) the cart with shafts *(charrette)*. The cart with shafts emerged simultaneously with the modern horse traction-harness, probably because with the new way of harnessing, one horse could draw the cart instead of the former two. Spreading from southern Europe northward, the cart provided with shafts superseded the clumsy, pair-drawn four-wheeled wagon. Naturally, the change-over did not take place overnight. It would have been impossible but for economic reasons, as the acquisition of the new type of cart was no simple matter. Besides, one has to consider the traditional conservative attitude of the peasants where changes were involved. In some places (e.g. Auvergne, the Pyrenees) the cart persisted as an ox-drawn vehicle, in others (e.g. Russia) the shafts were applied also to four-wheeled vehicles. On the other hand, the cart was often adapted to the existing requirements: if one horse proved insufficient, a second or even a third one was harnessed to the shafts to pull in tandem.

209

The wheelwright. In the early Middle Ages and even in the late Middle and early Modern Ages, the wheelwright constructed each vehicle separately. No 'serial type' was developed; consequently, the vehicles appearing in contemporary representations differ considerably from each other in form and structure. The making of the wheels was still regarded as the most complicated part of carriage-building. The wheelwright's trade developed from carpentering, and those engaged in it were held in great esteem; this appears most expressively from the old English sayings: "A bad wheelwright makes a good carpenter," and, more roughly put: "A wheelwright's dog is a carpenter's uncle."
The bottom of the farm-carts was made of planks or wickerwork; the travelling-carts or -wagons were covered with tarpaulin, matting or, later on, with leather, to protect the passen-

gers against scorching sun and rain or other rigours of weather. Thus the cover represented the only difference between the ordinary farm-cart and the travelling-cart of the higher classes.

Freight was transported both by carts and wagons. The new type of traction-harness multiplied the former carrying capacity of the vehicles. On flat land the carts and wagons could cover fifteen to twenty miles a day. In medieval England road transport was often preferred to that by river—despite the competition of the boats—because the time of shipment was always erratic owing to flood and drought. Timber was also transported by carts and wagons, naturally, not only in England but all over Europe, and the crop was gathered in by farm-carts. The *Cronicon Novaliciense*, the eleventh-century chronicle of the Novalese monastery which stood at the foot of Mont Cenis, describes the vast number of carts that brought in the wheat from the monastery farms. The train of vehicles was headed by an empty cart with a tinkling bell suspended on a rod. Naturally, this was not meant to increase the parade but rather to warn the devout that the freight which followed was 'sacred'—lest anyone should try to rob the carts and thus risk his salvation.

The war-chariot was hardly used at all; still, we know from Irish sources that it had not been altogether discarded even in the early Middle Ages. King Chuchulain's wooden vehicle, called a *carpat*, was a pair-drawn chariot; the warrior and his driver sat on soft cushions in it.

The earlier cult importance of the carriage diminished considerably in the Middle Ages. The spreading of Christianity and economic developments relegated the ritual carriage to the background. From the early part of the Middle Ages, the data referring to the use of wheeled vehicles for cult or religious purposes become scanty. There is, however, a seventh-century legend which tells us that, when Sigurd Ring (or Hring) defeated his uncle, King Harald Hildetand, in the battle of Broovalla, he had the dead sovereign buried on his carriage, but a saddle-horse was also placed in the grave, so that the King might choose between riding on horse-back and travelling by carriage to the Walhalla.

The Oseberg carriage. Regarding the famous ninth-century Oseberg carriage, scholars like Sigurd Grieg and Schetelig are of the opinion that it was a ritual carriage (Pl. XXXVIII). It is very effective at first sight, and only closer examination reveals its weak points. The carvings ornamenting the four sides of the vehicle are fairly chaotic and inordinate in style and form. The felloes are remarkably thin and broad; they extend

164

almost to the middle of the radius of the wheel and are connected with the unwieldy hub by short spokes. The method of harnessing employed is extremely odd and hard to understand. The carriage had two poles fixed to the body in such a way that one can only imagine that an animal, probably an ox, was harnessed to each of them on the outside. But how then did they fix the traces? Gösta Berg is inclined to believe that they were tied to the hubs of the front wheels, but this seems to us rather unlikely. The unusual structural features of the vehicle indicated that it was not used for practical purposes.

During the great migration of the fourth century, the nomadic tribes of the Black Sea steppes set out for the west. The Hungarians, inhabiting originally the Volga and Kama regions, wandered first to Bashkiria, thence to the territory between Kiev and Voronezh, and later, to west of the Dnieper, until eventually they came to present-day Hungary. From among the peoples migrating from Asia to Europe, they alone struck root here.

Logically, it appears beyond doubt that the hunting and fighting Hungarian nomads were followed by their wives, children and aged relatives on two-wheeled travelling-carts. As mentioned before, the same type of vehicle had been used also by the Central Asiatic nomads, and it is even possible that the wagon which developed through the combination of two carts was the accidental or consciously produced fruit of the experience of some originally nomadic tribe—Hungarian or otherwise—gained during their wanderings over hill and dale. Naturally, no actual find or representation of these carts or wagons survives: their material perished, and neither the wandering tribes nor the peoples of higher civilization they came into contact with made any representations for posterity. It is noteworthy, however, that in the Black Sea regions and in Asia Minor the light four-wheeled wagon was called *madjar*, while, originally, the present Hungarian term for cart, *taliga*, was used for a four-wheeled vehicle. The corresponding word in the Osmanli-Turkish language had the same meaning: it denoted a small, four-wheeled wagon, covered on the top, but open at the sides. Ethnographical investigations show that the four-wheeled caravan of the shepherds was also called a *taliga*, i.e. cart.

Literary sources confirm the logical arguments and linguistic inferences concerning the above. Thus, Emperor Leo the Wise records in his *Military Tactics* (about 894) that the 'baggage train' of the Hungarians was stationed at one or two Roman miles distance from the fighting-line. Eckehart, one of the chroniclers of the St. Gall monastery, refers several times to the Hungarian wagons in his description of the St. Gall booty campaign of 926.

We do not claim that the Hungarians had an exclusive or even a decisive role in the development or diffusion of the wheeled vehicle, but there is every reason to believe that they had a keen interest in this implement. It should be also borne in mind that the bowels of the Hungarian earth have yielded a surprisingly large number of carriage models from different ages, suggesting that the surface and vegetation of this territory was particularly suitable for the use of wheeled vehicles.

Chapter VIII

Highway traffic increases—and highwaymen flourish — The Crusades — The *Drang gen Osten* — Imperial travellers — Traffic regulations in the Middle Ages — Types of medieval vehicles — The *carroccio* — Wagon fortifications — The war-chariot with pivoted front axle — The carriage of Pope John — Further technical innovations — The suspended carriage-body — The coach — The state-coach in the Graz Joannaeum — The evidence of the Froissart Chronicle — Wedding-carriages — The carriage promenade

During the eleventh and twelfth centuries freight and passenger transport by road was further improved. It should be borne in mind in this connection that prior to the industrial revolution the horse represented the main source of power. Thus, despite the poor road conditions, more and more horse-drawn vehicles travelled on the highways, and with the growing traffic highway robbers also emerged in increasing numbers; their 'golden age' began in the twelfth century.

The highwaymen saw to it that, if the pot-holes, dust and mud of the roads were not enough to keep the traveller's attention engaged, they would not be bored. Clyn of the Clough, Adam Bell and William of Cloudesley—not to mention Robin Hood— were the most notorious 'entertainers' of the highways. In the thirteenth century, for example, these circumstances caused the Abbots of St. Albans to protect the London road with armed men.

That the situation was no better in Germany may be inferred from the fact that in 1156 the Holy Roman Emperor, Frederick I, permitted merchants to carry a sword in their wagon, so that they should not be defenceless if attacked; however, they were not allowed to gird on this weapon in a knightly fashion but only to keep it under the dickey.

In France, in addition to highwaymen, there was waylaying which was aggravated by various other forms of systematic' fleecing': the landed gentry extorted smaller or larger sums of money from travellers under different pretexts; they charged road tolls, pontage, dust money, and sometimes even freight and shaft taxes. However, in spite of these circumstances, traffic continued to grow.

The Crusades. A new type of traveller also appeared on the highways. Long winding processions of strange, armed men, the Crusaders, advanced on the roads leading from Western Europe to the Holy Land, with rows of carts and wagons jogging along beside their files.

167

It happened in the year 1095 A.D. that Pope Urban, preaching on a plain near Clermont, proclaimed a crusade for the liberation of the Holy Land from the Moslems. Peter of Amiens, a recluse eloquent of speech, gathered thousands of poor peasants under the sign of the cross. Poverty-stricken people who probably figured that they had little to lose were easily persuaded to undertake the adventurous journey. They hastily sold their cows and sheep and the scanty domestic appliances they possessed, and taking only the most necessary with them, clambered on to two-wheeled ox-drawn carts or long wagons, with their wives and children, to follow the long-bearded Pierre. Guibert de Nogent has left us an eye-witness's account of this mass conversion. About seventy thousand men, many of them in carts or wagons, proceeded through Aachen, Cologne, Austria and Hungary, along the river Danube to Constantinople, until in October 1096 they were dispersed near Nicaea by the Seljuks. About six further campaigns followed, in the course of which multitudes of carters, incited by a thirst for adventure and gain, also left France, Germany and Italy for the Holy Land. On the way there they carted the sick or tired crusaders or those unable to walk, while on the return journey they transported the booty, if any. Often, however, there was not only no booty to carry, but many of the men left their boots in foreign parts.

The Children's Crusade came to an even more dismal end. In 1212, a shepherd boy of Cloyes, named Étienne, declared himself God's own prophet destined to lead innocent children to success where the grown-ups had failed. The children soon set out from Marseille; they were joined by men, matrons and maidens. The procession was headed by Étienne in a carriage hung with rich carpets. He was followed by some thirty thousand pilgrims on numberless carts and wagons.

Naer Oestland willen wy ryden... Around the same time another surging crowd, similarly with a religious object in view, started in a different direction. Their declared mission, 'to convert the heathen', concealed, however, political aims, namely the Germanization of the Slavs. *Der grosse Treck* carried tens of thousands of Dutch, Flemish, Westphalian and Frisian colonizers *gen Osten*, to Silesia, Pomerania and Prussia. The reckless and adventurous spirit of the colonizers appears from the following Dutch folk-song: —

> *Naer Oestland willen wy ryden*
> *Naer Oestland willen wy meê*
> *al over die groene heiden,*
> *frisch over die heiden,*
> *daer isser een betere stee...*

Betere stee, that is "a better place", was what the wandering peasants longed for, and they were luckier in a way than the crusaders had been, for they did gain a foothold on the occupied territories, which they then held for centuries.

Imperial travellers also increased the heavy traffic. According to contemporary records, Frederick of Barbarossa covered nearly 1,875 miles (3,000 kilometres) between August 1157 and January 1158, travelling from Halle to Posen, thence back through Würzburg to Besançon, and again eastbound to Magdeburg, and finally, through Goslar to Regensburg. This corresponds to roughly 12 miles (20 kilometres) average a day, from which we have to deduct, of course, the time he spent in the various towns. Still, he could not do more than 19 miles (30 kilometres) on average by carriage, about as much as a good walker can cover in a day. The 44 to 47 miles (70 to 75 kilometres) daily average reached by mounted travellers makes it obvious that people on an urgent errand preferred the jolting of a horse to that of a wheeled vehicle.

The discomforts of travelling were further increased by frequent accidents: on the neglected roads the unsteady wagons often overturned with their occupants. In the *Chast de Couci* a lady complains as follows: —

> *Quar quant mes chars fu hier versés*
> *Ma chambariere y fu blecie...*

(For when my carriage overturned yesterday, my chamberlain was hurt...)

The Holy Roman Emperor Henry VII (about 1312–1313). From the travelling accounts of the Emperor it appears that the keep of the ladies accompanying him on his journeys often amounted to more than the pay of his soldiers. The mounted travellers were at that time followed by whole lines of *Kobel-* and *Kammerwagen* and even by *Kapellwagen*. The *Kobelwagen* (travelling-wagon) was a carriage-body resting on four wheels and covered by tarpaulin or leather; the *Kammerwagen* contained the travelling-beds and the baggage of the imperial household, the table-ware, the tents, wall-hangings, cushions and rugs. The *Kapellwagen* was a travelling-chapel with an altar, altar-cloths and the necessary devotional objects.

Traffic regulations in the Middle Ages. The growing highway traffic called for certain regulations. Thus, the *Sachsen- und Schwabenspiegel* (a German medieval book of laws) fixed the widths of the various types of roads, and the rules for avoiding and passing other vehicles. It ordered the *idele*, or empty vehicle, to give way to the loaded one; even the *min* (less loaded) had to clear the way for the *sverrer* (more heavily loaded vehicle).

We have to mention here two extraordinary German regulations, without knowledge of which our picture of the 'eventful life' of the medieval merchant on the road would be incomplete. According to the stipulations of one of them, towns vested with staple rights could force a merchant to unload and sell his wares, by making his passage conditional on his compliance. Such rights were granted to Cologne in 1259, to Görlitz in 1339, etc. The other regulation, the so-called *Grundruhrrecht* (a seigniorial right), stipulated that if a wagon was forced to stop on account of a broken axle, its freight passed into the property of the landowner whose estate the vehicle had been passing through at the moment of the accident, and whose land the broken shaft had touched.

In England a law enacted in 1285 provided for the widening of the roads of large market towns in such a manner that no trees, bushes or ditches were left nearer than at two hundred feet distance from the road-side. This measure was, naturally, directed against the highwaymen in the first place.

The Winchester statutes of 1285 provided that the highways were to be broad enough to permit the passing of two vehicles. The use of iron rims which expedited deterioration of the roads was forbidden in England and a similar prohibition applied to studded wheels, as they were perhaps even more destructive to the pavement (Figs. 210 and 211).

210

In France sometimes measures were elicited by special incidents. In the twelfth century the streets of Paris were so muddy that the author of a satiric doggerel apostrophizing the Latin name of Paris *(Lutetia)* asserted that it derived from the word *lutum* (mud).

210 Cart with studded wheels from **The Romance of Alexander**
211 Cart with studded wheels, carrying corn uphill
212 French travelling-wagon
213 Travelling German merchant with his cart

211

The story Rigordus wrote about the French king Philip-August gives us an idea of the thick mud which covered the streets of Paris and the foul smell that filled the air of the City. The King, sensitive to smells, was looking out of his palace window when a passing cart stirred up the thick layer of mud in the street. His Majesty fainted from the ensuing stench. Thanks to this incident, the street in front of the royal palace was paved in 1185. However, only a few months later the look and the smell of the place was the same as before, with the only difference that the mud was no longer bottomless: it was separated from the solid earth by a layer of stone.

Still, two hundred years later the street traffic in Paris was normal. A fourteenth-century manuscript of the legend of St. Denis, the first bishop of Paris, contains the picture of a *char de promenade* (Fig. 212) jogging along the paved embankment of the Seine. It is a covered wagon, but not rectangular in shape as it would appear on first sight, only the illuminator failed to render the semicircular curve of the cover—a special feature of the medieval covered wagon. The two horses in the picture are pulling in tandem, and as the traces are tied to the two sides of the wagon, it may be assumed that the vehicle was fairly narrow.

212

213

Types of medieval vehicles. In agriculture the use of the two-wheeled cart continued to prevail (Pls. XXXIX and XL, and Figs. 213–214). There was a time, in the twelfth century, when the cart was used only for carting, and it was regarded as shameful to sit in it because individuals sentenced to death were also taken to the scaffold by similar carts. However, this aversion to the cart as a means of travelling was not general; there are numerous representations of carts of this type carrying holy

171

214

passengers (Figs. 215–216). According to these, travelling on a two-wheeled cart could be, contrary to the usual practice, a distinction as well. The same can be said about the *tensa*-like transporting relics on Fig. 217.

216

Four-wheeled wagons were also in use at the same time. The contemporary miniatures, paintings, reliefs and woodcuts show us a wide range of such vehicles. Their load, structure and harnessing differ; virtually only the four wheels appear alike in all these representations. The Bayeux tapestry shows a simple wagon carrying a wine barrel (Fig. 218). The special feature of the vehicle on the bronze door of the Novgorod Cathedral is that it is provided with whipple-trees—swinging bars to which traces are fastened—the first to emerge in that period (Fig. 219). The peasant carriage in the *Sachsenspiegel* (Fig. 220) is also shown

215

217

PORTANT:ARMAS:ADNAVES:ETHIC
TRAHVNT:CARRVM
CVMVINO:ETARMIS:~

218

219

214 Late Saxon country cart
215 Cart with shafts
216 Detail of the façade of the cathedral
Borgo S. Donnino
217 Capital in the crypt of the Cathedral of
St-Denis
218 Detail of the Bayeux tapestry
219 Wagon with whipple-trees

173

220

with a whipple-tree, but this part of the vehicle is missing from a later representation (Fig. 221), although the carrying capacity of the illustrated wagon appears to be considerable.

Plate XLI, representing a French wagon, is extremely instructive, as it shows the structure of the vehicle with unusual preci-

221

222

sion. The outpeeping tip of the pivot (indicating that the wagon had a swivelling front axle) is clearly recognizable, and the details of the whipple-trees and horse-collar (hame) are most illustrative. A Polish cart carrying a diocesan and a Hungarian one transporting a wine barrel (Pls. XLII and XLIII, respectively) are presented here because they demonstrate the use of the car-stake (a south-eastern European feature) or stake-brace, which is a curved wooden part connecting the axle to the upper edge of the lower part of the wagon's inside mudguard. Their whipple-trees and smart way of harnessing also deserve special attention. We close our series of wagon illustrations with two curiosities: the one is a queer, allegorical representation of the foundation of Magdeburg by Otto the Great (Fig. 222); the other (Fig. 223) shows an interesting scene with a water-cart proceeding on the ground, an 'air-ship' in mid-air and a man running after the latter, crying *beita, beita!* (wait, wait!) in vain. Wagons were at first rarer than carts; in England they occurred only occasionally until the sixteenth century.

223

The travelling-wagon. Then, however, the wagon soon developed into a typically medieval passenger vehicle. In the beginning, the only difference was that an awning cover was applied, to make the wagon suitable for travelling. The protecting tarpaulin, fabric or leather was stretched on a semicircular frame made first of wicker and later (from the sixteenth century on) of bent rods.

224

220 Peasant with his carriage
221 On the highway
222 Allegory of the foundation of Magdeburg
223 Woodcut in Peter Attendorn's Directorium statuum
224 The family of Baron Guitschard travels to Bern

225

226

The vertical rods were strengthened with horizontal laths (of which usually three or five were applied), and the ends of the latter were ornamented with buttons.

The vehicle appearing in "Jacob's Journey to Egypt" in Rudolf von Ems's *Zurich World Chronicle* is interesting not only on account of its cover but also because the carriage-body is a suspended, swinging structure (Pl. XLIV). A panel in the choir of the Lübeck Church of the Holy Ghost shows St. Elizabeth of Hungary travelling from Hungary to Wartburg on a carriage provided with a whipple-tree (Pl. XLV). Exactly the same type of vehicle was used by Baron Guitschard's family on their journey to Berne in 1478 (Fig. 224). The fact that travelling was not an undertaking without incidents appears from Fig. 225. The use of the type of vehicle seen in this picture was not confined to the West. It appears also on a Czech stove tile (Fig. 226); although the representation is somewhat sketchy, the whipple-trees, foot-board and button ornaments of the carriage are clearly recognizable. In England the same kind of vehicle was called 'long wagon' or 'whirlicote'. When Richard II had to flee before the rebels in 1377, his whole suite followed him on horseback, but his ailing mother travelled in the queer vehicle known as the 'whirlicote'.

176

XXXIX Illumination from the "Très
Riches Heures"
XL Woodmen
XLI Illumination from the "Vie et
Miracles de Notre-Dame"

XXXIX

XLII Diocesan Philippus returns from the
coronation of Queen Kandake
XLIII Miracle of the gold in the stick
XLIV "Jacob's Journey to Egypt"
XLV "The Journey of St. Elizabeth of Hun-
gary to the Wartburg"

XLV

XLIV

XLVI The Florentine carroccio
XLVII The state-coach of Emperor Frede-
rick III
XLVIII Relief of a wheel on the sun-chariot
IL Frieze of the Hoysaleswara temple at
Halebid

XLVI

XLVII

XLVIII

IL

L Body of a bridal coach
LI German coach
LII Hungarian Kotschiwagen

L

LI

LII

The names for the different types of vehicles underwent constant changes also in the Middle Ages, which only increases the confusion about them. Thus, in the first half of the twelfth century, a large, horse-drawn vehicle, the *longa carretta*, referred to as 'long cart' by William Langland, emerged on the scene; it was a four-wheeled vehicle of a large carrying capacity (though, originally, the Latin word *carretta* meant a two-wheeled cart). The wagon with shaft came to England from Holland, as indicated also by its very name, the word 'wagon' being of Dutch origin.

In medieval Russia the most common vehicle was the *kolya*. According to the illuminations of the song about Boris and Gleb (1457), the *kolya* was a four-wheeled vehicle, but in other sources the same term is applied to two simple supports. From still other records we learn that in Kiev the *kolya* was used for carting. According to the Hypatios chronicles, the body of Prince Igor, a victim of the rising in 1147, was carried to the Babina market; there his bearers "found a man standing with a *kolya*, on which they placed the body and transported it to Podolye."

In the Crimea the Flemish Franciscan monk Wilem van Ruysbroeck (Rubruk) was offered the choice between a pair-drawn ox-cart and a pack-horse for the transportation of his baggage on his journeys in 1253–1255. However, the Constantinople merchants advised him not to take the open cart but to ask for a vehicle such as the Russians used for the transportation of furs.

In Hungary the cart and the wagon existed side by side. This is confirmed by records dating back to the twelfth century, but referring to even earlier events. The *Vita sancti Gerardi*, an eleventh-century document on the life and martyrdom of Bishop Gerard, describes how the heathen Hungarians overturned the bishop's wagon *(currus)* and, dragging him out of this vehicle, put him on a cart and thrust him in the deep. According to the Latin version: "*everterunt currum eius... ubique abstracto eo de curru eius in biga positum de monte Kreenfeld submiserunt.*" Thus, he was transferred from a four-wheeled vehicle into a two-wheeled one, for the term *biga* in the Latin text evidently means a two-wheeled cart. The legend rather justifies Gerard's habit of using a wagon *(currus)*: referring to his journey to the ferry at Pest, it emphasizes that "The bishop was small of stature, and, having exhausted all his strength in the service of God, he had to avail himself of a *currus*." This statement is, however, contradictory to another part of the legend, according to which, when Gerard was appointed as bishop of Csanád, a nobleman called *comes* Csanád took ten priests to the diocese in his own wagon.

It is very interesting in this connection that a law, proclaimed by King Ladislas I (St. Ladislas, 1077–1095), permitted the post-

carriers *(cursores)* to exchange their horses against any other horse they found under way, so that they might speed up their progress, but forbade them at the same time to unharness horses from the wagons of presbyters and members of the clergy for this purpose, which implies that the ecclesiastical officials and priests travelled by wagons.

Another type of Hungarian wagon. On his return from Jerusalem in 1433, Bertrandon de la Brocquière passed through Hungary. In an account of his experience during the long journey, he describes how in Hungary he often met "one-horse wagons *(chariots)* carrying six, seven, or even eight people. Some of these vehicles were covered; they were very nice and so extremely light that one could have carried the whole structure, including the wheels, on one's shoulders. The back wheels were much higher than the front ones, and the body was very comfortable to sleep and rest in." There is no doubt that the vehicle described had special features and was unique in type, as otherwise Brocquière who had travelled almost all over the then known world would not have devoted so much attention to it. The fact that he went into details in his account justifies the assumption that the wagon in question differed from all other wagons existing at that time.

The 'carroccio'. In most medieval wars the standard played an important role; the warriors kept an eye on it throughout the battles. As the equestrian standard-bearer could not carry it high enough for everyone to see, the standard was hoisted on a staff, and the staff was mounted on a vehicle. This innovation was introduced by the Italians. The *carroccio*, as the vehicle was called in Italian, is mentioned by Arnulphus, Archbishop of Milan, in his *Gesta Mediolanensium* of 1038; it is supposed to have been invented by Archbishop Aribert when Conrad II laid siege to and pressed hard on Milan. We know more about the structure of the Florentine *carroccio;* it was a platform on four wheels, with a staff in the middle on which the standard of the community was hoisted. The tip of the staff was ornamented with golden apples and palm leaves. The vehicle which was drawn by one of several pairs of white oxen carried a war bell, the *martinella*, which tolled when the chieftain ordered the army to attack, and fell silent to indicate a halt. The Florentine *carroccio* (Pl. XLVI) appears in various records as far back as 1167.

The flag-carriage is often mentioned also in Middle High German poetry under the name *Karrasche*. In battle the loss of the flag-carriage was tantamount to defeat. Thus, when the Prince of Löwen lost his *Fahnenwagen* in a campaign against Bishop Alexander of Lüttich (Liège), it meant that he had lost the battle, too. It was, in fact, enough to overturn the enemy's flag-carriage to seal his defeat. For this reason, the combatting parties attached stakes to the four corners of the vehicle, which they drove into the earth during the battle to prevent a turnover.

The importance of the flag-carriage was enhanced by its splendid make-up. In a novel about Troy, Benôit de Sainte-More describes the prodigious flag-carriages of the Trojans, evidently transplanting a custom of his own age into the past.

The wagon fortification, known in ancient times, was revived in the Middle Ages (Fig. 227). Thus, according to Matthaeus (Matthew) Paris's *Historia Maior*, the French formed a fortification of vehicles before the battle of Bouvines (1214). We know from Guiart des Moulins's records from 1304 that the Flemings also used wagon fortification in the battle of Monz-en-Pelve, but the real masters of its structure were the Hussites. In the battle of Tachov (Tachau) (1427) Holy Prokop, the Hussite chieftain, built a fortification from 3,600 vehicles and defeated the armies of Emperor Sigismund. Chunrad Kyeser added the following explanatory note to the illustration of a wagon fortification figuring in his codex: *Bellifortis* ('The Warhardened'): "During the exploits, the wagons were arranged side by side in a continuous line to form a closed unit."

The war-chariot with pivoted front axle. Human ingenuity proved inexhaustible in the development of further types of vehicles in the Middle Ages. The fifteenth-century German drawing shown in Fig. 228 represents an armoured war-chariot with clearly distinguishable swivelling front axle. The unwieldy struc-

ture, pushed by six horses, was steered from inside. The drawing being the earliest representation, in which the pivoted front can be distinguished beyond doubt, several writers on vehicles consider its date as the birthday of the pivoted front axle, though actually this technical innovation had a past of several centuries by that time.

The carriage of Pope John. The pivoted front axle appears even better outlined in the medieval satirical drawing (Fig. 229) illustrating a travelling accident of the ill-reputed ecclesiastic Baldassare Cossa, known also illegitimately as Pope 'John XXIII'.

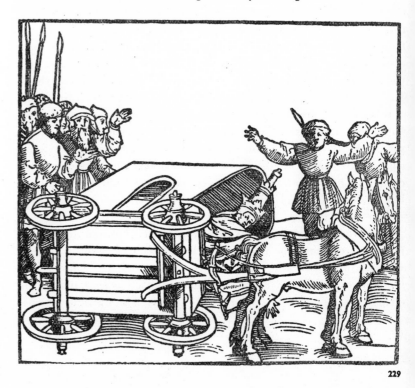

229

The misadventure must have occured in 1415 when the antipope travelled to the Council of Constance. The drawing is extremely realistic and instructive, as it gives a clear picture of the structure of the vehicle. It has no springs, nor is it provided with any device for the suspension of the carriage-body; it is further clearly discernible that the pivot was made of a single piece of branching wood—at least this is what one may infer from the asymmetrical form of the forked part.

Further technical innovations. Naturally, the first centuries of the second millennium also left their imprint on the cart and wagon. Written documents relating to this period are scarce, and the few which survive here and there are not very reliable.

182

Thus, according to the *Mainzer Chronik*, the spoked wheel was diffused in Germany by Willegis, Archbishop of Mainz, originally a wheelwright by profession. Lest he should forget his humble birth, painted wheels surrounded the inscription "*Willegis! Willegis! Deiner Abkunft nicht vergiss!*" (Willegis! Willegis! Remember your origin!) on the walls of his archiepiscopal palace.

The information we have on the diffusion of the whipple-tree in Europe appears to be more trustworthy. The whipple-tree belongs to the improvements which had been known in the Far East long before they were discovered in Europe. Its independent development here is supported by the fact that the Asiatic and European whipple-tree zones are separated by a wide geographic gap.

In Russia, on the shores of the Baltic Sea and in Siberia, the carriage with shafts persisted. For better steering the Russians invented another device: the shaft-bow, a distant relation of the bent shaft used by the Sumerians, which allowed the draught-animals a certain freedom of movement. It was used both with carts and sledges and is mentioned in the *Kalevala* (Song XVIII).

The car-stake also emerged in the Middle Ages, though at first only in a primitive form. According to the Hungarian paleontologist, geologist, geographer and ethnographer Ferenc Nopcsa it originated from southern Poland and the Ukraine.

An important document regarding the technical development of the cart and wagon was the *Hortus deliciarum* by Herrad von Landsberg (died 1195); it is an illustrated encyclopaedia of "everything worth knowing", which was used for the education of the nuns and pupils of the Hohenburg convent. Unfortunately, the original manuscript which found its way to the Strasbourg Library was destroyed by fire during the siege of the town in 1870, but part of the drawings it contained had been copied earlier. According to these, the innovations then known affected only the way of harnessing: the horse-collar and the primitive whipple-trees appear in these pictures. The heavy wagon carries not less than sixteen passengers. It may have been, of course, different in practice, and the representation should not be regarded as accurate beyond dispute; one can put anything on paper or parchment, and Herrad could fill the wagon in his picture with as many passengers as he cared to draw.

Camber may imply two different things in the case of vehicles. It may mean that the axle-pin is not the horizontal continuation of the axle but bends slightly downwards, as a result of which the wheel does not wobble or come off the pin on uneven, bumpy roads. This sort of axle-pin camber appears already on some of the ancient representations (on Greek vases). Cambering the spokes involves, however, a more complicated process which requires higher craftsmanship and technical knowledge. Here the camber means that the spokes are not flush with the hub and the rim but form a flat cone between these. Owing to the conical structure the wheel is less sensitive to lateral impact. The camber of the spokes amounts generally to a twelfth or a fourteenth part of the diameter of the wheel; it is an accepted rule that it should not exceed one-eighth part of the latter. The camber of the spokes offsets the drawback which otherwise the cambered pin would involve, for if the wheel were flat, the pressure of the spokes would not be perpendicular to the pin; the camber of the spokes represents a deviation from the perpendicular by as many degrees as the pin deviates from the horizontal.

All these innovations helped to render the wheeled vehicle more and more useful, and the practical importance of this implement increased as transportation grew quicker and cheaper. While under the Romans the high carriage charges about doubled the price of bulk goods each hundred miles, in the thirteenth century the same charges augmented the wheat price by only thirty per cent over a similar distance. The increasing requirements of the towns for produce called for large-scale deliveries.

The suspended carriage-body. The most important innovation—the full story of which would fill a separate book—was, however, the suspension of the carriage-body on ropes or chains. The first traces of its reintroduction—following the Thracian carriages—date from 1343.

It was in 1343 that Elizabeth, Dowager Queen of Hungary, travelled to Italy on a visit to her son Andrew, then king of Naples. The ties which united Hungary with Naples require some explanation, even if it means deviating a little from our subject, for it will help the reader understand the probable origin of the relations between the Italian and Hungarian carriages.

To begin with, we have to recall that, when Charles I of Anjou (1266–1285), son of Louis VIII and Blanche of Castile, and younger brother of Louis IX, conquered the Neapolitan Kingdom with the battle of Benevento and marched into Naples to ascend the throne, the ladies also took part in the procession on four-wheeled vehicles, called *carreta*. The chronicler of the event praises especially the queen's *carreta* which was covered with sky-blue velvet within and without; lilies embroidered in gold ornamented the inside of the carriage. After a series of sanguinary events and turns of fortune, the Angevins recaptured Naples, and Robert ascended the Neapolitan throne (1309–1343). His nephew, Charles Robert (Caroberto), son of Charles Martell, became King of Hungary. And Elizabeth, the wife—and from 1342 the widow—of Charles Robert, was the Queen who in the above-mentioned splendid *carreta* or *raeda* entered Naples in

184

1343. According to contemporary records, the vehicle was drawn by four horses and carried not less than eight ladies, in addition to the Queen, while other noblewomen followed in a *currus*. We could only make guesses as to the features of the *raeda*, so carefully distinguished by the eye-witness from the *currus*, were it not for the records of Johannes Archidiaconus de Küküllő, describing the funeral of Charles Robert a year earlier. In this document of 1342, the writer refers to a three-horsed, purple-coloured *currus mobilis* or *currus ostilarius*, by which he evidently meant a coach whose body was suspended on straps or chains. (Incidentally, the word *ostilarius*, or correctly *oscillarius*, is the equivalent of the Hungarian expression *hintáló szekér*, or *hintó* for short, which means a swinging wagon.)

According to the *Grande Encyclopédie*, the first coach *(carrosserie)* appeared in France when Isobel of Bavaria entered Paris in a vehicle of this type on the occasion of her marriage to the French King Charles VI in 1385. The second was a gift of Ladislas V, King of Hungary and Bohemia who sent a coach to Tours on the occasion of his proposal to Madeleine, daughter of Charles VII and Mary of Anjou. Villaret described the vehicle as *"un chariot branlant et moult somptueux et moult riche"* (a swinging coach, most sumptuous and rich). According to Villaret the vehicle was the object of general admiration, as no *voiture à sous-pente* had been seen in France until then. Instead of resting on the axles, like a wagon, the body of the coach was suspended on iron or wooden supports which emerged from the framework of the vehicle.

Strangely enough, this type of coach was not identical with the Hungarian *kocsi*, though the name it bore throughout Europe originated from the Hungarian term. The English word 'coach', the Dutch *koets* (formerly *cotsie* or *kotsie*), the German *Kutsche* (formerly *Gotschi*, *Gotschiwagen* or *Gutschi*), etc., denote a different vehicle than that understood by *kocsi* in Hungary. (This complicated issue will be dealt with in detail in the following chapter, for—although the earliest written reference to the *kocsi* in the Hungarian sense can be traced as far back as the end of the Middle Ages—most of the important data regarding the development of this vehicle date from the beginning of the modern times.) The French *coche* approaches nearest to the conceptual content of the Hungarian *kocsi*, though there are some essential differences between the two types of carriages covered by the above terms; this refers especially to the heavy weight of the French *coche*, which lent the vehicle a different character. However, it is not the only case where the same term has a different meaning in its place of origin to that understood beyond the boundaries of the country.

The state-coach in the Joannaeum of Graz. There is a splendid state-coach (Pl. XLVII), preserved in the Graz Joannaeum, which was manufactured in Wiener Neustadt around 1450 for the personal use of Emperor Frederick III and his wife, Elinor of Portugal. The richly carved and gilded coach was used by the Emperor at his coronation in Rome on March 16th, 1452, and on the day of his wedding there. Whether the body of the carriage simply rested on axle bolsters or was suspended is still an open issue. Dr. Jürgen Smolian, an authority on the history of the wheeled vehicle, believes that it was of the suspended type, and he reconstructed the vehicle in a drawing according to this theory. Against this, Frau Dr. Gertrud Smola, Director of the Joannaeum, does not consider the reconstruction correct, for in her opinion the body of the coach bears no mark of any suspension. However, it is not difficult to decide the matter: we may start from the fact that the suspended carriage-body was no lon-

230

ger a curiosity at that time (1452); in fact, it was a structure well known at the court of Frederick III, and since they knew about the Italian coach fashion, it is perhaps not unrealistic to suppose that they had the new type of coach built for the Roman journey to keep pace with what was regarded as the *dernier cri* in vehicles.

The evidence of the Froissart Chronicle. The question whether this historic object was a wagon or a coach may perhaps be decided best on the basis of the Froissart codex of Breslau. There are three miniatures in this manuscript, which represent vehicles. The first shows Isobel of Bavaria entering Paris; the second, the entrance of a princess (Fig. 230); the third, the funeral of King Richard II of England. It is evident from these illustrations that both types of vehicle were current. The hearse of Richard II had a suspended body; the carriage of the princess was only slightly different in structure, probably wooden springs were used for the suspension of its box; that of Queen Isobel was carried litter-like by two horses. Against this, the carriage-body of the vehicles in the background appears to have rested directly on the axles, at least as far as this can be seen from the miniature drawings. It is presumed therefore that the passenger compartment, the most valuable part of the carriage, was treated in different ways, according to the smoothness of the road, the inclination of the passenger to nausea and the occasion of the journey. It was very likely that the body of the coach of Frederick III was transported from Wiener Neustadt to Rome on a wagon, for this type of vehicle was not practical for longer journeys; it was a sumptuous object meant mainly for display.

Wedding-coaches. Towards the end of the Middle Ages, the coach began to assume the special rôle of increasing the splendour of parades, weddings and funerals. Numerous documents render account of the pageantry of such events, but most of them treat the subject in a stereotype manner. We would quote here the one describing the entry of Beatrice of Naples to Hungary: —

> The Princess, then bride-elect to Matthias Corvinus, King of Hungary, came to Buda in 1476 with a large suite. The bridegroom-King, accompanied by three thousand mounted noblemen, went to meet her at Fehérvár where she arrived in a gilded coach covered with gold-embroidered green velvet. The members of the Princess' suite travelled in seven richly gilded coaches, each of which was drawn by six horses; the coachmen wore velvet suits with gold buttons. Matthias brought with him two coaches from Buda, which were even more magnificent than those of his bride-elect; after the Fehérvár festivities they entered Buda in the Hungarian vehicles.

Sumptuous weddings and carriage parades were organized also by Lodovico il Moro in Milan. Bandello counted sixty four-horsed coaches on a single parade day. He also tells us that the finest coaches were manufactured, gilded, painted and upholstered in

187

Milan. The splendid vehicles rocked slowly along the lively streets, so that the ladies might make a show of their jewellery and fine clothes. If there was congestion in the traffic, loud chatting began between the passengers of the coaches and the gentlemen on horseback.

The driver's seat. From the beginning of the twelfth century, the drivers rode the first horse on the left side before the wagon; this is why the horse on the left is still called *nyerges* (saddler) in Hungarian and *Sattelpferd* in German. Prior to that period—and of course also afterwards—the driver sat sometimes on the edge of the wagon or on a plank, but the dickey-seat as such did not yet exist.

India. In this chapter, too, we have to point out the more or less independent development of carriage-building in the Asiatic countries, especially in India, during the period corresponding to the European Middle Ages. Essential changes can be observed in these parts in the ritual use of the carriage. The rustic mural paintings which survive in Pari, the famous Orissan place of pilgrimage, illustrate the special rôle vehicles had played in religious ceremonies. The appearance of Vishnu, the Hindu god, in the form of Jagannath drew—and still continues to draw—thousands of pilgrims to Pari, to take part in the procession which carries the divine statues from the temple to a summer site, on ceremonial cars. The mural paintings and the so-called Pari pictures represent also such ceremonial vehicles.

231

Temple vehicles carved from stone. The carved temple cars or rather 'car temples' were developed from the ritual vehicles which played such an important rôle in the Hindu cults; they can be regarded partly as buildings, partly as works of plastic art. The temple of Konarak, for instance, constructed around 1240, stood on twelve pairs of wheels. One of them, decorated with reliefs of high artistic quality, is presented here in Pl. XLVIII.

188

232

The Hoysaleswara temple in Halebid (thirteenth century), though not built on wheels, bears reference to the wheeled vehicle. One of its friezes represents a battle scene from the *Ramayana*. The chariot of the archer figuring in the picture deserves special attention; it is best compared to the dray of our times (Pl. IL).

China. The Chinese wheeled vehicle retained its traditional form also in the centuries corresponding to the European Middle Ages: mostly carts drawn by a single horse harnessed to a pair of shafts were used; at least this is what the representations of reliefs and paintings indicate. Only a few exceptional representations show that attempts had been made to harness more than one draught-animal to a vehicle. Occasionally four-wheeled wagons are represented, but it is evident at the same time that the Chinese did not know the pivoted front axle until European culture penetrated into China; in fact, no turning front axle has been found on any of the Chinese carriages of this period. Nor did the Chinese cart have a perch or a pivot.

The vehicle shown in Fig. 231 may be regarded as the typical Chinese cart. It is interesting to note that the same mode of harnessing appeared in Europe only centuries later.

What Marco Polo saw in China. Marco Polo who visited China at the end of the thirteenth century described the traffic in 'the great city of Kinsay' in his famous itinerary as follows: —

In the main street of the city you meet an infinite succession of these carriages passing to and fro. They are long covered vehicles, fitted with curtains and cushions, and affording room for six persons, and they are in constant request for ladies and gentlemen going on parties of pleasure...

Other Asiatic territories. Burma, Thailand, Cambodia, Laos, Vietnam, Indonesia and Japan of today have developed partly under Indian and partly under Chinese cultural influence; thus the various forms of wheeled vehicles also spread to the East from these two empires. Variants of the Indian and Chinese vehicles can be seen, for example, in the famous reliefs of the magnificent temples of Angkor (Fig. 232) and on the Boro Budur shrine in Java.

189

233

190

The discovery of America — The goods van and the cart at the beginning of the modern times — How the wagon developed into the coach — A 'celestial' carriage—The suspension of the carriage-body—Matthias Corvinus as the inventor of the *kocsi* — The rôle of Ippolito d'Este — The researches of Conte Gozzadini — A counter-opinion advanced by K. Titz — Witnesses and testimonies: Tommaso Dainero, Cuspinianus, Herberstein, Avila y Zuñiga and Hortleder — State-coaches and town-coaches — Roads and journeys — Other dangers of travelling — The carriages of German princes — Nuptial carriages — The spreading of pleasure drives — The carriage in France — Montaigne about the *coche* — Literary scraps — The introduction of the mail-coach service in Germany and in France — The coach and the cart in the British Isles — The interruption of road-building — The diffusion of the wagon — The increased recognition of the wheelwright's trade

The discovery of America created a new situation also in the field of transport, as the search for condiments, gold and precious stones was diverted from the Middle and Near East to the newly discovered continents. The ports which had formerly handled the maritime traffic towards the Levant of the East, lost their earlier importance, as a result of which the traffic on the roads leading to these ports also diminished. On the other hand, the Spanish and Portuguese ports (Cadiz, Seville, Lisbon), and later Antwerp, Amsterdam, Rotterdam and London, became traffic centres of steadily growing importance. The fact that more than two hundred vehicles passed daily through the gates of Antwerp gives a fair idea of the traffic this town had to cope with in its heyday. The number of loaded carts coming from Germany, France and Lorraine amounted to over two hundred a week, while that of peasant carts and corn wagons was estimated at ten thousand a week.

What were these wagons and carts like? The question may be answered by a series of illustrations. The woodcut shown in Fig. 233 represents wagons in front of the gate of Lübeck; they hardly differ from the ordinary peasant wagons of our days. A Nuremberg woodcut of moralizing content (Fig. 234) shows

234 German woodcut of moralizing content: the education of children

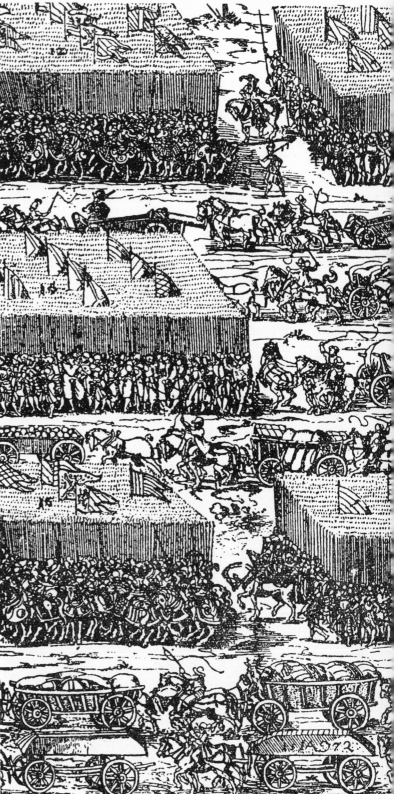

a regular peasant wagon, the only difference being that horses are harnessed to both ends of the vehicle: in its legend Hans Sachs condemns parents who, because of their different ideas about upbringing, try to influence their children (the six standing in the wagon) in different directions. Jost Amman's woodcut (Fig. 235) shows a long train of wagons. The range of carts is perhaps even richer and more diversified. They figure in various representations, for example the French woodcut illustrating timber-vendors in Fig. 236, the German *genre* picture showing a pie-baking oven mounted on a cart (Fig. 237) and the illustration taken from a Swiss chronicle, representing the loading of looted or stolen paraphernalia onto a simple cart drawn by a skinny nag (Fig. 238). But the cart, and sometimes the wagon, too, were allotted also the sad role of carrying the condemned to the scaffold (Fig. 239). The two types of vehicles—the cart and the wagon—can be studied together on Lucas Cranach's woodcut representing the siege of Wolfenbüttel (Fig. 240).

236

237

236 Paris timber-vendors
237 Pie-vendor with his cart
238 Ransoming a Swiss village
239 Cart carrying a condemned woman to the scaffold

239

How the wagon developed into the coach. In sixteenth-century woodcuts, paintings and reliefs one can easily follow the stages of development which led gradually from the peasant wagon to the coach. The former needed but little modification according to Fig. 241; it was enough to put a tarpaulin awning over the body (Fig. 242), and there it was, ready for travelling. The simple

238

240

240 Siege of Wolfenbüttel
241 Detail from a stall in the Cathedral of
Amiens
242 Covered German travelling-wagon
243 Merchants travelling to the Frankfurt
fair

241

242

type of wagon, called *Rollwagen* in German (Fig. 243), was much
in use at that time. In his *Rollwagenbüchlein* (publ. in 1555), Jörg
Wickram, a *Meistersinger* of Colmar and scribe of Burgheim,
describes how during the long journeys the travellers endeavoured

243

197

to dispel their boredom by telling funny stories and interesting anecdotes under the awning of the wagon. The wagon seen in an illustration of Edmund Spenser's *The Shepheard's Calendar* appears to have been a somewhat finer but by no means more comfortable vehicle (Fig. 244).

In Fig. 245 two travelling-conveyances are facing each other: an unwieldy travelling-wagon and a litter. Their passengers are, however, of greater interest: Emperor Charles V is seated in the litter; he is seen taking leave of John Frederick the Magnanimous, Prince-Elector of Saxony whom he had led captive in the battle of Mühlberg (1547). We also know the exact date and place of the Prince-Elector's release: 2nd September, 1552, near Linz. In the picture John Frederick is seen uncovered, shaking hands with the Emperor; a travelling-wagon in the background is waiting to take him back to his own country. Clumsy covered wagons stand also in St. Peter's Place in Rome (Fig. 246), while the Pope is giving his blessings from a balcony. Six such wagons may be counted among the dense crowd, with grooms standing ready on the footboard of some of them.

A 'celestial' carriage. The vehicle figuring in Hans von Leonrodt's book illustrated by Hans Schäufelein and printed in Augsburg in 1517 is unusual in form, but it was not an ordinary carriage from the point of view of its destination either: the picture

244

425

represents a 'celestial' carriage, made of "carefully selected, expensive timber", in which "those who lived and died well" could go straight to heaven. The structure of the vehicle—though only partly visible in the drawing (Fig. 247)—is clearly recognizable: it is that of a simple box wagon, both ends of which rest directly on the axle. From the easily discernible hand-grip and front ring it may be concluded that such carriage-bodies—which evidently had a terrestrial use, too—were simply placed on the frame of a farm wagon to form a travelling-carriage. The accurately drawn harnessing and the clearly distinguishable whipple-trees also point to the fact that the artist had a real carriage for model.

The suspension of the carriage-body was gaining ground in the course of the sixteenth century. The essential feature of what the Germans called *Kutsche* and of the similar carriage (the English 'coach') was that its structure incorporated some device (of straps, chains or springs) which, fitted between the carriage-body and the axle, reduced the jolting of the vehicle. It is usually a heavily built, decorated carriage, necessarily provided with a cover. First semi-cylindrical awnings made of tarpaulin or leather were used; later this was replaced by a canopy-like top, which still later developed into a box-like carriage-body.

246

Other types of vehicles. At the same time, the coach with a suspended body and a semi-cylindrical roof was also in use throughout Europe. Several sixteenth-century coach-bodies (without wheels or chassis) survive, but all these lag behind the *Festwagen* (festive carriage) of the time of Frederick III almost by a century. One of them, a bridal coach (Pl. L), was presented by John Frederick the Magnanimous, Prince-Elector of Saxony (referred to in this chapter earlier) to his fiancée, Sibylle of Cleve, on the occasion of their wedding on 9th March, 1527. We have already mentioned the two sixteenth-century coach-bodies now

248 A state-coach of Veronese origin
249 Side elevation of state-coach on Fig. 248
250 A state-coach body

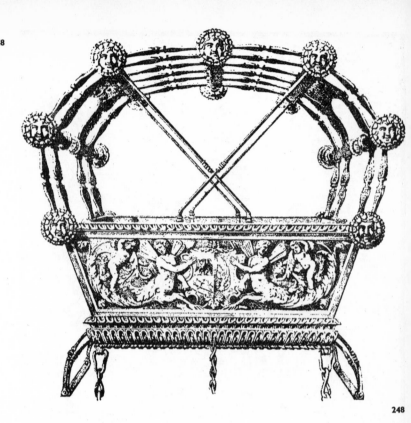

248

249

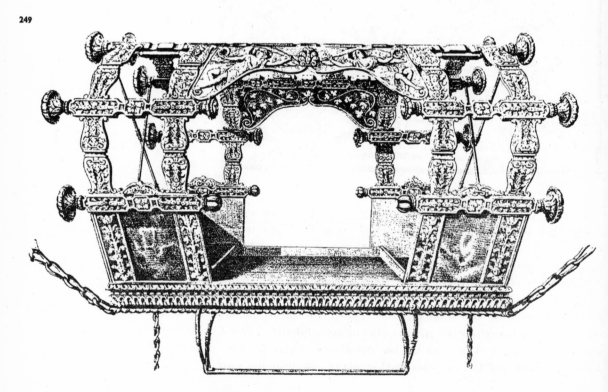

kept at the Serego-Alighieri palace in Verona, dating from 1549 and 1572, respectively.

The suspension of the carriage-body meant a further improvement which we shall discuss in detail later; here we would only mention that the oldest document which has come down to us regarding the use of this structure, called the 'coach' are German woodcuts and a book already produced by printing. Hans Tirol's woodcut (Fig. 251), representing the carriage parade of distinguished ladies on the occasion of the Augsburg Congress in 1530, does not show precisely how the back part of the ornate covered wagon was suspended; but in the background of a woodcut from the *Trostspiegel*, executed by a German artist called 'the Petrarch Master', it is clearly discernible that a suspension structure was applied to both pairs of wheels (Fig. 252). The way only the rear part of the carriage was suspended appears clearly from one of the illustrations in *Kurtze gegrundte Beschreibung des Pfalzgrafen bey Rhein hochzeitlichen Ehren Fests*, a book printed in Munich at Adam Berg's in 1568 (Pl. LI).

250

The first authentic representation of the Hungarian *kocsi* dates from 1568 (Pl. LII). It appears in an Augsburg manuscript, entitled *Chunteruet Buoch*, which contains a coloured drawing introduced by Jeremias Schemel as follows: "*Weiter volgt hernach ein ungarische Gutsche, wie si soll geordnet und mit aller zugehör gerist Werdenn.*" (And hereupon follows a Hungarian coach as it should be complete with all its fittings installed.)

The drawing completes the information the reader could gather hitherto on the appearance of the Hungarian *kocsi*: it shows that its body rested on the axles; the wicker frame-work of the vehicle was higher at the back than in front; cushions and sacks filled with wool made the carriage-body more comfortable for travelling.

Searching for the inventor of the Hungarian *kocsi*, we strike upon the name of a king in the first place, for it is said that the vehicle was originally devised by Matthias Corvinus (1458–1490). Although there may be a good deal of exaggeration in this attribution, fed by the flattery due to a king everywhere and at all times, yet it is undeniable that Matthias was very partial to the *kocsi* which he used in spite of the fact that he owned some splendid saddle-horses and—as we have seen from the foregoing—a large number of ornate coaches, too. The King's Italian biographer, Bonfini, mentions in his *Rerum Hungaricarum Decades* that Matthias travelled with unbelievable speed, by fast wagon, covering as much as 100,000 steps (about 47 miles; 75 kilometres) a day. Bonfini also remarked that Matthias had been fond of both riding and carriage races since he was a young boy. By some fortunate chance, there exists a copy of the Bonfini biography which Johannes Listius, Bishop of Veszprém (Hungary)

(died 1577), had provided with marginal notes while in his possession. The above quoted passage bears the following remarks of the bishop partly in Latin and partly in Hungarian: "*Bizony kochis nem volt—Romanus enim ille mos iam tum desierat, nisi forte dicere velit, curru kochy vectum, cuius Rex primus Inventor fuit.*" (Truly, he was no driver [meaning the King]—The Roman fashion had long been forgotten by then, unless he [Bonfini] meant that the King travelled on a coach called 'kochy' whose first inventor was the King himself.) According to this, Listius who still had the possibility of obtaining first-hand information from the King's contemporaries (Matthias died in 1490) regarded the dead monarch as the inventor of the *currus kochy*.

It is beyond the scope of this volume to decide the above question, so let us leave it to the interested scholars. We can, however, subscribe to the view that the light and fast rolling carriage of the type described above had been invented in Hungary and was, for some reason or other, called *kocsi*, 'wagon of Kocs'. It is quite possible that the vehicle had been developed from the earlier farm wagon by the wheelwrights of Kocs; whether the King had anything to do with it is a question we better not pry into at this point. Why just Kocs should have had the opportunity to achieve this creditable result in carriage-building is explained by the fact that Kocs was situated on the Vienna–Buda road, along which King Matthias had established the first mail-coach service in Hungary. (In 1485 the King transferred his seat from Buda to the Austrian capital conquered shortly before that date, but he kept travelling to and fro and considered it of major importance to maintain close connections between the two cities.) There were resting and feeding places at every four or five miles along this road, one of which was in the village of Kocs. (The present Vienna–Budapest high-road no longer touches the village.)

Association of Ippolito d'Este with the Hungarian 'kocsi'. Conclusive proofs of the important rôle played by the Hungarian *kocsi* are supplied by the household records of Ippolito d'Este, nephew to Beatrice of Naples who was the wife of Matthias Corvinus. On the insistence of the Queen, Matthias had appointed the hardly six-year-old Ippolito as Archbishop of Esztergom. The child-Archbishop kept a large court at his residence; the account books of his household, now preserved in the archives at Modena, were kept by Italian scribes who also settled in the town of Esztergom. One of these historic records contains on page nine the following entry: "*1487 in Castello di Strigonio* [the Italian name of Esztergom]: *Per una careta de Kozo.*" Further on, *caro de Coki, carette da cozo, Cozy* and *cozi* are mentioned several times. It requires little imagination to guess that these terms are variations of the Hungarian *kocsi*, according to the sound it produced in the Italian ear.

We know from Conte Gozzadini's researches that it was the same Ippolito d'Este who introduced the Hungarian *kocsi (carro da coccia)* in Italy, in the town of Ferrara when he returned there as an adult around 1509. This is confirmed by the sixteenth-century writer Pirrho Ligorio who in his work entitled *De vehiculis antiquorum* states that "*Il cocchio fu portato prima in Italia dal primo signor Ippolito, Cardinale di Ferrara, da Ungaria.*" (The coach was first brought to Italy from Hungary, by His Eminency Ippolito, Cardinal of Ferrara.)

Lucrezia Borgia, the beautiful sister-in-law of Ippolito d'Este, addressed a letter to the archbishop in Ferrara on 17th November, 1509, with the following request: —

> My Lord and master having advised me this morning to meet the Duchess of Urbino with all possible dispatch, greatly I need a *carrettone* for my personal use, and not knowing whom to turn to in full confidence, except your Reverend, I have decided to request you to help me out with *l'Ongaro* until I return...

The word *l'Ongaro* may of course have meant the Hungarian coachman whom Ippolito d'Este took with him from Hungary (and of whom mention is made earlier in the letter). However, the context leaves no doubt that it refers here to the *carrettone*, for the Duchess explicitly says, "greatly I need a *carrettone*" and not that she requires a coachman.

The term *kochy* figures repeatedly also in the 1494–95 Latin household records of Wladislas II, successor of King Matthias. According to an entry dated 1st May, 1494, oranges and lemons were transported by order of His Majesty, "*per currum kochy*" to the royal castle in Visegrád, and we come across the word *Kochy* and *currier de Koch* (wagon of Kocs) also under several other items of the account books.

According to K. Titz, the Czech linguist, however, *kocsi* is not a Hungarian word but only an early popular derivative from the Czech noun *koči* or the still earlier adjective form *kotčí* (i.e. *kotčí vuz*—wagon) which meant a vehicle provided with a *kotec*, i.e. a covered body. He argues that the Czech term *koczy* can be traced back as far as 1469, whereas the earliest occurrence of the corresponding word in Hungarian dates from eighteen years later.

In our opinion the precedence of written occurrences does not in itself decide the question, for the wagon of Kocs had existed long before the date of the first extant written document referring to its use. The fact that Italian scribes of Esztergom used their own idiomatic variants corresponding to the Hungarian word *kocsi* as early as 1487 demonstrates that the term must have been deeply rooted and widely used in the Hungarian language by that time.

Multitudes of data prove that this was actually the case. The present volume does not afford space for all the documentary references pertaining to this question or for the details connected with the few selections quoted hereunder; thus we have to confine ourselves to indicating the sources of our information on the subject. Tommaso Dainero—who as ambassador of Ercole d'Este, prince of Ferrara, visited Wladislas II, king of Hungary, at Buda in 1501—spoke highly of the then fashionable *carro da coccia* in his report to the Prince, stating that he found it an agreeable and rapid travelling conveyance. (He covered the distance between Vienna and Buda—167 miles [267 kilometres]—in a night and a day.) Cuspinianus, rector of the Viennese University and an outstanding scholar and diplomat who visited Hungary on twenty-four occasions, states in his description of the meeting between Emperor Maximilian I and the Hungarian, Czech and Polish kings, of which he was an eye-witness in 1515, that many of the Hungarian noblemen arrived on fast wagons, "*quibus nomen est patria lingua: Kotschi*" (called *Kotschi* in their native language). In a speech held in 1526, the same Cuspinianus referred to a certain Hungarian fast wagon, "*qui vulgo gotschi ab oppido passim nominantur*" (which is commonly called by the name *gotschi* after the respective town).

The next witness we wish to cite was the Austrian statesman and historian Freiherr Siegmund von Herberstein (1486–1566) who had discharged important diplomatic duties in the service of the Emperors Maximilian and Charles V. On 20th April, 1518, he travelled to Moscow through Hungary in a *Kotschi* which he states "was so called after a village situated about ten miles from Buda." According to the details contained in his description of the 'wagon of Kocs', the vehicle was drawn by three horses; there was little or no iron fitting on its structure, and it carried four passengers besides the coachman. The fact that in 1525 Herberstein travelled also from Wiener Neustadt to Prague "*auf Cotschien*" indicates that the use of this conveyance spread rapidly to the neighbouring countries.

Emperor Charles V also used the 'wagon of Kocs'. Luis de Avila y Zuñiga, the Spanish historian, writes in his *Commentarios de la guerra de Alemaña hecha por Carlos V en 1546 y 1547* the following: "*Por que la noche ere larga y rigidissima, se puso a dormir en un carro cubierto, alos quales en Ungría llaman coche, por que el nombre e la invención es de aquella tierra.*" (Since the night was long and cold, he went to sleep in a covered wagon, called *coche* in Hungary, since the name and the invention came from that country.) Friedrich Hortleder also writes that the Emperor Charles V "went to sleep in a Hungarian *gutschwagen* because his gout troubled him."

207

The Hungarian 'kocsi' made its way to the West; naturally, its use spread first to the neighbouring Austria, whence it infiltrated into other countries of the Holy Roman Empire. We cannot stress sufficiently, however, that this *kocsi* was of the type seen in Pl. LII. It is presented in an adapted form in A. Guldenmund's woodcut (Fig. 253). It shows the main features of the Hungarian

253

vehicle: the high-backed, light wicker-work body resting on the axles and the three horses harnessed abreast. At this stage the changes in the structure were still only of minor importance: a protecting cover was added to the wicker-work body at the back; the sides were decorated with carpets; the cushion or sack or wool was slipped into a tassled velvet case; the wheels appear to have been fitted with iron tyres; between the spokes the profile of the felloe was thinned by carving. (Schemel was not skillful enough to bring out this latter detail in his illustration.) The harnessing had been slightly altered; the vehicle was still drawn by three horses, however, the third horse was no longer tied to a separate pole but to the main swingle set (unless Master Guldenmund had a finger in the modification appearing in the picture). The horses, covered with decorated horse-cloths, were not of Hungarian breed, but the clothing of the coachmen was characteristically Hungarian.

State-coaches and town-coaches. After the first century of modern times, no respectable European court could do without a collection of coaches if it cared for its reputation. As usual, fashion passed from the court downwards also in the case of the coach; however, it did not descend beyond the aristocracy until the end of the sixteenth century, when it reached the ranks of the nobility and higher bourgeoisie.

Roads and journeys. At the beginning of modern times the use of the coach was confined to urban roads if the danger of getting stuck or overturned was to be avoided. Even in towns, the streets were paved only here and there, but they were still in

208

relatively good condition compared to the amazingly deteriorated and neglected highways. In the streets at least the larger pot-holes were filled up, but on the highways such repairs were seldom carried out. It was therefore a custom in Germany that, if someone undertook a longer journey, he engaged hands for the trip to help extricate the coach if it got stuck in the mud. Poles, faggots and ropes were also taken along for this purpose. To illustrate the German road conditions it is perhaps sufficient to cite a single example: in 1571 there developed on the Marburg–Frankfurt road a pot-hole of such depth that a farm labourer who happened to fall in found his death at its bottom. This was too much to be tolerated, so the road-master arranged for the repair of the 'slight unevenness' of the road: it was filled up with five hundred faggots.

Other perils of the road. Besides the bad road conditions, other perils, too, threatened the bold who ventured on a longer journey. Such travellers had to be prepared to meet dangerous robbers, especially if their road led through big forests. Desperate bandits who did not recoil even from murder lay in ambush along the roadsides. In spite of every pursuit against them, and even after the destruction of their fortresses, the robber knights carried on their activities even after the middle of the sixteenth century. If one wanted to avoid becoming the victim of a highway attack, one had to pay escort money to the landowner of the region, who then gave armed escort to the traveller. If the protection thus provided did not prove adequate, then the landowner who guaranteed the traveller's security paid damages for the goods or other valuable objects which had been taken. The escort money was no paltry sum; thus it is quite comprehensible that the sixteenth-century Leipzig merchants bound for Frankfurt to attend the fairs there tried to save the substantial ransom by out-witting the bandits: they avoided the main roads and took the less frequented byways to get their ware to Frankfurt.

The carriages of the German princes. We know from a contemporary record that, on the occasion of the big tournament organized by Joachim I, Prince-Elector of Brandenburg, in 1509, his consort appeared at the festival in a gilded wagon and not in a coach, while twelve noble ladies paraded in simple, although crimson-lined wagons. Historic records of 1530 still mention only the *Frauenkobel* which was a wagon with a tarpaulin covering. The Bavarian Princess Jakobäa and her ladies-in-waiting owned several expensive carriages, among them some gilded ones, too. They are described in the earliest inventory of the *Hofwagenburg* (court stall) dating from 1600. According to this document an old gilded *Frauenkobel* and three other carriages for the ladies-in-waiting stood in the carriage-house of the court. As the inventory does not call these vehicles *Kotschiwagen*, it may be presumed that they were actually wagons of the decorated type.

Wedding-carriages. In the sixteenth century the sumptuous bridal carriage represented an essential, almost indispensable requisite of princely or aristocratic weddings. It became a general custom for the bridegroom and his family to meet the bride outside the town or on the riverside, if the latter arrived by boat, and to lead her and her escort into the town in bridal carriages forming a procession similar to the Italian *trionfi*.

The memory of an especially splendid wedding is kept alive by Nikolaus Solis's engravings representing the bridal procession of Prince Wilhelm of Bavaria and Princess Renata of Lorraine at Munich, in 1568. The pictures show the expensive coaches with which the bride and bridegroom have mutually presented each other. Though the carriages display much similarity with the *Kobelwagen* developed from the covered wagon, yet their bodies no longer rest directly on the axles but appear to be suspended on straps or ropes. Heinrich Wirre has put into rhymes his admiration for these coaches. In turns, he sang the praise of the wheelwright, the cutter, the blacksmith, the painter, the harness-maker, the gold-plater, the upholsterer and every other craftsman who by his work contributed to the perfect manufacture of the coach. We also know from contemporary records that, when Johann Wilhelm III, Prince of Jülich-Cleve-Berg, led Jakobäa, daughter of Margrave Phillibert of Baden, to the altar in 1585, the bride who arrived in Düsseldorf by boat on the Rhine entered the town in a *Gutzwagen* drawn by six horses.

The four-horsed 'behangener Wagen' (suspended wagon), in which Wolf von Barby appeared at the Speyer Reichs-Assembly in 1544, was not yet called a *Kutsche* in the respective records. That such suspended, swinging wagons were still quite unusual at that time is evident from the fact that Wolf von Barby had to ask for special permission to use one.

The term *behangener Wagen* is used for the new invention also in Johann Coler's *Oeconomia ruralis et domestica* (Rural and Domestic Economy) which appeared between 1591 and 1601. In this the writer states that there are wagons with suspended carriage-bodies which are covered, but not all covered wagons are of the suspended type. These are the most practical vehicles for travelling. Then—continues Coler—there are coaches *(Kutschen)* whose tops can be put up or left open; in the latter case one can look around comfortably in every direction. The *Kutsche* he refers to was actually the type of conveyance we now call a landau. It was already used by distinguished travellers at the close of the sixteenth century. An Austrian archduke is seen in one on a representation dating from 1593; however, the body of this vehicle was not suspended, nor did it rest on springs (Fig. 254).

254

Pleasure-driving spread like an epidemic, and the comfort of the coaches increased with it. Instead of serving practical purposes, driving became a favourite pastime, an occasion for parading and showing off. In other words, the carriage became an excellent instrument of prodigality. Excessive indulgence in this pleasure sometimes required the interference of higher circles, and even the clergy had to fight against it from the pulpit. The liege lords, too, had every reason to disapprove of the comfort offered by the coach, for their interests demanded that they should be able to lead their liegemen into battle on horseback at any given moment. They foresaw that the nobility would lose the habit of horse-riding and thus become less suitable for military service and unable to stand the rigours of war. The German princes could not stress enough that the nobility ought not to indulge in coach-driving but practise horse-riding instead. In 1588 Julius von Braunschweig had to introduce prohibitive measures to forestall the further spreading of this pastime, for he feared that "the manly virtues, dignity, courage, honour and loyalty of the German nation were impaired, as carriage-driving was equal to idling and indolence." By the end of the sixteenth century, pleasure-driving assumed such measures that, according to the German satirist Johann Fischart, the *Gutsche* relegated horse-riding to the background, and its excessive use caused the decline of saddle-horse breeding in Germany.

In France the German word *Kutsche* took the form *coche* which originally meant a large travelling-wagon, a vehicle similar in semantic meaning to that covered by the second sense of the German term. However, in 1550 only three such vehicles were known of in Paris: one belonged to Catherine de' Medici, another, to Diane de Montmorency and the third, to Jean de Laval-Boisdauphin. (The latter owed it to his corpulence that, although a man, he had a carriage, for he was so fat that he could neither walk nor ride a horse.)

The coach presented by Emperor Ferdinand to the Maréchal de Vieilleville on the occasion of the latter's visit to the Viennese court as envoy of the French king, Charles IX, in 1562, was still an object of great admiration. The vehicle which was lined with crimson velvet was drawn by four snow-white Turkish horses whose mane and tail were also dyed red; the clothing of the driver and the groom was Hungarian in style, but in colours it was adapted to the coat of arms of the Vieilleville family (yellow and black).

Owners of this type of conveyance could not, however, boast of travelling at a high speed. The Comte de Brienne-le-Château, for instance, needed four days to cover the distance between Brienne and Paris, about 120 miles (190 kilometres). In outward appearance the coach, in general, showed considerable improvements.

Whence the French designation 'coche'? In the French translation of the chronicles of the Hungarian bishop Broderith (Brodarics), published in Paris under the title *Histoire des troubles de Hongrie* in 1594, we read the following: —

Paul Tomori, Archbishop of Kalocsa, who was not content with warning the king several times of the coming of the Turks, travelled in all haste to the king's residence, changing several times the small light wagon called *Kotcze*, after the place whence it originates, which he used for the journey. A marginal remark added to this passage reads: "Hence the name of *coche*."

Montaigne about the 'coche'. Let us quote a passage from Montaigne's Essays, Vol. V, Book 3, Chapt. 6, on the

infinite variety, which histories present unto us, of the use of coaches in the service of war... so that it is wondrously strange, how we have lost all true knowledge of them. I will only allege this that even lately in our fathers' time the Hungarians did very helpfully bring them into fashion and profitably set them to work against the Turks, every one of them containing a *Targattier* and a *Musketeier*, with a certain number of harquebuses or calivers, ready charged, and so ranged that they might make use of them all, all covered over with *pavesado*, after the manner of a *galliotte*. They formed the front-line of the army with three thousand such coaches, and after the cannon had played, passed them to discharge and shoot off a volley of small shot upon their enemies before they could know or feel, what the rest of the forces would do, which was no small advantage. If not this, they mainly drove those coaches amid the thickest of their enemies' squadrons, with the purpose of putting them to route and making a way through them. This quite apart from the use they might make of them, in any suspicious or dangerous place—to flank their troops marching from place to place or in haste to encompass, to barricade or to cover or fortify any lodgement or quarter.

Literary scraps. Another amusing literary relic relative to the travels of a Frenchman in Italy is a collection of poems by Joachim du Bellay, canon of Notre-Dame in Paris. This excellent poet accompanied his uncle, the Cardinal Jean du Bellay, to Rome in 1551 and remained there for five years. He put his impressions of the city into verse under the title *Regrets*. The following is a quotation from this work:

> *Celui qui, par la rue, a vue publiquement*
> *La courtisane en coche ou qui pompeusement*
> *L'a pu voir à cheval en accoutrement d'homme*
> *Superbe se montrer; celui qui, de plein jour,*
> *Aux cardinaux en cappe a vu faire l'amour,*
> *C'est celui seul qui peut juger de Rome.*

(He who has seen the courtesan in the street publicly driving in a coach or haughtily riding a horse, attired in man's clothes; he who has seen her in broad daylight make love to cardinals in ecclesiastical garb, he alone can judge Rome.)

A short quotation from Ariosto's *Cassaria*, mocking at the ladies of Italy, may also fit in here. It runs as follows:

> *...uscir si sdegnano*
> *Di casa a piedi, ne passar pur vogliono*
> *La strada, se non hanno al cullo il dondolo*
> *Della carretta, e le carrette vogliono*
> *Tutte dorate e che di drappi sieno*
> *Coperte e gran corsieri che le tirino.*

(...they are loth to leave their homes on foot, nor will they even cross the street unless they have a rocking gig beneath them, and their gigs they must have fully gilded and draped with precious stuffs, and want them drawn by sturdy chargers.)

The above lines cover all the characteristic features of the coach: the swaying movement, the gilding and the carpet covering.

The introduction of the mail-coach service in Germany and in France. In Germany, the international mail-coach service was founded by the von Taxis brothers, Franz and Joseph, whom Maximilian I (1493–1519) appointed Postmaster Generals. The French mail-coach service was initiated by Charles IX (1560–1574). To facilitate passenger transport, the King licensed the

213

255

public carriers *(coches publiques)*. Henry III (1574–1589) followed in the wake of his predecessor. At the Blois assembly of the *états généraux*, the Third Estate, however, protested already against the concessions granted because, while earlier anyone was free to keep a wagon, by the time of the assembly the licensed owners provided for the passenger transport at higher prices and in a less satisfactory manner.

The glass-windowed carriage. In 1599, the Maréchal Bassompierre brought the first glass-windowed carriage to Paris. By that time the development of this vehicle proceeded in two directions: fine workmanship and artistic execution were aimed at to enhance its outward appearance, and every effort was made to render the vehicle also more comfortable for travelling. The well-to-do traveller who did not wish to risk the questionable cleanliness of roadside inns spent the night in his coach on the way. Travelling-beds and bed-clothes were taken along for longer journeys.

The coach in England. It is generally accepted view that the coach was introduced to the British Isles by Guylliam Boonen, a Dutch coachman in the court of Queen Elizabeth I, in 1564. The Queen preferred to ride on horseback, but she was not averse to parading in her plume-capped, curtained coach either, even at the risk of 'coaching pains from being knocked about'. The term 'coach' can be traced back in the English language even further: it is mentioned by Dr. Peter Vannes, England's ambassador to Venice, in his report on the death of Lord Courtenay, dated 18th September, 1556. In this he writes amongst other things that the invalid lord refused to take a boat to Padua, but since he also wanted to spare his own horses, he travelled by "certain waggons called *coches*, very shaky and uneasy", according to Dr. Vannes's judgement.

The English wagon is similarly of continental origin, having come to the British Isles from Holland. (The English term 'wagon', too, is derived from the Dutch language.) While the coach was adopted by the court, the nobility and the bourgeoisie, the farmers favoured the wagon which gradually supplanted the cart. However, the English were not content with taking over these vehicles as they were but—true to their traditions—endeavoured to improve the adopted forms. The wheelwrights of the British Isles developed a lighter and more comfortable carriage-body, so that in the sixteenth century the coach was already in use as a public conveyance in England. Later the so-called stage-coach became a popular and widely used passenger transport vehicle.

255 Wheelwright's shop

214

In Hungary carriage driving was, one might say, a veritable national custom; in the sixteenth century it was so much in fashion even among the lesser nobility that, for love of comfort, many a nobleman went to war in a coach instead of on horseback or on foot. In view of these circumstances it had to be decreed by law that officers were to join the army on horseback or on foot, as befitting camping soldiers, and *non in kocsi* as was their wont.

Road-building showed precious little progress at this time throughout the world. Although in England the General Highways Act of 1555 demanded that parishes keep the roads in good repair, records from the time of the Tudors prove that it brought but poor results. According to these documents a steady rainfall was enough to turn the English highways into actual mires; to draw a heavily loaded wagon on such roads required sometimes as many as ten horses. The trouble was that the Highways Act did not go beyond decreeing four days obligatory road-repair work a year per head, and the amateurish work of the roadmenders, acquainted only with the most primitive techniques of the trade, could hardly have been of much practical value.

The spreading of the wagon. The cart which formerly played a dominant rôle on the highways was gradually superseded by the wagon. The spreading of the latter was due to the widely adopted technical innovations and improvements (the pivoted front part, the whipple-tree) which offset the advantage easy steering had represented earlier in the case of the cart.

Increased recognition of the wheelwright's trade. With the perfection of the cart, the wagon and the coach, naturally, the manufacture of these vehicles required more and more skill. Both the coach-builder and the wheelwright had to work with increased accuracy and elaborate care. This contributed to the appreciation of their trade, in proof of which we close this chapter with the presentation of a woodcut from Jost Amman's *Ständebuch* (Fig. 255).

215

Chapter X

The slow and gradual development of the coach — The growing popularity of the state-coach — Henry IV meets his fate in a coach — The coach park of Louis XIV — The etiquette of coaching — Ambassadors and envoys — The further diffusion of the coach — Rising coach prices increase the fortune of coach-makers — Further luxury vehicles — The *berline*, and the *cabriolet* — Simple carts and wagons — The travelling-carriage of the Dutch — Special vehicles and oddities — Streets, roads and highways — The mail-coach service — Travelling by mail-coach — Urban traffic in the seventeenth century — The appearance of the hackney and of the omnibus service

The seventeenth century brought several innovations in coach-building: the carriage-body was suspended higher; the ungainly, clumsy carriage-box of the sixteenth century was gradually replaced by a lighter, more comfortable and more attractive structure. The big, cage-like box was reduced to more acceptable and tolerable dimensions; later, doors and windows were put on the openings of the carriage-body, and, finally, the windows were glazed.

The slow and gradual development of the coach. Its various stages, though not clearly defined, are quite distinguishable in contemporary representations. The engraving representing a Nuremberg rifle meeting (*Stadtschiessen*, Fig. 256) shows a heavy coach with thick felloes; it has neither doors nor windows, but figures standing behind the vehicle can be seen through its openings. The coach in Fig. 257, seen passing through Covent Garden in the time of Charles I, was neither light nor of an attractive form either. But the vehicles, in which London society fled before the plague in 1630 (of which a somewhat inaccurate drawing is presented in Fig. 258), were definitely less clumsy and more airy (if but for their open sides). An English travelling-coach is seen in an

256

257

259

engraving by John Dunstall (Fig. 259). The ink drawing by Willem
Buytewech (Fig. 260) shows a travelling-coach with leather curtains. It appears from the above representations that in this period the passengers did not sit looking forward but sideways,
enjoying the view through the openings of the vehicle. And here
we come to a sudden leap in the development of coach-making: a
glance at the line engraving dating from the time of Charles II

260

(Fig. 261) will suffice to see that it brought radical changes. A similarly light, coupé-like box-carriage (Fig. 262) is represented in D. Loggan's *Oxonia illustrata* (1675).

259 An English travelling-coach
260 Travelling-coach with leather curtains
261 English coach
262 Detail from D. Loggan's Oxonia illustrata

261

The growing popularity of the state-coach. Technical progress was so to speak the *sine qua non* of the development which ensured the coach an outstanding rôle in the royal and aristocratic courts of Europe for the three hundred years that followed. In the seventeenth century it was no longer a sporadic occurrence but a regular custom for both the female and male members of the court—princes, aristocrats and even ambassadors—to parade in coaches. However, in spite of the fact that the coach became an indispensable requisite of royal splendour, it did not stand

262

219

263

by the dozen in the coach-houses of the courts, at least not at the beginning of the seventeenth century, not even in the court of the French king.

France. A letter by Henry IV (1589–1610) to his favourite Minister, Sully, proves plainly and beyond doubt that the French

Kutsche Heinrich IV. König von Frankreich und Navarra worin er 1617 den 4 May in Paris von dem verruchten.
Ravaillac erstochen wurde.

264

court had but a poor supply of coaches. It appears from this document that Sully fell ill, and as he lived in the arsenal, a long way from the Louvre, Henry needed a coach to call on his sick Minister. However, he was prevented from fulfilling this philanthropic duty because—as he pleads in his letter—just then Maria de'Medici, the Queen, was using the royal coach.

But let us put the clock back a little further: The engraving presented in Fig. 263 represents a minor accident Henry IV, King of France, suffered on 9th June, 1606, in the ford of the river Seine, near Neuilly. The artist was anxious to illustrate as convincingly as possible the fright caused by this mishap but neglected the structure of the coach, of which little can be seen. The vehicle evidently belonged to the more developed type; we must, however, bear in mind that the engraving was made long after the event had taken place.

The accident may be regarded as an ill omen concerning the fate of Henry IV, for only four years later he was stabbed to death in a coach by François Ravaillac while driving through a lane in Paris. Several drawings and engravings have been made to record the event. In some of them the vehicle is shown as an obsolete box-type structure, with the carriage-body resting on the axles; in others it is represented as a fashionable coach (Fig. 264). It would, however, be an error to draw far-reaching conclusions from seeing the King in an outmoded carriage, for the artist was evidently no eye-witness of the accident; he had to rely on his imagination and scanty knowledge of carriage structures, and may have represented the tragedy incorrectly.

Under the reign of Louis XIV, France took the lead in European coach-building, as in many other fields of art and craft. The plans for the decoration of the *carrosses* came from the greatest masters, so that the coaches of the period are still regarded as unique of their kind. The model of a coach used by Louis XIV himself is preserved in the Cluny Museum. It gives an

263 Accident of Henry IV
264 State-coach in which Henry IV was killed
265 Model of a coach, style Louis XIV

265

221

excellent picture of the then new features of coach-making: the suspension of the rear part and the revolving axle with low wheels, which enabled the turning of the front part of the vehicle under the bent perch supporting the box (Fig. 265). Louis XIV himself was fond of pleasure-driving and sumptuous parades. The coach fitted well into the idle, pleasure-seeking life which the court led amidst perpetual merry-making, dancing and music, as if the world were a fairy-castle.

The etiquette of coaching. Naturally, the coach was not only a means of transport but also a sign of rank. Cunningly conceived, fine differences in its outfit revealed the position of its owner. The royal princes, princesses and grandchildren enjoyed the privilege of using a crimson cover which they were permitted to nail to the top of their coaches, while dukes could only spread similar covers loosely over theirs. Serious men were not above entering into hair-splitting disputes over their respective rights. Prince Condé, for instance, claimed to be entitled to tack down his coach-cover; on being refused this right, he flew into such a rage that he had the cover thrown off his wife's coach altogether. The vehicle entered the court without the crimson spread, to the general consternation of all those present. For riding *dans les*

266

carrosses du Roi, one had to prove one's noble ancestry back to the fourteenth century.

But France was not the only country with such absurd rules of etiquette. In Germany even the number of horses was strictly regulated: the coach of a nobleman was drawn by four; that of a count or duke, by six; while members of the royal family drove in eight-horsed coaches. Everyone was closely and jealously watching over his privileges; in fact, we know of a national assembly in 1683 which had to be cancelled because no agreement could be reached as to whether the *Reichsgrafs* were to appear in four or six-horsed vehicles.

It appears from the above that the mere possession of a coach meant distinction and prestige. But it is equally evident that the more distinguished a person was, the more magnificent his coach had to be. The most sumptuous coach belonged to the king, but his ambassadors were also obliged to live in great style; thus when the Earl of Castlemaine presented his credentials in Rome in 1687, he drove up with ten coaches, each of which was a masterpiece of coach-building. According to contemporary records, the one planned by the eminent artist Ciro Ferri (Fig. 266) "alluded to the sea". Its carriage-body was held by four Tritons and was so richly decorated with gilded garlands of roses, thistles, lilies and acorn that the structure almost gave way under their heavy weight. The coach was covered with crimson velvet; one hundred and twenty yards of material being used for this purpose.

The delegate of the French court had to be at least as elegant. When Prince Longueville had to represent the King at a congress of sovereigns in Münster in 1646, Mazarin wished him to take with him his wife, the celebrated beauty, Marie-Ann de Bourbon. The Princess was feted at Münster as the 'Queen of the Congress'. A contemporary record describes her entrance to the town as follows: —

On 26th July, at about five or six in the afternoon, the richly attired Princess entered Münster. Trumpeters marched at the head of a procession of pages, equerries and noblemen; they were followed by sixteen Swiss halberdiers, a litter and further trumpeters; then came the coach of Prince Longueville and his consort, with thirty footmen marching around the vehicle. Body-guards and fourteen coaches, drawn by six horses each, followed the princely carriage.

The Dutch painter Gerard Ter Borch also went to Münster on this occasion, in the hope of obtaining important commissions from the dignitaries assembled there. That he was not disappointed in his expectations appears from the fact that he painted, together with Gerrit de Haen, a picture representing the arrival of the Dutch ambassador, Adriaen Pauw, in Münster (Pl. LIII).

The popularity of the coach knew no bounds. Now the bourgeoisie began to hanker for it. The shipping contractors and merchants, who had grown rich during the period, did not want to remain behind the aristocracy. By the middle of the century the four-horsed coach was no longer such a rarity as fifty years earlier: it became a concomitant of prosperity. As time went on, men of lesser income also endeavoured to acquire one. Samuel Pepys wrote in his diary in 1667: "I have had it much for me now; in degree or cost, to keep a coach, but contrarily, that I am almost ashamed to be seen in a hackney." After several months of hesitation Pepys chose "a little chariot, very genteel and sober". He drove out, "it being"—he writes—"a mighty pleasure to go alone with my poor wife in a coach of our own to a play and make us appear mighty great, I think, in the world." Apparently the vehicle was smaller and lighter than a real coach; still he found great satisfaction in his acquisition which he did call a coach. In December, 1668, he wrote: "I was abroad with my wife, the first time that I ever rode in my own coach."

As a present, the coach was appreciated even by the highest royal personages.

The Turkish historian Evlia Chelebi describes the journey and reception of the Turkish ambassador and his suite in Vienna after the conclusion of the peace-treaty at Vasvár in 1664.

According to one point of the treaty, Emperor Leopold and the Sultan, Mohammed IV, were to send ambassadors to each other early in the following year. The Sultan sent Mohammed, the Rumilian *begler-bey*, whose suite included Evlia Chelebi. When they arrived near Vienna, negotiations started concerning the formalities of the delegation's entrance into the town. Chelebi describes these discussions—with some exaggeration, no doubt—as follows: —

In the morning the Chief Commissary and the Second Vizir, accompanied by Mikel, the interpreter, appeared before the Pasha, kissed the ground and said: "Our Emperor sends his greetings and leaves the formation of your troop entirely to your discretion." They brought with them an eight-horsed vehicle, decorated with precious stones; it was the coach of the Emperor himself, and all who saw it marvelled at its splendour.

But the Pasha said: "I will not mount a coach: we are Ottomans and will enter the town on *koohylan* horses, playing *dshirid* [throwing javelins and catching them], as is our custom; in Istambul only women sit in such a vehicle; we do not want it."

"Sultan, you know best," replied the delegates yielding.

But after all, the Pasha did take the coach to cross the bridge over the Danube when the Emperor received him in audience: he mounted his *koohylan* horse only in the castle grounds.

The exterior of the coach. It also appears from the above illustrations that technical progress stamped its mark on the exterior of the coach from the beginning of the seventeenth century: a high dickey-seat was developed for the driver in the front part of the vehicle, while the back was provided with a 'bridge', which later became the foot-board of the grooms (who originally attended only to duties about the coach). At the bottom the carriage-body was first supported by two perches; by the end of the seventeenth century, however, it was reduced to one which was practically concealed under the coach; the latter was suspended by wooden or steel springs.

The invention of the steel spring represented a decisive turn not only in the development of the seventeenth-century coach but also in technical evolution in general. This invention is unequivocally associated with England. Though, according to certain views, the first experiments were carried out by Sir Harry Blount on the basis of Turkish examples, there is no doubt that the steel-springed coach, ensuring smooth, sway-free travelling, originated in Great Britain, whence it spread all over the world.

Types of coaches. In the seventeenth century coach-building followed two different trends in Europe: in the northern states closed forms were developed to suit the weather conditions; in the south the open or semi-open types were predominant. In addition to these two main types, several others were simultaneously used. The one with an adjustable top, which could be opened or closed (Fig. 267), represents rather a transition between the above-mentioned two styles; its origins can be traced back to the sixteenth century.

In large state-coaches Italy set the fashion: the masterpieces of coach-making, known as the *carrozzas*, came from Italy. On

267

225

these the barrel-shaped top was replaced by a canopy-like roof; the carriage-body was first cubiform or of a longish rectangular shape, but later it narrowed downwards, so that the sides of the box assumed a trapezoid form. The outside of the coach was covered with red, crimson, blue or—according to the Spanish etiquette—gold and silver embroidered black velvet. In Germany simple or fancy leather was used for the same purpose, according to the stylishness of the vehicle.

The prestige of the coach-builders increased further. It is obvious that under these circumstances coach-building developed into one of the most profitable trades. The coach-maker became a veritable contractor, controlling a whole army of craftsmen: wheelwrights, joiners, hammersmiths, locksmiths, saddlers, painters and varnishers formed the pyramid topped by him. In 1677 the Company of the Coach and Coach-Harness Makers was established in England, and the prestige of the organization reflected that of the whole guild.

Other luxury vehicles. The *berline* is said to have been invented in 1660. Roubo, the famous coach designer, writes that "This second variety of the modern vehicle was a product of the Prussian capital after which it is named." According to others, it was invented by one Philippe von Chieze of Piemont, Quarter-Master General to the Prince-Elector of Brandenburg. Generally, the first version is regarded as correct. The characteristic feature of the *berline* is that it is a four-seater. Fig. 268 shows a *berline*

268

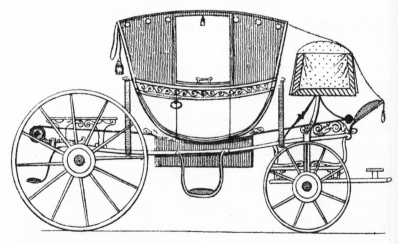

whose strapping partly supports the bottom of the body, besides restraining its lateral sway. The perches are curved high enough for the front pair of wheels to pass under them when taking a curve, so that the vehicle is able to turn almost in its own length. Thus the two side perches have made room for the wheels; the

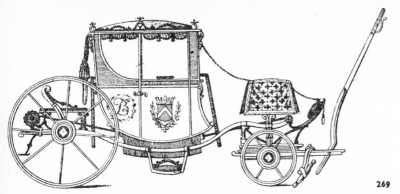

268 Berline
269 Halbberline
270 Hungarian wagon

269

driver's box, however, had to be built rather high up on account of this structural arrangement. The ancestor of the urban coupé has been developed from the *berline* by simply discarding the front part of the latter (Fig. 269). If put on two wheels, the same type of body formed a *poste chaise*. Later this denomina-

270

tion was used for the four-wheeled country chariot without a driver's box, so that its meaning is varying, obscure and often confusing, as most coach names are. The two-wheeled gig appeared at the end of the seventeenth century; it rapidly struck root owing to its lightness and comparatively high speed. The gig served as a starting-point for the development of various open and closed types of vehicles.

The original *cabriolet* also dates from the seventeenth century, according to Ramée's researches *(Histoire des chars, carrosses, etc.).* It was a pair-drawn vehicle with the driver riding one of the horses.

Simple carts and wagons. The carts and wagons had an established structure by this time and—apart from certain minor details—did not undergo further changes till the twentieth century. If in spite of this we mention here the Hungarian wagon (still called *kocsi* in the native tongue), it is because the four engravings in Anton Ernst Burckhard von Birckenstein's *Ertzhertzogliche Handgriffe* (1698), executed by Justus van der Nypoort, cover every contemporary variation on this type of

271

228

vehicle. They include a wagon driven from the back of a saddle-
horse. One vehicle is drawn by three horses, another by two,
while a third—a sorry reminder of lamentable times—is pulled
by two peasants who, having no horses, are trying to save their
family from the Turks in this manner (Fig. 270). In a still more
stirring picture, Turks are seen transporting the heads of the
decapitated in a Hungarian wagon (Fig. 271).

272

The typical travelling conveyance of the Dutch was the light
vehicle they developed from the farmer wagon; it was sometimes
a simple, sometimes a more luxurious carriage (Figs. 272 and
273). The latter—still a springless vehicle—may be regarded as
the ancestor of the open coach widely adopted later.

273

Special vehicles and oddities. Ever since the existence of the
carriage, there have always emerged unique pieces which differed
from the common, everyday type. It appears that from the
seventeenth century on, such special carriages occured more
frequently. As a matter of curiosity we present here a few of these
oddities.

Johann Hautsch, a Nuremberg mechanic, constructed a carriage which moved 'automatically' with the aid of manually
operated cog-wheels and levers (Fig. 274). In front, the richly
carved frame was decorated with an open-mouthed dragon which
could turn its eyes, while trumpeting angels could be seen on the
two sides; if the crowd dared come too near, the trumpets were
sounded, and if this was not enough, the dragon spurted jets of
water on the excessively curious. Hautsch paraded in the streets
of Nuremberg in this carriage in 1649. Its speed was two thousand
steps an hour. The Swedish crown-prince Charles Gustavus visited
Hautsch and bought the vehicle from him for five hundred

274 Johann Hautsch's 'automatic' carriage
275 The 'automatic' carriage of Stephan
    Farfler

Reichstaler. When the Prince ascended the throne, he found the carriage decorous enough to take part in the coronation parade.

Stephan Farfler, a legless watchmaker in Altdorf, near Nuremberg, also heard about Hautsch's carriage and decided to make a similar vehicle for himself. He succeeded in this undertaking, as appears from Fig. 275.

The long established custom of carrying the condemned to the scaffold in a cart or occasionally in a wagon (Fig. 276) survived also into the seventeenth century. The unfortunate woman in our picture was executed for witchcraft in Augsburg on 23rd March, 1669. The woodcut is of special interest because of the peculiar form of the wagon and the unusual way of harnessing illustrated therein. The vehicle looks like a rustic version of the landau, made especially for this lamentable service. The odd harnessing confirms this assumption: it was usual for such vehicles to be drawn by a single horse between shafts.

This brings us to the end of our survey of the carriage types known in the seventeenth century. In conclusion, and as a transition to the next section of this chapter devoted to journeys of illustrious personages, we should like to give an abstract of the meticulously detailed information on vehicles and on various ways of travelling, recorded by Péter Apor, the Transylvanian historian and writer, in his *Metamorphosis Transylvaniae*. The author tells us the recollections of his youth, as an eye-witness of the end of the seventeenth and the early part of the eighteenth

274

230

centuries. Although his retrospective account refers to Transylvania, it is valid—with slight modifications and minor time differences—also for the whole of Europe. Apor writes: —

The nobility used small leather-covered carriages for travelling; they
were drawn by two horses if the journey embarked upon was to be a short
one, and by four, if longer distances were to be covered. The vehicle was
either of the suspended type or just rested on the axles. Coaches were rare;
two sorts of these were known: a kind of landau with a top opening and folding
two ways, which was the more expensive structure, and a vehicle, the
Hungarian name of which referred to the spindle-shaped ends of the bars
of its framework. The top of the latter one was supported by ornate carved
columns. If a family owned coaches of both types, then that one of the first type
that was used by the master and the one with the spindle-shaped bars, by the
mistress of the house. The horses were driven from a saddle and not from
a dickey; the driver was assisted by postilions who marched before or around
the coach. The cushions, covered by carpet, served as a seat under way.
The garments and other belongings of the squire and the mistress were
packed in a large box in the rear of the carriage; their underwear and linen
went in another box in front. It was also a habit to make a pot of cabbage
for the journey, but occasionally roasted meat also formed part of the fare

276

under way. When the company found a nice grassy plot on route, they got out of the carriage for their meals, especially in summer. As good wine was not everywhere obtainable, the travellers also took their own wine along, in bottles or in wine-bins. The squire and the mistress occupied the back seats; if there was a child of three or four present, its place was between the parents; bigger children, especially girls, rode with their grandmother in the front seat; the ladies-in-waiting, sometimes as many as four of them, sat sideways, squeezed into the carriage just at the footstep. On the footboard behind the carriage, a jackman and a footman stood behind the squire and the mistress, respectively. The footman carried the squire's golden wash-cup, face-towel and comb in a leather case round his neck. Servants on horseback rode before the coach, and a groom led the off-horse at the back.

From another source we learn about the escort and the number of carriages an aristocrat travelled with. (The example cited refers to Gábor Bethlen, Prince of Transylvania, 1580–1629.) His train of carriages included a landau, a kitchen-wagon, a buffet-wagon, a drinks-wagon, an ice-wagon, a food-wagon, a footmen's wagon, a fodder-wagon and a camp-wagon; naturally, mounted escort followed the train.

Even so travelling was no pleasure. Though the escort provided for the comfort of their master or mistress in every respect, they could not protect them against the bad road conditions. We know, for instance, that the coach, carrying the ladies-in-waiting of Sophie, Grand-Duchess of Hanover, to Florence, overturned nine times on the way, so that when the ladies left for Modena, they preferred to walk beside the vehicle, rather than sit in it. No wonder that Jean de la Bruyère, the famous author of *Characters*, also hated travelling by coach. In his opinion, the burgher who harnessed his six horses to a coach was but *un fat* who wanted to show off.

232

Streets, roads and highways. Still, we have to distinguish between the coach owners who wanted to 'show off' only in town and those who risked their neck on the highway. Though in the big towns paving was practically unheard of, yet the ground was fairly firm in the streets, and the puddles, gutters and dirt meant no serious obstacle to carriage-driving. The situation on the highways was different: here the pot-holes had not yet disappeared. Only Holland devoted more attention to her roads. In France first Paris and Toulouse, later Paris and Alsace were connected by a highway whose construction was carried out with forced labour, to the great embitterment of the population.

One should not believe, however, that the French roads improved forthwith. Though every text-book teaches that Colbert, the genial Minister of Louis XIV, concerned himself most intensively with road-building, his expert, Gautier, preferred to leave the task of road-rolling to the travellers; thus the drains and the elevation of the middle of the roads were of but little use.

It was only in 1681 that the Sun King was at last allowed to travel after the larger pot-holes on the road had been filled up with brush-wood. The King's journey from Versailles to Bourbon l'Archambault, i.e. over a distance of 156 miles (250 kilometres), took ten days. $15^1/_2$ miles (25 kilometres) a day is a poor accomplishment, indeed!

Mme. de Sévigné achieved notable results when she reached Rochers in nine days; 25 miles (40 kilometres) a day were regarded already as an admirable performance. At the same time, however, she warned her daughter against travelling by coach: —

"Believe me, my child," she wrote in a letter, "you must not challenge nature. You have to pass where no coach has ever passed before; go on horseback or take a litter like others do; think of the calamity a broken arm or leg or an injured head would mean."

And yet, the French roads appear to have been better than the English; at least this is what John Evelyn wrote in 1644: —

The way from Paris!... as indeed most of the roads in France, is paved with a small square freestone, so that the country does not much molest the traveller with dirt and ill way as in England, only 'tis somewhat hard to the poor horses' feet.

As to travelling in Germany, the following inscription, found by Pfarrer Hartmann in an inn before the gates of Hamburg, throws some light on the reluctance it evoked: "It is fine to leave to-morrow but still finer after to-morrow; stay on here; I will do so myself." No doubt, many a traveller followed this sound advice.

People who had no horse or carriage of their own either had to walk or make their journeys dependent on opportunities offered. Friedrich Lucä, later chaplain to the Prussian court, wanted to study six months at the Frankfurt-on-Oder university. However, he had scarcely arrived there when he turned back, availing himself of a possibility to ride in a wagon. "God has disposed otherwise," he wrote. "An empty wagon bound for Brieg was foreordained for me as a remedy." So Lucä returned home, lest he should get stuck in Frankfurt or have to walk all the way back.

The above example shows that the need for a stage-coach service was becoming more and more pressing; the demand of the steadily growing camp of travellers not possessing private carriages had to be satisfied some way or other.

The regular stage-coach service was developed gradually; in Germany the first line was started by the Taxis family between Hildesheim and Bremen via Hanover, in 1640; soon all the main routes were covered with a network of coach services. But they soon encountered competition: Johannes Geiger, a Stuttgart burgher, obtained permission from the Württemberg government to run a *Landkutsche* service to Heidelberg and Ulm once a week. The Taxises fought heroically against this rival, but in spite of their efforts, further competitive enterprises started up now in Nuremberg, now in Jena. The setback caused by the Thirty Years War in the economic life of Germany retarded also the development of the stage-coach service for a long time. The poor coachmen had a hard time during the war, for both deserters and regular soldiers found the stage-coach easy prey.

In England the public coach conquered the highways, in spite of many difficulties. Official passenger transport can be traced back as far as 1500, when slow stage-wagons carried goods and passengers. Under Charles I the stage-wagons were banished for some time in order to protect the public roads from excessive wear. According to a nineteenth-century authority, in 1605 so-called 'long wagons' or 'machines', covered with matting and curtains for the protection of the passengers, ran between London and Canterbury, and some other big towns. The scheduled stage-coach appeared only around 1640. With this service two days were needed to travel from London to Oxford, and six, to reach York in winter. It was regarded as a record-breaking speed when in Cromwell's time the so-called 'flying coach' covered the London–Oxford distance in thirteen hours.

In France public coaches began to run on the highroads under Charles IX, and by 1647 they connected forty-three towns with Paris.

Travelling by stage-coach involved a great many inconveniences. The travellers crowded in the vehicle sweated in summer and shivered in winter. They never knew beforehand whom they would be shut up in the close compartment with. Talkativeness was a natural concomitant of this confinement. La Bruyère writes: — "Let the man whom chance has made your neighbour in

277

a public vehicle talk away; you will soon get to know his name, that of his friends, family..." If the miserable traveller peeped out of the carriage, he saw but a dusty or muddy highroad, according to the season, with now and then a covered wagon, a cart or a van jogging along beside walking peasants, pilgrims or travelling journeymen. The clumsy carved carriages, swinging

278

235

on straps or just jolting on wheels, pulled with difficulty by four or six horses, were an even rarer sight. If the vehicle of a prince of royal blood or some other distinguished person proceeded along the road, a whole army of guardsmen, mounted soldiers, footmen and postilions surrounded it in fancy uniforms. Only the rattling of the heavy coaches, the cries of the drivers and now and then the sound of the post-horn rose above the rumbling of the stage-coach. The post-horn was not a decorative symbol or an evocative instrument: it served very practical purposes, namely, every other vehicle had to make way for the stage-coach on hearing its sound. It looked like a small circularly bent cornet without valves and produced the following tones: —

The tune to be brought out was not discretional either: the extra mail, the express mail and the ordinary mail-coach each had its own notes. The alarm signal was G B flat C. The horn was continuously sounded from the moment the coach passed through the town gates until it reached the local post-house.

Urban traffic in the seventeenth century. According to historic data, there were but a couple of hundred coaches in use even in the largest towns of Europe. In Paris 310 to 320 were counted in 1658, yet time and again people complained of the commotion in the streets and of the noise caused by the traffic which—they alleged—both dazzled and deafened the passers-by. In 1680 Friedrich Mathias writes about Vienna as follows: —

> The streets, continually crowded with people, horses and wagons, are often a menace to the safety of the pedestrians. The drivers and litter carriers keep shouting "Look out! Look out!" and while you avoid one, you bump into another of them.

The hackney-coach (or hackney, a four-wheeled coach drawn by two horses and seating six persons), probably contributing to the anarchy of the urban traffic, was also a product of the seventeenth century.

In England the hackney (Figs. 277 and 278) appeared about 1610 and soon became a veritable scourge, for it made such a terrific noise in the narrow streets of London that eventually the authorities had to introduce special regulations for their control.

It is said that by 1625 there were as many as twenty hackneys in London. They were stationed before the better-class inns for hire. However, their number rose so rapidly that Charles I restricted their use by passengers to areas at least three miles outside the confines of the town; even this privilege was subject to the hackney-owner's keeping four good horses available for His Majesty at all times.

As recorded by many, the French *fiacre* owes its still surviving name to St. Fiacrius, or rather to a house-sign representing this Scottish ⸝aint. It decorated a Paris house in the Rue St.-Martin inhabited by Monsieur Sauvage, the father of the Paris *fiacre*. Although according to some other data it was a certain Monsieur de Givry of Paris who applied for and obtained the privilege of maintaining a passenger service with two-wheeled, one-horsed vehicles, Sauvage is regarded as the more probable initiator of the *fiacre*.

An omnibus service (but not so called) was also started in Paris. The elegant horse-drawn vehicles used for this purpose could carry eight passengers each; they ran on five different routes, and the fare was five *sous;* hence the name *carrosse à cinq sous* (five-*sous* coach). The opening of the service was celebrated with great ceremony, and the first passenger it carried was no other than Louis XIV himself who—it is said—made several further trips by omnibus later, in the gay company of his friends. However, the enterprise failed in less than ten years. It is alleged that it was the high fare that caused its ruin.

The above completes our *tour d'horizon* in the seventeenth century. From our specific point of view, the spread of coach travel may be considered the most outstanding development of the period, but the appearance of the hackney also belonged to the important episodes of the sixteenth and seventeenth centuries.

Chapter XI

The eighteenth century brought the carriage to its zenith, at
least as far as the quantity of vehicles and the variety of their
types are concerned. The coach-builders racked their brains
partly to make the coach a finer, more comfortable and desirable
vehicle, and partly to keep the craze for carriages alive or
promote its further diffusion. And indeed, the wildest ideas took
on and became the rage of the carriage fiends.

It is practically impossible to get a full picture of the wide
range of novel types of luxury carriages produced in the eighteenth century. Yet the drawings which have come down to us
from outstanding coach-builders and designers of the age, like
Felton, Garsault and Roubo, further, the oil paintings and etch-
ings, and even the coaches seen as staffage in contemporary
vedute, give us a fair idea of their great variety.

The outlines of the carriages became more and more daring
and sweeping, while repeated modifications enriched the vocab-
ulary of the carriage experts with new terms. 'The right carriage
for the right occasion!' is perhaps the best summary of the
coach-builders' aspirations. Felton, the famous eighteenth-century representative of the trade, expressed the classical opinion
of the British coach-builders roughly as follows. The carriage
should always be built to suit the place it is destined for; the
builder must therefore consider whether the vehicle is meant for
town, country or the Continent; whether it would be heavily
loaded, or used on stony or smooth roads; he must also bear in
mind that jolting on cobble-stones in town practically shakes
the framework of a carriage asunder.

Most of the changes introduced were, however, only super-
ficial; the eighteenth century hardly produced any structural
innovations. The main objective was to remodel and bring to a
perfection the old types. The most important modernization was
the improvement of the springs, which was to reduce the jolting
of the vehicle. Seventeenth-century experiments led to the
development of the Daleme springs. It was an invention which

238

combined the steel springs with suspension. The carriage-body was still suspended on straps, but steel springs were inserted between the straps and the body. The French regarded Daleme as the inventor of the carriage spring, but there are also other versions current concerning the origin of this device. This invention was so to speak completed by the introduction of the C-spring which can, in fact, also be traced back to the seventeenth century. (The French called it *ressort à la Polignac*, claiming that it was invented by a Frenchman of that name.) Although the device spared the passenger from jolting over pot-holes and is said to have lent the coach the 'gentle sway of a boat', its lengthwise swing unpleasantly increased the traction resistance, so that the English drivers called the carriage equipped with this type of spring a 'horse-catcher'. Reaction did not fail to follow the innovations: according to a newspaper item of 1773, an inventor had set himself the objective of eliminating the springy effect of the various straps, steel springs and chains, and re-establishing the "healthy, violent shaking" of the carriage. And as he believed his invention to be important to everyone who valued his life, he charged no less than 2,000 thalers for a carriage of the 'new system'. However, the springs were improved further; the lengthwise swing was successfully reduced; the Daleme-type springs lent the coach a motion comparable to the gentle rolling of a boat.

The English as top-rankers in carriage production. In the eighteenth century the English advanced to the vanguard in carriage-designing and -construction. The old, clumsy English vehicles were replaced by elegant, artistically light and finely shaped carriages. This positive change was due to several reasons. One of them was that in England the roads were very good, compared to those of the Continent ("the general goodness of our English roads", as Felton put it). Moreover, the carriage—as we also know from Felton—was a distinguishing mark of the taste and rank of the proprietor. The English became especially masterful in introducing and bringing into vogue, again and

279

279 Coach with a perch

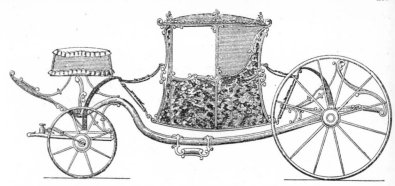

again, new varieties of coaches. Without aiming at completeness
—for which not even a separate volume would suffice—we wish
to enumerate in the following some of the more important proto-
types of English carriages.

281

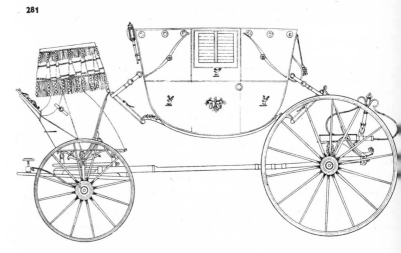

We wish to remark here that in our following discussion of carriages in general we have in mind the eighteenth-century English
customs in the first place. The mutual influence, however, prevailing between various countries in that age manifested itself
rapidly also in the field of vehicles, so that what is valid for the
British Isles holds good—*mutatis mutandis*—also for the western
and central parts of the Continent. The few decades difference
in time—occurring now in favour of England, now in that of the
Continent—will cause no confusion. The fact is that, with the
few exceptions pointed out separately, even the coaches running
in the streets of St. Petersburg were similar to those seen in
London at that time.

The perch and the crane-neck. We have to begin by saying
that the luxury coaches of the period may be divided into two
main categories according to whether the gears of the under-

280 Coach with a crane-neck
281 English town-coach
282 Elegant Spanish travelling-coach
283 Post-chaise

carriage were connected by a perch, i.e. a straight or slightly bent pole (Fig. 279) or by a so-called crane-neck consisting of two parallel iron rods bent in such a way as to allow the front wheels to pass under them (Fig. 280). The perch had the advantage that it was light; the crane-neck, that it permitted the coach to turn even in narrow streets. Coaches destined for travelling on the Continent were all of the crane-neck design.

The coaches were built either for town use (Fig. 281) or for travelling (Fig. 282). The town-coach served for official and social calls or other special occasions; the use of the travelling-coach requires no comment; we may only add that, in addition to the coach, the post-chaise and occasionally the landau were also used for journeys. The post-chaise may be best described by saying that it was like a coach, the front third part of which had been cut away (Fig. 283).

283

The landau, mentioned already in the previous chapter, was not an eighteenth-century invention, only its name dates from that period. Opinions differ as regards the origin of the latter. According to one version, Emperor Joseph I travelled in a vehicle of this type to the siege of Landau; another version claims that the same emperor had a similar vehicle made in Landau.

241

Goethe believed the latter; referring to a coach of this kind in his *Hermann und Dorothea*, he says: — "It was manufactured in Landau." A third version, however, keeps up the memory of Landow, the English inventor of the type of coach in question. It would be difficult to decide which of these stories is correct and at all circumstantial. The only point of interest is that the landau differed from the coach in that its top could be opened (Fig. 284); thus it was particularly suitable for use in summer,

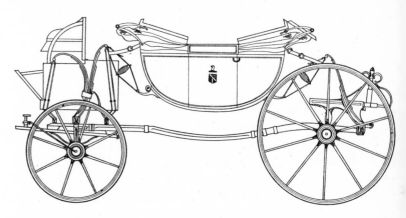

but when the top was closed, the landau replaced the coach also in town. Briefly, it was a 'two in one' conveyance, favoured also for less formal occasions and for drives in parks. In this respect it was similar to the vehicle known as the 'sociable' (Fig. 285) which owed its name to the fact that it could carry several people. The landau was used not only in parks but also for excursions into the country and even for transporting the domestics if a squire moved from one of his residences to another.

285

From among the owner-driven carriages we would mention the phaeton (Pls. LIV and LV) in the first place. It was a two-wheeled vehicle whose body was suspended so high that according to a current joke you had to climb into it from a first-storey window. There were phaetons with perch and phaetons with crane-neck. Owing to their high centre of gravity, both types were unstable and therefore fairly dangerous to drive (perhaps the perch-type was the safer of the two). Later the four-wheeled carriages were called phaetons as well.

286

The curricle which was also a two-wheeled vehicle was used for short journeys. The gig differed from the curricle in that it was drawn by a single horse, instead of a pair (Fig. 286). The *cabriolet*, developed from the gig, was the favourite vehicle for driving about in town. It was an elegant, easy-running two-wheeled vehicle with a light body. The spokes were generally painted red and yellow for decoration; the seat was covered with blue cloth and was protected by a hood made of shining black leather, kept open with the aid of a gilded, compass-shaped lever. If the vehicle belonged to a person of position, a livery servant stood on the footboard behind this structure. The *cabriolet* was extremely fashionable in the eighteenth century and caught on especially in Paris. Ramée wrote about it saying: "...there is nothing new [meaning in the field of carriage-building], only the *cabriolet; it is the rage of all Paris.*" In higher-class houses not only the young master but also the head steward and the major-domo had their own *cabriolets.* The gentlemen of the robe, businessmen, dentists, dancing-masters and fencing-masters used the same type of vehicle to go about their tasks as the dandies did to show off. Even ladies could be seen driving *cabriolets;* according to Babeau, they did it out of sheer Anglomania.

However, the *cabriolet* was not only a fashionable but—from the pedestrian's point of view—a dangerous vehicle. It being a light and fast carriage, its owners tried to overtake and cut in on all carts, wagons and cabs, and even on the stately *berlines* and coaches, just for the sheer fun of it. They drove past between them so recklessly—without heeding the side-walks which at that time were still level with the drive-ways—that the pedestrians were all but run over before they knew where they were. Frightened, they pressed themselves against the wall to let the *cabriolet* dash past.

In view of these circumstances the pedestrians demanded the banning of the *cabriolet.* However, it was only in Metz that they succeeded in carrying their point, and even there only partially: the use of the *cabriolet* was subjected to conditions, namely either a man had to precede the vehicle to warn the pedestrians, or a postilion had to ride on one of the two horses it was drawn by.

The similarly popular, though not quite as fashionable whiskey was a queer sort of vehicle: a huge structure rose from its four

284 Landau
285 Sociable
286 "The Runaway"

243

wheels to carry a light body suspended on springs. The carriage-box of the whiskey was supported between the two cranes by horizontal springs. The chariot was the pendant of the post chaise, destined for town use and social purposes. Actually, it was the ancestor of the 'town coupé'.

As mentioned more than once in this book, the carriage denominations were not universally applied; they changed Proteus-like and were often confused and varied also according to the country by which they were adopted. For instance, the name of the popular French vehicle, the *barouche*, derived from the Latin *birotus* which meant 'two-wheeled'. Against this, the *barouche* (or *birouche*, as it was sometimes called) was often a four-wheeled vehicle. The Italians called the same type of coach *baroccio* or *biroccio*, while its German equivalent was *Barusche* or *Birutsch*; in Vienna this was distorted to *Pirutsche*, but the word no longer had exactly the same meaning as the French original.

Travelling in France. The unwieldy French travelling-coach was built to accommodate whole families, including the more intimate domestic servants. Its huge body kept swaying throughout the journey, as, owing to its considerable dead-weight and the combined weight of the passengers and luggage, the builders were afraid to suspend it on steel springs—still fragile at that time—lest their breakage should cause some serious accident with injuries, etc. The seats of this private coach, accommodating eight to ten persons, ran all round the carriage-body, so that those on the sides blocked up the doors; thus the latter could be opened only after removal of the side-seats. Its body was seven feet long and five feet broad. The seats had to be placed inside the carriage-body. The vehicle had no glass window but only leather curtains. Later the French built even larger and clumsier travelling-coaches which they called *gondoles*. In this vehicle the number of seats was raised to twelve; the body was divided into two compartments, one of which could be entered from the back.

Both in Great Britain and on the Continent distinguished passengers travelled in their own carriage even when the mail-coach ensured already sufficient comfort and speed. They only availed themselves of the relay facilities. Private coaches were still so highly respected that when Lord Ferrers was condemned to death, he was allowed to drive in his own six-horsed state-coach to the place of execution on 4th May, 1760. An English country gentleman could not exist without a coach, for it was the only means of transport he could use for going to town. It is considered an important development in England that the eighteenth-century Englishman grew tired of sitting at home; people began to go to the seaside for at least a couple of weeks or months

244

a year and to attend the more notable horse-races. The 'grand tour' had also become an accepted custom by then, and the travelling Englishman was a notorious figure on the Continent.

In Spain the new style of coach did not catch on. True, it would not have been in keeping with the conventional mule-drawn Spanish carriage which had persisted since the time of Charles V. It was a low, wooden box with small windows and broadcloth curtains, and nobody could or would depart from the tradition it represented. The number of mules used was also restricted: only the king was allowed to harness six animals to his carriage, the grandees had to content themselves with four, and everybody else, with two.

A short trip in Germany in 1721. The following authentic report on the journey a burgher of Schwäbisch-Gmunden made to Ellwangen requires no comment. The whole distance involved was only about 25 miles (40 kilometres). Our good man started out with his wife and maid-servant on a Monday at daybreak, after having had mass celebrated the previous day "for the successful accomplishment of the planned trip." But after hardly an hour's journey, the carriage got stuck in the knee-deep mud, and the whole company had to get out to give the *Planwagen* a push. In the first village the coachman drove into a dung-pit, as a result of which the wife fell from the carriage, bruising her nose and face on the iron bands of its roofing. For the next approximately six miles' (ten kilometres') section of the journey, they had to hire three forehorses. But the road was in such condition that even so it took them six hours to reach their next station. Early next morning they continued their journey, but hardly had they left the village of Hopfen behind them at noon, when the carriage overturned in a puddle. Those of the party who only got muddy could call themselves lucky, for the maid broke an arm, and the driver dislocated a hand— not to mention the broken axle and the foundered horse. The following day they were obliged to hire a wagon and leave the carriage, the driver and the girl behind in Hopfen. The evening bells were ringing on the third day by the time the travellers, jarred to the bone, reached Ellwangen, their final destination.

Famous state-coaches. The most outstanding carriage at the Viennese *Wagenburg*—a carriage museum established after the downfall of the Austro–Hungarian Monarchy (1918) to preserve the historic vehicles of the Viennese court—is the so-called *Imperialwagen* (Imperial Coach, Pl. LVI). Its rich carving is the work of unknown eighteenth-century wood-cutters; its inner tapestry of red velvet was embroidered in a corresponding style by Viennese gold-embroiderers. This fabulous coach, built without a coachman's box, weighs 92,400 lbs. (4,200 kilos). It is decorated with allegorical figures representing the virtues. According to tradition, the pictures had been painted by Rubens, but there are no authentic data that would corroborate this attribution (which anyhow cannot be reconciled with the date of origin of the vehicle). The only thing we know for certain about this vehicle is that it was restored by Franz X. Wagenschön *(nomen est omen!)* in 1763. In its full splendour it must have presented a superb sight indeed when, drawn by eight white stallions, it rolled majestically through the streets of Vienna, surrounded by *Vorreiter* and *Stangenreiter* in gala dress and by wigged, ostrich-plumed orderlies in gold-laced uniforms. It was this coach the imperial family used on every important occasion—be it a court, domestic or state event—including coronations.

The coach of the Lord Mayor of London is one of the famous British coaches with a story of its own. It was used first by Sir Charles Asgillon on his installation in November 1757. The whole vehicle is covered with rich carving (Fig. 287). "The most superb carriage ever built" is, however, the British royal carriage designed by William Chambers; the paintings on its walls were executed by Giovanni Battista Cipriani in 1761 (Pl. LVII). It is interesting to compare the drawing published by Ginzrot (Fig. 288).

That the British set great store by the coach appears also from the fact that they wanted to send one to the Emperor of China through the British envoy George Macartney. Historic records tell us, however, that the presentation proved a failure.

George Macartney was appointed British envoy to China after he had been made an earl in 1792, in the hope that he would be able to establish trade relations with that country. To win the goodwill of the Emperor, Macartney delivered him a state-coach on behalf of His British Majesty. However, the Chinese sovereign regarded the gift with critical eyes: he objected in particular to the highly built driver's box. How could anyone have such an absurd idea as to seat a man in front of, and even higher than the emperor?— he asked. Eventually he informed Macartney that he "set no value on objects strange and ingenious," and declaring that he had all he ever wanted, refused the royal presents, including the famous coach.

The coachman in the dickey was an eyesore not only to the Emperor but also to many others. Peter the Great wanted to push through the election of the Pschov metropolitan, regarded as a 'westerner', as patriarch. However, all his efforts in this direction remained futile; he could not break the resistance of the conservative popes of the Orthodox Church who brought three grave charges against Peter's candidate: (a) that he spoke

barbaric tongues (Latin and French); (b) that his beard was not long enough; and (c) that he made his driver sit in his own carriage (i.e. in the driver's-box and not on a saddle-horse).

The Spanish aristocrats preferred to put their drivers on a saddle-mule (which replaced the horse in Spain), to seating them in a dickey; this was so because a Duke Olivarez once talked of some highly important state secret in his carriage in a loud voice, and the coachman not only overheard the conversation but passed it on, causing serious consequences by his gossip. (Naturally, the court used the conventional coach, too.)

Keeping a coach was a great luxury. To quote but a few authentic French data: In the time of the *Régence* (1715–1723), the price of an equipage—a coupé or a *berline*—was 800 to 900

287 The coach of the newly installed Lord Mayor
288 The British royal state-coach

Staats-Kutsche worin die Könige von England ihre Auffahrt ins Parlament halten.

francs, that of a pair of horses amounted to about the same figure, while the harness cost 120 to 130 francs; this made a total of about 1,800 francs, to which should be added 25 *sol* a month for the coachman's wages, 40 for the rent of the stable and coach-house, and finally, the costs of the hay, straw and oats required for the animals. But the coach or sports-carriage, once possessed, was a source of great pleasure. For could one imagine anything more delightful than driving to the Bois de Boulogne or taking part in some carriage parade, especially in the Longchamp pleasure-drive in the Holy Week?

"The pilgrimage of the coaches"—this is how Sophie la Roche called the Paris custom which took the upper ten to the Longchamp convent in the Bois de Boulogne during the Holy Week. On March 26th, 1785, about eighteen hundred vehicles took part in this parade. It was an excellent opportunity for Sophie to study the various types of carriages at her ease, for the soft sand of the wood prevented fast driving. The fashion of the year was a white, blue or green ground with silver or gold borders. The white *cabriolets* of some of the young gentlemen were bordered with painted garlands of roses and forget-me-nots. Pink *cabriolets* went with silver decoration and silver harness.

Hyde Park and Kensington Gardens. For the gazing London crowd, the roads of Hyde Park were the best place to watch the parade of fine coaches and other vehicles, followed by dandies on horseback. Yet the main scene of eighteenth-century high life was Kensington Gardens, the continuation of Hyde Park to the west. Here the rakes and dandies walked, lingered and flirted with their ladies, the latter exhibiting their toilettes and beauty. Sometimes as many as a thousand coaches could be seen along the splendid carriage drives leading through Hyde Park into Kensington Gardens. The ladies sitting behind shining plate-glass windows resembled paintings under glass. Some of them drove their phaetons themselves, using a white whip.

Italy. In the old quarters of the bigger Italian towns, the streets were so narrow that it seemed practically impossible to drive through them. Yet many a coach lined up in the late afternoons on the roads that proved suitable for parading, like the Corso in Rome, the Marina di Chiaia in Naples (frequented from the end of June to 8th September, on Sundays, Wednesdays and Fridays), the Marina or the Cassaro in Palermo, along which the vehicles passed at least twice on such occasions. Thus the ladies could have themselves admired in the above mentioned towns just as well as if they paraded in the Avenue des Acacias or the Avenue du Bois de Boulogne in Paris. Italy was perhaps the strongest rival of Paris in public displays (Fig. 289). The famous

248

Roman carnivals were a match for the pageantries held in the French Capital. The coaches, decorated with flowers and garlands, were driven in two rows back and forth between the Piazza del Popolo and Piazza di Venezia.

At the same time the mud in the side-streets of Rome was knee-deep. An anecdote about how Pope Benedict XIV (1740–1758) tried to put an end to these evil conditions tells us that, when the Pope—who was still the secular ruler of Rome at that time—learned that the prelate in charge of keeping the streets clean was spending the money allocated for this purpose in quite a different way, he drove in his coach to the side-street the prelate had the habit of visiting daily (with a certain discreet object in view), precisely at the time the latter was due to appear there. Ecclesiastic discipline demanded that the clergyman who met the Holy Father knelt on the spot to ask for his blessing. Well, the Pope was in no hurry to give it on this occasion but, through the open door of his coach, called upon the prelate—kneeling in the mud—amidst lengthy and edifying admonishments, to fulfil his duties more faithfully. We understand that his sermonizing did not go unheeded.

Traffic in the bigger towns, then forming the centres of Continental life, was still most chaotic. Dandies with a poor knowledge of driving and lady-drivers anxious to attract attention threatened the safety of the pedestrians. In Paris, among the

249

many amateurs, a certain Mlle. Rosalie, a member of the Comédie Italienne, also tried her hand at the reins—and in a whiskey (or wisket) at that. This queer vehicle was actually a highly mounted *cabriolet* on four wheels. One of the lady's cavaliers—so runs the contemporary report—undertook to walk in front of the vehicle to warn the passers-by in a loud voice of the coming danger. It appears, however, that a curb-stone—which must have been deaf—did not side-step, and the whiskey ran against it. The pretty driver of the vehicle would have dived head-first in the mud at ten steps distance, had not a young gentleman caught her in his brawny arms. Thus—concludes the sympathetic writer with a touch of hypocrisy in his tone—she luckily escaped with but a few bruises which, however, only her most intimate devotees got a glimpse of.

The *Chronique Scandaleuse* also published an apocryphal letter of complaint signed by a certain Monsieur Denis Topineau of Paris; it concerns a lady whose surname is not mentioned, but whose first name happens to be also Rosalie. According to this letter, Monsieur Topineau had been knocked down by a coach in a side alley of Boulevard Saint-Honoré, so that he could scramble to his feet only with the aid of some passers-by. When he recovered from the shock caused by the accident, the kindly and decent people who helped him up from the dusty pavement told him that the misadventure had greatly amused the lady, the coachman and the groom in the carriage; they also revealed that the owner of the vehicle was a certain Mlle. Rosalie, the well-known Paris prostitute. Monsieur Topineau finished his letter in an indignant tone saying: — "Being a prostitute does not entitle one to knock down honest people in the street."

Voltaire himself also joined the exclusive camp of carriage-owners, if but for a short while. It so happened that one fine day Voltaire who—be it said in his excuse—was only seventeen at that time received one hundred *louis d'or* from the Duchess of Richelieu for the correction of some poems. With this pretty sum in his pocket, he found himself in the Rue St-Denis at an auction where, seized by a sudden impulse, he bought a carriage for the money, with horses and coachman's livery included. An unemployed coachman happened to be hanging around just there; Voltaire engaged him without hesitation and bade him put on the livery and take the reins. It was already difficult to make a start with the vehicle: the Rue St-Denis was so badly congested with traffic that it took them half an hour to slip into the row of carriages. But scarcely did they drive 300 feet, when the coach overturned. This was more than enough for Voltaire. The next day he returned to the auction and put up his carriage for sale. The experience cost him fifty *louis d'or*.

However, there were some tragic cases, too.

The famous botanist Tournefort (1656–1708) found his death under the wheels of a Paris *fiacre*, as Karamzin tells us in his travel diary. He adds that Tournefort had journeyed so much in the world that in the meantime he forgot how one had to skip chamois-like from cobble-stone to cobble-stone in Paris to avoid the mud and the advancing carriages.

Traffic in the main thoroughfares of Paris was indeed confusing, as things were at that time. No 'rule of the road' was ever heard of: the vehicles ran on the right or left side of the roadway in both directions, at their will and pleasure. The poor passers-by, pedestrians not possessing a carriage, could do nothing but watch the procession of equipages from the pavement or—if they had to cross a road—run for their lives, trying to evade in a panic the onrushing carriages and obeying, willy-nilly, the rude advice of bawling coachmen. The streets swarmed with various types of vehicles: dashing coaches, *fiacres*, wagons, carts and litters thronged the thoroughfares. One may well imagine what it meant if a six or eight-horsed coach appeared in such traffic.

But if the king—a Louis—came to the Capital from one of his castles, such problems did not arise. Then the traffic was stopped to give way to the royal procession. French or Swiss guards lined up along the route; the *cortège* was opened by mounted civic guards; they were followed by ten six-horsed coaches carrying the court dignitaries and some other, eight-horsed ones with the princes of the blood. Then, behind a hundred Swiss guards marching to the roll of drums with flying colours, came the king's coach—an extremely richly decorated vehicle of somewhat antique effect and style. It was surrounded by footmen holding the reins of the horses and the knobs of the carriage doors, and by a swarm of mounted pages and stable-boys of the royal household. The outlines of the characteristic Bourbon profile of the king were discernible behind the carriage windows.

At coronation ceremonies the coaches continued to maintain their outstanding representative rôle. We need hardly mention the still live traditions associated with the English coronation coach: they are well known to all. On the Continent, the greatest pomp was displayed at the coronation of French kings and German emperors. Specially significant coronations, involving the enactment of some important political decree, were similarly sumptuous, also in respect of coaches. As an example we could cite the coronation of Frederick III, Prince-Elector of Brandenburg who, under the name of Frederick I, was crowned king of Prussia in Königsberg (now Kaliningrad) on 18th January, 1701. Although it seems almost unbelievable, according to certain records, the transport of the royal suite and their luggage required a total of thirty thousand horses, relays included. It is more

credible—and we believe it too—that at the King's Berlin entrance on 6th May of the same year, sixty-three six-horsed
coaches took part in the procession. Another unusual coronation
was that of Maria Theresa in 1740. She succeeded Charles VI to
the throne against the original Hapsburg rules of succession and
—as history has shown—against the will of some of the European
rulers. Actually, she was never crowned empress and bore this
title only after her husband. When she ascended the throne on
22nd November, 1740, only the archducal bonnet was placed on
her head. Being an expectant mother, she did not sit in the state-
coach on this ceremonial occasion but had herself carried in a
litter in front of it. This precaution reflects on the comfort the
coach might have afforded.

The only carriage parade for ladies in the Vienna court was
also arranged by Maria Theresa, in 1743. The ornate vehicles
of the ladies followed a specially designed course. Maria Theresa
had eight exquisite, shell-shaped carriages built especially for
this occasion, one of which has remained intact until today.
(Fig. 290).

290

Maria Theresa's 'counter-emperor', the Bavarian Prince-Elector Karl Albrecht, ascended the imperial throne in January 1742.
His years of Prussian reign were few, but he was not aware yet
of his fate when he entered the ancient imperial coronation town,
Frankfurt, in his coronation coach which also came from Paris
(Pl. LVIII). It was an old-fashioned vehicle, outmoded both in
form and execution, but probably so ordered by its owner. Its
too rich decoration and ungainly shape created a somewhat de-
pressive effect compared to the graceful style prevailing in the
middle of the eighteenth century.

Although there are detailed reports available on the coronation
of Francis of Lorraine, husband of Maria Theresa, in 1745, yet
we prefer to describe the election of their son and successor,
Joseph, as king of Rome. (Later he became Emperor Joseph II.)
Our choice is justified by the fact that the report we have on this

252

event comes from the highly illustrious eye-witness: Goethe. The then fifteen-year-old author was deeply impressed by the King's coronation procession.

"Hardly any of the suites," he wrote, "consisted of less than twenty henchmen and two state-coaches, but some numbered even more. The Prince-Electors of Cologne and Trier took part with more than twenty state-coaches each, while the Prince-Elector of Mainz had as many alone. However, His Imperial Majesty [Francis] outshone everyone as was proper in his position. The grooms, the led horses, the horse-furniture, the ornate rugs and horse-cloths arrested the eye. Sixteen six-horsed coaches, carrying the imperial chamberlains, privy councillors, the Lord Chamberlain and the Master of the Horse closed this part of the procession."

The parade of the envoys and prince-electors has been described by Goethe similarly at length.

Goethe himself was fond of driving, too. He travelled to Switzerland and, the first time, also to Italy, by mail-coach. Later he was presented with a *Halbchaise*, a comfortable carriage well fitted with springs, by his friend Karl August, the Prince of Weimar. He used this conveyance in the French campaign of 1792 but somehow lost it in the great turmoil of the war. All the greater was his pleasure when, riding along a highroad, he suddenly recognized his *chaise* in a stray vehicle. "With the trunk stowed away undisturbed in its old place, it was a most welcome sight," writes Goethe in his diary. Later he bought himself a large equipage, a four-seater landau, also well fitted for the rough roads. But when he left for Italy on 3rd September, 1786, Goethe availed himself of the mail-coach.

Hired coaches. People who did not have enough money to buy a coach hired one. At least in Paris it was an easy matter: the *carrosses de remise*, available for this purpose, were well-kept, varnished coaches, driven by properly dressed coachmen. They were much finer vehicles than the ordinary hackney *(fiacre* or *Droschke)* which could be hired for single journeys in town; in fact, they were accepted also at court. Sign-boards, bearing the inscription *Loueur de carrosses* (coaches on hire) hung above the door of many a house in the Faubourg Saint-Germain. The charges were 10, 12 or 15 *livres* a day or 12 to 15 *louis d'or* a month, to which one had to add a tip for the coachman. In 1786 the *Voyageur à Paris* estimated the number of hired coaches in use at 650; in 1789 the *Encyclopédie méthodique* put it at 800.

Theoretically, *fiacres* should have been available in Paris at the stands day and night. In practice, however—as we know from the German traveller Schulz—they were nowhere to be found when most wanted. (In this they resembled our present-day cabs!) And yet their number ran to 2,000. According to another contemporary observer, "these awful boxes did not go any faster than a pedestrian." If we add moreover that the horses were skinny and the cabman ragged, the fare of thirty-six *sous* for the first hour, and thirty for the second, appears to be pretty high.

Towards the end of the reign of Louis XV the cabmen decided to demonstrate against an impending reform and proceeded to Choisy where the court happened to be staying. The security officials were in a blue funk at the sight of the 1,800 *fiacres* approaching at a trot, for they thought the revolution had broken out. Louis XV was scared, too, on hearing the news. Eventually the officials managed to disarm and send home the demonstrating cabmen with promises; but their spokesman was taken to the Bicetre for mental examination. ('Bicetre', distorted form of the English word 'Winchester', was so called because the place once belonged to the bishop of Winchester. From 1656 it became a famous lunatic asylum.) It is hard to say why—whether on account of the changed times or because of the growing stock of private *cabriolets*—but by 1794 the number of the Paris *fiacres* diminished to 800.

The 'Droschke'. The Prussians who had travelled in Russia spoke with so great enthusiasm of the *Troschke* in use at St. Petersburg that the Prussian King Frederick William I had twelve *berlines* and *Halbberlines* made for cab service in Berlin. Externally these carriages did not resemble the St. Petersburg or Warsaw *Troschkes* at all; in fact, the only characteristic they had in common was that the Berlin vehicles, too, were to be used as cabs. In spite of these circumstances the denomination *Droschke* was adopted for the cab throughout Germany. They were painted yellow, and the fare was fixed at four *Groschen* per passenger. But although the cabs stood ready for service, there were no cabmen to run them, for the low fare meant a sure deficit from the very beginning. The first applicant came forward only when a government subsidy of ninety *Talers* a year was assured. Then, on individual initiative, they even had three further *Droschkes* built.

By 1769 the number of the Berlin *Droschkes* increased to thirty-six; later it diminished to twenty. Around 1780 they gradually disappeared from the streets, for the carriages grew more and more worn and the horses more and more lean, which made the passengers avoid this shabby means of transport. In 1794 the service ceased altogether.

Urban public service does not show any development of consequence in the eighteenth century either. The first traces of public vehicles in London date from 1772. The *Public Advertiser* of 18th January of that year mentions a "new contrived coach" which against a fare of sixpence carries the passengers from

Charing Cross to the Royal Exchange; the same fare was, naturally, charged for the journey back. There was room for fourteen passengers inside the carriage, and two more could sit next to the driver. In Paris the *carrosse à cinq sous* ceased to exist, and no other public vehicle replaced it in the city. But while no organized passenger transport existed within Paris itself, the suburban roads carried a lively traffic. The number of public vehicles, *voitures publiques à prix fixe* running along them, was especially high when the court stayed at Versailles or at one of the royal castles around Paris.

The vehicles used for passenger transport between Paris and Versailles were the so-called *carabas* which ran twice a day. The *carabas* was a six-horsed, cage-like, long wagon resting on four or six wide wheels; it could carry as many as twenty to twenty-four passengers. Everything resounded with its noise, wherever it passed. "One could not tell whether the clatter of the horseshoes, the rattling of the carriage, the shouting of the driver or the cracking of the whips kicked up the bigger din," says a contemporary eye-witness. Getting on the vehicle was not easy either: "A steep iron ladder," writes Mercier in the *Tableau de Paris*, "forced the ladies, young and old, to show at least their thighs to the curious passers-by." On Sundays the *carabas* was replaced by the *guinguette*, a vehicle covered with a canvas roofing. It trotted quietly with its load of Sunday excursionists. But among the vehicles going to Versailles the *pot de chambre* was the ugliest and the least comfortable of all. It was quite open; six passengers could travel inside; two were seated next to the driver, two on the roof, and a further two held on to the side-basket. The latter were the most pitiable of the lot: true, they only paid twelve *sous* for the Paris–Versailles trip. Besides the above, similar vehicles, called *galios* or simply *coches* ran to St. Cloud and Fontainebleau.

The *journalière*—a scheduled service started between Berlin and Potsdam in 1745—was the pendant of the Versailles public vehicle. First it ran once a day, later, twice a day, there and back. The speed of this vehicle roused general admiration: it covered the Berlin–Potsdam distance in four hours!

Waylayers. The robbers and malefactors of the eighteenth century also formed bands and used open force. Italy, Germany, England and France were all alike in this respect. The one had her Rinaldo Rinaldini or Lipo Tullian; the other, her Nickel List, Mandrin, Cartouche, or other known or unknown highwaymen. The highway robberies were, however, not confined to coaches travelling alone, without any escort. The often valuable packages transported by mail-coach, *Postwagen*, *diligence*, or whatever they were called, made these vehicles the favourite targets of the attacks. By the middle of the century mail robbery assumed such measures in England that in 1765 the death penalty was imposed for this crime and for stealing a letter containing a bank-note or bill.

The development of the stage-coach. In England the stage-coach—which did not carry any mail—still presented a rather depressing picture at the beginning of the eighteenth century. It was generally a clumsy, quadrangular structure, carrying four to eight passengers huddled together on its wooden benches. But gradually the situation improved. The jolting of the carriage was reduced by steel springs, and the seats were made somewhat more comfortable. The old vehicles which were little different from the ordinary carriers' wagons were used now only by people of small means.

At the eagerly awaited stops the passengers could at last stretch their stiff legs. Sometimes they listened to the harness-master who, busying himself with the horses, told them the doubtful news he had picked up partly from the passengers and partly from the drivers of the stage-coaches.

The year 1784 and the name of John Palmer meant a turning-point in the history of passenger transport, not only in England but also elsewhere. Up to that time the situation was that, officially, the mail was carried only by post-boys, on horseback; actually, however, the post-coaches (so called only because they were most numerous on the post roads) and the stage-coaches also delivered letters, although this was illegal. John Palmer, the owner of the Bath theatre, hit upon the idea of combining the stage-coach and the mail. He immediately approached the Postmaster General with his suggestion, pointing out to him how much safer and cheaper it would be if the mail were carried by the passenger coaches instead of by riding post-boys.

John Palmer's reform put new life into the stagnant passenger service. On August 2nd, 1784, a stage-coach, manufactured especially for this purpose, made a trial trip between Bristol and London. The results were gratifying, for the vehicle covered seven miles an hour. The combined stage-coach and mail service proved a great success. Gradually the speed was further increased; it reached eleven miles an hour, and the coaches ran day and night. As they carried also the mail, they were called mail-coaches. The Continental equivalent of the mail-coach was the *diligence* or, at a smaller scale, the German *Stellwagen* or *Eilwagen*. The mail-coach was protected by a guard, usually an ex-serviceman who, armed with two guns, sat in front to keep an eye on the road and catch sight of the waylayers in good time. No passenger was allowed in the dickey so as not to hinder the guard in performing his duties. The coachman was also armed with pistols.

LIII

LIV

LV Sir George Armitage's phaeton
LVI The Imperialwagen
LVII The British royal state-coach

LVI

LVIII The imperial coronation coach of the
Bavarian Prince-Elector Karl Albrecht
LIX 'Egyptian' berline
LX The state-coach of Prince Dietrichstein

LVIII

LIX

LXI

LXII

LXIII

LXIV

LXV

LXVI

LXIV Model of Shillibeer's omnibus
LXV The phaeton of the 'King of Rome'
(Napoleon's son)
LXVI On the Vienna Ringstrasse

The use of the mail-coach spread with unbelievable rapidity. At the beginning of August 1784, it ran only on the London–Bristol line, but by the end of the same month the service was extended to Norwich, Nottingham, Liverpool and Manchester, and in the following year Leeds, Milford, Gloucester, Swansea, Hereford, Worcester, Birmingham, Shrewsbury, Holyhead, Exeter, Portsmouth, etc., were included in the network. In 1786 scheduled mail-coaches ran also between Edinburgh and London; the trip which earlier had taken six days and six nights was reduced to only two days and three nights. However, there were people who did not approve of this rapidity, and some even raised the question whether such a high speed was not detrimental to the human brain. It was rumoured that men and women who travelled at such abnormal pace died a sudden death, due to a brain affection, on their arrival in London. A German writer, Joachim Campe, complained that, owing to the high speed, he saw nothing of the countryside while travelling from Yarmouth to London.

Another German, Georg Christoph Lichtenberg, wrote that travelling in a mail-coach was an opportunity not only for a dangerous exchange of glances but often also for a scandalous entanglement of legs causing a giggling in both parties and a confusion of souls and thought, so that eventually many an honest young man who only wanted to travel from London to Oxford went straight to the devil instead. Whether Lichtenberg intended this as praise or criticism of the mail-coach is difficult to tell.

Comparing the English mail-coach to the German, Lichtenberg complimented the German Postmaster General on not adopting the English service system. By this the Postmaster ensured the triumph of virtue—he said—for if a London girl ran away with her lover, she could be in Scotland or France by the time her father woke up, and an author required no trick to bring the lovers to safety; it was enough for him to take them as far as Charing Cross or Hyde Park Corner. On the other hand, if a German father realized her daughter's absence only on the third day of her escapade and knew that the lovers had taken the mail-coach, he could overtake them at the third station on horseback.

But even though, according to Lichtenberg's sarcastic statement, the English mail-coach failed to ensure "the triumph of virtue", it did spread rapidly. By 1797 there were already forty-two mail-coach routes established in England. Their total length amounted to 4,110 miles, and the maintenance of the mail-coach service cost the government £12,416 sterling a year, i.e. about half of the amount paid for the post-horses and riders earlier. In addition to this service, special passenger transport by post-chaise, with postilion and horse relay facilities, was still available

257

at the post-houses for individual travellers. The carriage-body of the post-chaise, or chaise for short, was suspended on straps and springs and carried a single person only.

The Continent lagged far behind the excellently organized English mail-coach service which functioned with the punctuality of well-oiled clockwork. In the first half of the century, the French used the *messagerie* service only if they could not escape it. Not only the vehicles but the roads, too, were extremely primitive; the latter should have been maintained by *corvée*, that is, forced labour required of the peasants without any compensation. The further a stretch of road lay from Paris, the worse condition it was in. Passenger transport was, however, essentially improved in 1774 when Louis XVI entrusted Turgot with its finances. Turgot was not content with putting the *messageries* under state control but reorganized the whole service. To the great disappointment of the innkeepers, the vehicles, now called *turgotines* after the Minister, ran also in the night and rolled past many a post-station without stopping. The journey from Paris to Rouen, Reims, Amiens or Orléans shrank to a single day. Turgot also modernized the carriages, so much so that the new type of *diligence*, swaying on springs, ran almost as smoothly as private *berlines*. Yet, in spite of these improvements over earlier conditions, the *turgotine* was still far from being a graceful vehicle. It could not be, if only for the fact that a large number of passengers had to be crammed into this "rolling prison", as someone called it. At least ten persons sat packed together; the smaller parcels, hat-boxes, etc., were placed inside the carriage, the bigger luggage was piled on its top. There was room for three further passengers on the driver's box; half price was charged for this 'high position' which, though not comfortable, provided a fine view.

Passengers of smaller means continued to use the *diligence* which was slower and less comfortable than the *turgotine*.

The Frenchman desiring to travel but not possessing a carriage of his own could, by then, choose already between various means of transportation: if he found the *turgotine* beyond his means (for it was expensive, indeed) and was prepared for some shaking, he could take the very primitive *fourgon* or *chariot* or travel by *carrosse publique* which, though somewhat better than the first mentioned vehicles, was still less comfortable than the *turgotine*, by far. But if he was willing to pay more, he could always hire a *chaise de poste* which stopped anywhere and at any time, according to the wishes of its passenger; it was an elegant, light carriage, with a body suspended high on strong springs.

The German counterpart of the mail-coach was a simple peasant wagon even at the beginning of the eighteenth century.

258

It ran only from one station to the next, where the passengers had to change carriages. Through-traffic between more important stations was introduced only towards the end of the century. The *Postkalesche* of the Prussians, put into service in 1700, did not actually resemble the type of vehicle later generally known under that name. It was but a kind of long wagon, without suspension or springs. Prussian mail-coaches were covered only on the main routes. An edict issued by Frederick I in 1712 reproves the Prussian mail-coach service, stating that, if things went on in that fashion, the coaches would soon be no better than a carrier's wagon; they did not keep to the time-table either, and the postilions had the cheek to put extra passengers and luggage secretly into the already completely filled carriage, overburdening it to such an extent that very often it got stuck, bringing shame on the royal mail service. In 1720 the speed of the mail-coach was fixed with Prussian accuracy at a mile per hour, but the service failed to meet even this modest claim on its performance. In 1732 Frederick William I objected to the mail being three to four hours late. Henri de Catt, reader to Frederick I, King of Prussia, had it from the King himself that a certain Monsieur Cogolin, travelling from Potsdam to Berlin, hoped to make his postilion drive faster by using his stick. He was, however, soon bitterly disappointed in his hopes, for the postilion got off his box, unloaded the luggage on the roadside, dragged the Frenchman out of the carriage and gave him a good beating, whereafter he drove off like one who had done a good job. The unfortunate Frenchman trudged the rest of the way to Berlin carrying his trunk on his back. He went to complain to the King, but, on top of it all, Frederick only laughed at his adventure. It was, however, a general complaint that the Prussian mail-coach was not only slow but unreliable.

As a contrast we would cite here a decision taken by the authorities of Kurmainz: according to this, the town refused to grant transit permission to the Prussian mail-coach because it drove too fast, and thus the innkeepers, bakers, saddlers, smiths, brewers and wine-coopers along the highroad had no profit from it. The situation, however, improved in time: the mail-coach was painted yellow and was generally 'modernized' to the extent that its carriage-body was at last suspended on chains or straps; a canvas roof was put over it, and more care was being devoted to the outward appearance of the vehicle. When the weather was bad, the canvas or linen side-curtains were also let down, though this left the travellers in complete darkness. Moreover, the Prussian mail-coach lost its balance too easily. An overturned mail-coach was quite a usual sight. Nevertheless, a Berlin press censor once rejected a short story because it contained a sentence reading: "At nine o'clock the mail-coach ran along

291 Stage-wagon
292 The criminal Schwarzbeck carried on a cart to Bern

the *Friedrichstrasse* and overturned at the corner of *Leipziger Strasse*." He argued that the accident described might reflect badly upon the Prussian royal mail service.

In a book entitled the *Letters of a Russian Traveller*, Nikolai Mihailovich Karamzin gives a fairly realistic picture of the mail-coachmen. According to him the mail-coachman of Saxony differed from his Prussian colleague only in the colour of his coat —which was blue instead of yellow—but they both spared their horses, had a weakness for roadside inns and used rude language.

Regarding the rudeness of the coachmen, Knigge, the famous instructor in deportment, gives the following advice in his book entitled *Über den Umgang mit Menschen:* —

292

Don't be economical at the wrong moment if you are on a journey. Give the postilions an ample, though not exaggerated tip! They will tell each other at the stations about it; you will advance quicker and thus benefit in a way by your liberality.

More of Knigge's advice runs as follows: —

The postilions are wont to drive rapidly through the towns. But this habit has its advantages, and one should not protest against it. Namely, if anything is fragile on the carriage, it is better if it gets broken where help is near than on the open road. But if the vehicle stands the test fast driving on cobble-stones represents, then there is hope that you will eventually reach your destination.

"The martyrs of the highway." This is what Macaulay called the carriage passengers. In bad weather—he wrote—the travellers had to face as many dangers as if they were crossing the Arctic Ocean or the Sahara. This was, naturally, valid not only for England but for the Continent, too. The coaches jolted and bumped on the roads everywhere, so much so that the old and broken did not dare face the tortures of this conveyance. Benjamin Franklin, for instance, took a litter from Passy to Le Havre when, at the age of nearly 80, he set out to return to America in 1785, after a stay of more than eight years in France.

Let us add to the above that, on 17th April, 1785, Schiller arrived in Leipzig "confused and broken"—to use his own words—after "a journey without precedent." "The road to you, dear friends," he wrote, "is as downright miserable as the one they say leads to heaven."

Ceremonies and etiquette. To characterize the age, we are recording in the following some of the more amusing rules of eighteenth-century etiquette. We know from numerous documents that at the French court accurately specified and strictly observed etiquette prevailed also in respect of carriage-keeping. One of the famous and notorious *honneurs du Louvre* which gave rise to so many delicate situations permitted the beneficiary lady to have a red velvet *imperiale* with gilded railings on her coach and, in case of court mourning, to cover it with black cloth and use four horses for driving.

The hearing of the case of a German count who drove about in a six-horsed coach, although according to certain authorities he was entitled only to a four-horsed one, was started at the *Kammergericht*—a special institution of the court of the Holy Roman Empire—in 1711 and dragged on for four years. Eventually, Emperor Charles VI put an end to the proceedings, pleading (and evading a decision) that "in view of the importance of the matter and of the circumstances connected therewith", he could not take the responsibility of passing a judgement. We cannot refrain from quoting here a statement by Lady Wortley

261

Montagu who, under the rule of Charles VI, spent a great deal of her time at the Viennese court and thus, no doubt, had first-hand information on the subject. She said: "Even their amours are carried on with great phlegm, they are never lively but on points of ceremony."

Maria Theresa's ambassador to Paris, Count Wenzel Anton Kaunitz, arrived in the French Capital on 12th September, 1752. At 9 o'clock that morning the eight-horsed state-coach of the King drew up before the house of Count Dufort, the introductor of foreign ambassadors. Dufort got into the vehicle and drove to Marshal de Balincourt, for etiquette demanded that a French marshal should attend the presentation. They reached Kaunitz's residence at half-past ten. After certain ceremonies the carriage line was formed as follows: Dufort, driving in a six-horsed coach, headed the procession; he was followed by Balincourt, also in a six-horsed vehicle; then came the six coaches Kaunitz had brought with him: the first was draped in gold, the second in silver, the third in crimson, the fourth in blue, the fifth in green and the sixth in pale yellow. After these came the coaches of the King, the Queen and the Dauphin, followed by the coaches of *mesdames* and those of the Duke and Duchess of Orléans, Prince Condé, Count Charolais, and the Prince and Princess Conti.

Wagons and carts. If asked why one or the other type of wagon or cart had gained ground in certain countries more than in others, we have to confine ourselves to generalities and explain the problem with the influence of geographic and economic factors. There are no rules we could refer to: the French farmers of the Auvergne, for instance, used the four-wheeled wagon on the mountain roads because they considered it more stable; at the same time most highland farmers elsewhere swore by the two-wheeled cart because it was lighter, easier to turn and, they said—more stable! One should not believe, however, that a two-wheeled vehicle spared the road more than a four-wheeled one, for a decree passed in France at the beginning of the eighteenth century indicates the contrary: it forbade the use of carts in every town for the very reason that the two-wheeled vehicle damaged the roads more than the four-wheeled wagon. In England the stage-wagon (Fig. 291) was used for long-distance traffic. The development of British farming demanded transport vehicles of bigger loading capacity than the two-wheeled cart. Three to five ton vehicles were adopted in general; their type depended on local requirements, the quality of the soil and the farming habits of the people. There were two main types in use, the box-wagon and the bow-wagon. From among the box-wagons generally used in Western Europe, the Lincolnshire wagon was the most typical in England. The body of the bow-wagon used in the west of England was much shallower than that of the box-wagon.

As regards the two-wheeled vehicles, the most common type used in the whole of Western Europe in the middle of the eighteenth century were the tilt-cart and the tumbril. Owing to the great prosperity in the Lowlands of Central Scotland towards the end of the eighteenth century, the English farmers also sent their sons to Scotland; thus the Scottish cart spread all over Britain and even to the Continent. It was a very light vehicle that could be drawn by a single horse, although its loading capacity was quite considerable. The carriage-box measured five feet six inches in length, four feet six inches in width and one foot four inches in depth.

Finally, we have to mention the special cart in which criminals were transported to prison, and those condemned to death, to their place of execution. An example of the first mentioned use

293 Some 18th-century carriages:
1. Travelling-cabriolet with four wheels
2. Travelling-calash without iron accessories
3. Travelling-calash on horizontal springs
4. Country calash

293

A.° 1800. Reise- Cabriolet auf 4 Räder. fig. 1.

Nach M.r de la Roche Jaquelin's Angabe in Petersburg.
A.° 1820. verfertigte Reise Caléche, ohne Eisen fig. 2.

A.° 1810. Reise - Caléche auf Horizontal -Federn fig. 3.

A.° 1819. Land Caléche mit Vorfall. fig. 4.

Fig. 292 shows a criminal called Schwarzbeck, otherwise Bierli, with his lover, Zillen, on their way to prison in a two-wheeled vehicle constructed for this purpose. The best-known example of the second use is the tumbril which carried Marie Antoinette to the *guillotine*. This 'rolling coffin' was a well-known vehicle in the French Revolution; the Paris tradesmen closed their shops when it passed the Pont Neuf and reached the Rue Saint-Honoré.

Fig. 293 gives a sample of eighteenth-century types of travelling-carriages.

Chapter XII

Classicism and the Empire style—the artistic trends prevailing at the beginning of the nineteenth century—influenced coach-designing and manufacture both on the Continent and in Great Britain, not only as far as ornamentation and lines were concerned but—indirectly—also from the structural point of view, bringing lighter solutions. The heavy and clumsy *grande-carrosse* disappeared completely, recurring only on exceptional occasions, in pageantry (Fig. 294), as the whim of some eccentric, or as the extravagance of 'potentates' wishing back the old times. In the Empire period a lady of fashion was simply unimaginable without a coach; in fact, a truly distinguished aristocratic lady was not content with only one: unwritten rules of society demanded that she have a coach for pleasure-driving in the morning, another for making calls in the afternoon, and a third to drive —let us say—to the Opera in the evening. However, coach-designing was no longer determined by a desire for dazzling pomp or by primitive ideas of excessive decoration to achieve splendour but by a demand for elegance, fine lines and—along with these— practical advantages and higher speed (Figs. 295 and 296).

294

294 The coronation coach of Napoleon

295

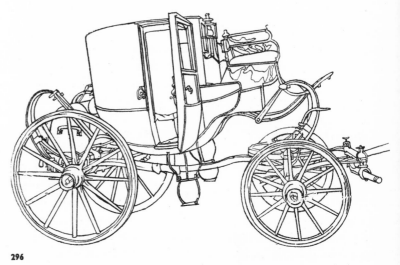

296

Speed could be increased in two ways: by reducing the net
weight of the vehicle and by the proper application of already
existing technical devices. The reduced weight of the carriage
made it possible for a lighter type of horse, bred under British
influence in growing numbers also on the Continent, to be used
for pulling. Technical development also continued: in 1804
Obadiah Elliot invented the elliptical spring which, surpassing
the C-spring, practically revolutionized the manufacture of
coaches. As the new spring was fitted directly between the
bottom of the coach and the axles, it made the suspension device
and the straps superfluous. Soon after the invention of the elliptical spring, around 1820, Hobson reduced also the height of the
coaches. Another important innovation which greatly contributed
to the outward elegance of the coach was the discarding or con-
cealment of the perch or centre pole joining the front and rear
wheel axles of the vehicle. As high-grade steel was already known

266

and produced at the beginning of the nineteenth century, the formerly used perch was replaced by steel rails concealed on the two sides of the carriage-body, so that the body frame itself formed as it were the connection between the front and the rear axles.

Various carriage forms. Coaches showed certain national characteristics in every country; the different features blended into each other to some extent only because the products of famous coach-builders did not always remain within the boundaries of their country of origin but went to distant lands. In spite of these circumstances the carriage experts have established certain 'national' features. According to them the English coach, for instance, was characteristically flat-roofed and had straight side-walls; the typical French coach had a slightly convex roof and curved side-walls, while the roof and side-walls of the German coach were strongly curved.

Looking through the model-plates and catalogues issued more and more frequently by the growing number of intensely employed coach-builders of the nineteenth century, we gain the general impression that both the designers and the manufacturers strove to vary the existing types of coaches and light carriages as widely as possible. The names invented for the diverse new types of luxury vehicles also bear witness to no little imagination. The language they derive from is in itself indicative of the origin of the respective model. To begin our review with the vigorously persisting types of carriages which survived the eighteenth century: the name *calèche* (calash) points to French origin, yet according to linguists it comes from the Serbian *kolica*, a diminutive form of the similarly Serbian word *kola* = carriage. The Germans, who also adopted it (Fig. 297), used the form

295 The state-coach of the Empress Josephine
296 Travelling-carriage from the biedermeier period
297 Four-horse German Kalesche

297

267

Kalesche, but this term was applied both to vehicles of the French *calèche* type, that is, a coach resting on C-springs and provided with an open body curved at the bottom, and to a simple, light two-wheeled vehicle. The English calash was not always identical with the French *calèche* either; although sometimes it did denote a similar vehicle, it was often applied to the *barouche* and occasionally even to a quite different type of carriage. However, all the vehicles called *calèche*, calash or any other name deriving from this term had two characteristics in common: they were all light and dainty, and had an open body. At the time of the French Restoration (1814–1830) the Duc d'Aumont made the *calèche* increasingly fashionable by introducing a new way of driving, called *à la d'Aumont*. The innovation did not affect the structure, only the harnessing: the *calèche* was drawn by four horses without reins, two of which were ridden by postilions. This type of coach served well for pleasure-drives, festive entries, ceremonies, etc. Sovereigns of the time are often represented in such vehicles in nineteenth-century engravings.

Another relic of the preceding century was the *berline* (Pl. LIX), a vehicle of German origin; it gained ground all over the civilized world but did not survive beyond the first few decades of the nineteenth century.

On the other hand, the *barouche* which was of French origin without doubt persisted as a promenade vehicle throughout the century. Its body and frame were usually painted in dark colours; the lining was mostly of satin, and connoisseurs of the time were of the opinion that it had to be of a somewhat lighter shade than the carriage itself. As this type of vehicle was only suitable for driving in fine weather, it was used exclusively by distinguished and rich people who could afford the luxury of keeping different carriages for special occasions.

Perhaps just because of its limited use, the *barouche* was gradually replaced in the rows of promenade carriages by the modernized landau. The origin of this vehicle had already been discussed in this volume. Whether we accept the British or German version, it is indisputable that the landau was a more practical vehicle than the former fashionable types and did not remain much behind them in respect of elegance either if it came from a good workshop. A fine landau was expected to have special quality springs; the rule was that a slight pressure with the hands on the seat should be enough to make the carriage-body swing. The new type of landau was also painted in a dark colour like the *barouche*, but the lining was to be of the same colour marocain if one cared for style.

The conservative character of the *calèche*, the *berline* and the *barouche* is evident if only from the fact that they were all suspended on C-springs. This old spring arrangement was maintained by conservatism also on a coupé-type town carriage until the end of the century (Pl. LX).

In the meantime two-wheeled types were also further developed. One of them has come down to the twentieth century in the form of the *tilbury* (Fig. 298).

298

The invention of the elliptical spring was followed by the appearance of a series of new types of vehicles. Let us mention first of all the brougham (Fig. 299), a carriage of undoubtedly British origin: it was introduced by the coach-builder firm Robinson and Cook who in 1838 manufactured the first specimen for Lord Brougham, then Lord Chancellor. It deserves priority in our enumeration if but for the fact that this town coupé was the first to which the new principles of coach-building were applied: not only was the carriage-body fixed on elliptical springs, but the perch was fully discarded and the body so suspended that the bottom part between the seat and the driver's box was sunk deep enough to permit easy entrance from the ground. It was a most ingenious innovation. The remains of the first coupé

299

269

built in this way are preserved at the London Science Museum. The brougham is the ancestor of the typical nineteenth-century coupé; its lineal and collateral descendants crowded the drive-ways of the larger towns of the past century. Let us therefore review some of them.

The shelbourne landau, characterized by its straight outlines, was so called after its inventor, the Earl of Shelbourne, while the sefton landau which had a more curved design owed its name to the Earl of Sefton.

The *landaulet* was a sort of 'cross-breed' which came into fashion in the second half of the century. Its nominal association with the *landau* is misleading, since its form lacks the very characteristic feature of the latter vehicle, namely that four passengers could be comfortably seated in its body, two on each seat, facing each other. It maintained, however, if only in a rudimentary form, the convertible and perfectly closing roof over the main seat. It was a practical but not a 'classic' vehicle.

The semi-closed luxury carriages with a folding roof—which, however, could not be converted into completely closed vehicles—may claim the phaeton as their ancestor. Certain varieties of them became known on the Continent as the victoria (Pl. LXI) and the milord in the second half of the century. The English names clearly show that true or imputed British origin was regarded as a first-class recommendation, even if the forms that gained ground on the Continent under English labelling did not actually come from the island kingdom, nor suited the taste of the English. This appears particularly from the names of the various types of carriages in vogue in the second half and especially in the last third of the century. Experts said, for instance, that the so-called mail-phaeton looked "as if it had been invented specially for the pleasure-drives of distinguished young married couples." It was particularly popular in London and Vienna and was used also by members of the court in both cities. Similar carriages also of English name were the spider, with or without a roof, and the stanhope. For ladies driving alone and for juvenile drivers there was the governess-cart, while the dog-cart, as shown by its very name, was originally used for carrying the dogs to shoots; later, however, it was developed into a regular light one-horse carriage.

Another fashionable type of carriage bore both the French name *char-à-banc* and the English name 'break'. It existed in open and in closed forms, and varied slightly also in other respects, e.g. in the length of the benches or their lengthwise or crosswise arrangement, etc. This type of vehicle was considered particularly suitable for training young, freshly harnessed horses and also for the purposes of shooting-parties. In the strict sense of the rules—which, however, were not always observed—the body of the *char-à-banc* was to be painted a dark colour, and the lower parts, red or yellow; the seats were to be covered with beige cloth or natural coloured leather.

The park coach, known popularly as the drag, served special purposes. It was particularly favoured for use at driving parades. Seen from the outside, it resembled the mail-coach, but while the mail-coach carried folding tables, crockery and travelling requisites in the compartment reserved for the luggage, the inside of the park coach was developed into a small ladies' saloon. The ladies were accommodated in the closed compartment, the gentlemen had to ride on the breezy top or behind the rear end of the carriage.

There were, of course, also some geographically specialized carriage types in use, such as, for instance, the American carriages.

The American carriage manufacturers were very active indeed and produced a wide range of vehicles on the European pattern. Larger scale coach manufacturing can be traced back in the U.S.A. to 1813: it was then that Lewis Downing began working in Concord, New Hampshire. His coaches won great fame; the New Hampshire Historical Society refers to them in one of its publications as follows: "No American product ever gained a wider patronage or ever gave better service than this Concord Coach... To him [Downing] we may well look back with pride."

The Americans followed the European styles consistently and steadily but allowed the influence of the lighter French carriages (e.g. Pl. LXI) to prevail over that of the English vehicles which were considered somewhat awkward and not very convenient for use on freshly broken roads. At the same time, however, they endeavoured to adapt the overseas types to their own taste. The results were rather ambivalent. Seen with the eyes of a European, the American carriages may have appeared ugly and tasteless, but their lightness and durable structure were recognized everywhere.

In America the most typical carriage was the buggy whose origin can be traced back to 1826. Its designer used the German wagon as a model for the frame, on which he put a light, tray-type body. The name of the vehicle had been borrowed from a light English carriage which, however, hardly resembled its American namesake. For one thing, the American vehicle had four small wheels, the English, two large ones; the springs, too, differed in the two structures. An interesting characteristic of the American buggy was that its elliptical springs were mounted at right angles to the travelling direction, both under the front and rear parts of the body, a solution similar to that used in the early T-model Ford cars—this is at least what we can gather from the available contemporary drawings and photographs. The buggy owed its extreme lightness to the fact that its frame and wheels were made of hichory cane. Hickory wheels were exported from America to every part of the world; those manufactured on the basis of the Sarvan patent were considered by experts as the most perfect of their kind. Count C. G. Wrangel, an expert of the age, was of the opinion that the quality, durability and finish of these wheels were unmatched by any other product in the world. G. A. Thrupp, the London coach-builder, wrote in 1877 that the buggy owed its low cost to mass production, the use of machines and "the educated dexterity of the American workman always ready to adopt any improvement."

However, Jacques Offenbach, the famous light-opera composer who happened to be in America the same year, seems to have thought differently about the American carriage, for he described it as follows: —

> The New York body-builders have specialized, it would seem, in building bizarre vehicles which may be divided roughly into two categories: the one kind is an extremely heavy, huge closed coach with a medieval, landau-type bulky body which comfortably holds quite a number of passengers. But how ugly these rolling houses look! The small window cut in their back, with its constantly fluttering curtain, makes them only more ungainly. In contrast to this, the other type is extremely light. It has a tiny box with or without a hood and can hold two persons at the most. Four large, thin and fragile wheels make the carriage look like a huge daddy-long-legs. The buggies—as they are called—often run with their hood up, and as the latter has holes in it on all sides, it looks as if it were tattered, lending the whole vehicle a very miserable aspect. Young girls of the best families are often seen in a buggy, driving a strong pair of horses alone.

Carriages on the Continent. The term *troika*, used for the typical Russian carriage, is quite commonplace. Still, some readers may be surprised to learn that it does not denote the vehicle itself but only the special way of harnessing its team of three: the horse in the middle, trotting under the *duga* (a kind of bent yoke) is flanked right and left by a galloping horse each.

The coaches used by members of the Russian high society were more or less like those serving similar purposes in Western Europe; only here and there did they alter the European form to suit local requirements. La Garde describes the elegant Moscow coach of the beginning of the nineteenth century as follows: —

> The vehicle was drawn by four horses with long manes; the heavy-bearded driver on the box wore a caftan embroidered in gold and held at the waist by a Kazan belt. The saddled horse was ridden by a boy of thirteen or fourteen who cried out from time to time in a drawling voice partly to encourage the horses and partly to warn the passers-by. Grooms clad in splendid livery, including a triangular hat with silver trimmings, stood on the foot-board behind the coach.

Hungarian landowners in the nineteenth century generally used a four-in-hand, but not infrequently they harnessed even five stallions to their yellow or pale green coaches, lined with blue cloth. The coachman on the dickey had a twirled-up, waxed moustache and wore a Hungarian costume with a crane-feathered round hat. Big landowners had the habit of driving out of their castles in this fashion even if they were bound on a journey by mail-coach: social convention demanded that they use their own carriage till the first post-station (Pl. LXII). It was also customary for them to hold the reins themselves. The most famous gentleman driver was Count Móric Sándor whom people called 'the devil rider', though 'devil driver' would have been a more correct nickname. As in nineteenth-century Europe Hungary represented one of the last bulwarks of feudalism, the prevailing conditions manifested themselves, naturally, also in the character of the coach parks kept by the big landowners. The vast territories of the estates—comparable only to Russian landed properties of the time—the many opportunities for hunting, the abundance of game and the fact that the manor houses lay remote from the railway stations at places difficult to reach made it necessary for a series of different carriages to be kept available for various occasions. This applied in a way even to the requirements of smaller estates. The types of the vehicles alone amounted to several dozen; among them the light basket-carriage which was suitable for use on rough, undeveloped roads, and various forms of wagonettes were particularly common.

The Polish also developed a special light carriage type, the *bryczka* which was used also for night service. Sometimes the Hungarian farm wagon was also drawn by five horses. The interesting method of harnessing used for this purpose is clearly discernible in Fig. 300.

301

302

To illustrate some of the more current types of Asiatic carriages of the nineteenth century, we present two Indian ones in Figs. 301 and 302: the first is a simple vehicle, the second, the covered carriage of a rich Hindu lady. Fig. 303 shows a Bashkir wagon in front of a *yurt*.

The nineteenth-century mail-coach. After this cursory review of the various types of vehicles, we have to come back again to the mail-coach, the most typical and popular means of transport in the first half of the nineteenth century. Poets have sung in different tones about it, and novelists found it a suitable scene for important episodes in their stories. The dim interior of the mail-coach was a source of romance, not only in literature but often also in reality. One could travel by various types of mail-coaches, and the fares differed widely, according to the service used. The best style was to travel individually, in a post-chaise or a *berline*. The ordinary mail-coach was shared by a number of passengers who were, however, distinguished according to whether they travelled inside the vehicle, on the imperial or beside the coachman (Pl. LXIII and Fig. 304). The inside of the mail-coach was considered the best place; the seats on the imperial were taken only by people wishing to enjoy the scenery and the fresh air, while the box-seat was attractive only to horse-experts or youngsters of David Copperfield's age. It was on a box-seat that David suffered one of his 'first falls' in life, which he describes as follows: —

301 Indian cart drawn by a zebu
302 Rich Indian woman on a carriage drawn by zebus
303 Bashkir wagon in front of a yurt

274

"That ain't a sort of man to see sitting behind a coach-box, is it though?" said William [the driver] in my ear, referring to the horse-coper behind him. I construed this remark into an indication of a wish that he should have my place, so I blushingly offered to resign it... When I booked my place at the coach-office, I had had 'Box-Seat' written against the entry and had given the book-keeper half a crown.

There are many other expressions in the English language which remind us of the old-world mail-coach. But when we speak of 'driving a train' or use the terms 'booking-office', 'book-keeper' or 'guard', we forget that a train is not actually 'driven', the tickets we buy are not entered in any kind of book, nobody keeps a record of them, and the guard no longer carries a blunderbuss, like his one-time ancestor.

Some curious information on travelling by mail-coach at the beginning of the century can be gathered also from *Tom Brown's Schooldays*. The journeys described in this book are also interesting, though not unique of their kind, but Tom's account of the breakfast he had during a twenty-minute halt at a roadside inn, famous precisely for its breakfast, is unusual indeed. Here is the menu of his meal: pigeon pie, ham, cold beef, kidneys, steak, bacon and eggs, buttered toast and muffins. How difficult to consume it all in twenty minutes!

The departure of the mail-coaches at eight in the evening presented a colourful spectacle which always attracted crowds

303

of people wanting to see the rows of handsome, light carriages, painted a typical red and decorated with the glittering gilded arms, and the fine horses with short-cut tails, four in front of each vehicle; they were so well trained that the first pair obeyed the slightest pull of the reins. Then onlookers admired the always clean and smart, brilliant scarlet uniform of the conductors and drivers with the hallmarks of their trade, the post-horn and the whip, in hand. The carriages followed each other in an admirable order.

We often come across the mail-coach in literature. In his *Don Juan*, Byron sings the praise of the English mail-coach (Fig. 305) and at the same time has a dig at the driver of its German counterpart.

The Germans themselves did not deny that their mail-coach service was still wretched. German literature contains no end of sarcastic and angry outbursts about it. The Saxon post got the worst of the wordy battles and newspaper campaigns, though the Prussian post could not boast of praises either. Adolph von Schaden, for instance, describes the Prussian travelling conditions in 1822 as follows: —

304

276

50 MILES to LONDON

If your chest is not made of metal, your entrails of copper and your most precious organs of platinum, we strongly recommend you not to undertake a journey by what is called a common mail-coach, for it is very common indeed. Its decrepit box lies directly on the axles, and the hardness of its seats reminds one of British steel. Paved highways exist only near the Capital [Berlin], so if you have to travel by ordinary mail-coach in other parts of the country, you risk breaking a couple of ribs on the miserable roads. The extra mail-coach is not much better either, for the vehicles they put you on resemble the tumbril of the condemned to a T. The ordinary mail-coach advances with a slowness that defies description, stopping at every station for hours. Personally, I once made less than eight miles in twenty-four hours, travelling in a conveyance of this sort. (Fig. 306.)

Conditions improved with the establishment of the Prussian *Schnellpost* or *Eilpost* (rapid service) which profited from the experience gained with the English mail-coach and imitated it in many respects. Thus it combined the passenger transport with the forwarding of the mail and adopted also the technical innovations used in England. The first test run was started between Berlin and Magdeburg in 1819.

When the first *Eilpost* carriages appeared on the highways, crowds of men, women and children thronged to the town gates to admire the new wonder vehicle, for it differed as much from the old German mail-coach as a modern electric express train differs from a small local railway drawn by a rickety old locomotive.

It took seven years to develop the whole network, but on 18th January, 1828, Karl Ferdinand Friedrich von Nagler, the Prussian Postmaster General, could report to the King that, after a series of difficulties, he had succeeded in establishing a daily *Eilpost* service between Paris and Berlin, and one scheduled to run three times a week between Berlin and St. Petersburg, reducing the 1,812 miles (2,900 kilometres) journey between Paris and St. Petersburg from the former 24 to $15^1/_2$ days.

But Börne wrote a curious satire on his journey from Frankfurt to Paris in 1821, *Monographie der deutschen Postschnecke, ein Beitrag zur Geschichte der Mollusken und Testazeen* (Monograph of the German Post-snail, a Contribution to the History of the Mollusks and Crawlers). It contains a statistical analysis, according to which more than one-third of the time required for the passage from Frankfurt-on-the-Main to Stuttgart was spent waiting: the passengers had to tarry three hours in Heidelberg, and three hours and ten minutes in Heilbronn.

However, let us not confine ourselves to the evils of the mail-coach but cite also a famous romantic story—a true one at that—which runs as follows: in 1827 Archduke Johann of Austria undertook a journey by express mail-coach. When the unexpected traveller reached Aussee, neither the postmaster nor the coachman on duty was there to receive him. Only the postmaster's daughter was at home. Fearing that her father would

279

get into trouble on account of this irregularity, she tumbled into the postilion's uniform and got on to the driver's box herself. The Archduke soon discovered the deceit but was not angry at all. He fell into conversation with the girl, and the end of the story was that he married Miss Anne Plöchl, the daughter of the postmaster of Aussee!

The romantic atmosphere surrounding the mail-coach did not, however, improve the awkwardness of this vehicle. The situation changed only after the introduction of the express service (Fig. 307)

307

which opened up a new chapter in the history and economics of the German post and roused the Biedermeier petty bourgeois from his stagnation and torpidity.

The Austrian post took the German express mail-coach as a model. In 1826 Christian Friedrich Adolf Rost tried out the newly established Leipzig–Vienna service in the company of two friends and left us a record of his experience. According to this document, the party had to change three times on their way to the imperial capital. First they travelled from Leipzig to Dresden in a comfortable six-passenger carriage; this they had to change for a superannuated court drag which was not only less comfortable but also considerably slower. It carried them from Dresden to the Czech frontier gate at Peterswalde; here they had to wait for the coach from Prague, by which they were to continue their journey. In Prague they changed once again, this time for a more impressive piece of structure: it had two sections divided by a wall, separating the male and female passengers. Rost soon discovered that there was a small trap-window in the partition, through which conversation was possible; it also helped to make a little draught in the fairly stuffy carriage. However, at night he could stand the stale air no longer: he climbed on to the driver's box, where he enjoyed the sunrise in the open. Arriving in Stockerau he was received with the cheerful news that the coach going in the opposite direction had been attacked by robbers the night before. Four of them boarded the carriage as passengers, while two others lay in ambush on the road. They bound the conductor and the postilion hand and foot, and got away with the money orders and the cash. One may well imagine in what state of mind Rost went through the rest of the journey. But eventually he arrived safely in Vienna, without any special trouble.

The nineteenth-century French post endeavoured to profit by the English experience but did not come anywhere near the English mail-coach, as far as its comfort or elegance was concerned. Besides, it was unsafe. A committee studying the statistical data for *diligence* and railway accidents in 1853–54 established that the ratio of fatal accidents for transport by *diligence* was one to every 335,430 passengers, as compared to one to 1,703,000 passengers for transport by rail; the ratio of non-fatal accidents was found to be 29,870 to 479,800, in favour of the railways. The *diligence* was not a very attractive vehicle in appearance either. In spite of these circumstances, as a French mail-coach it did have a certain atmosphere of its own that rendered not only its passengers but also its drivers romantic figures. In the *Postillon de Longjumeau*, Adam's once popular and even famous opera, the postilion of the mail-coach, in his royal blue

308

281

jacket with red trimmings, yellow leather trousers and huge boots, was staged as a swashbuckling hero. The French *diligence* looked like a huge yellow ark; it jerked and jolted along the highways and cobbled streets with a terrific noise.

The Spanish mail-coach resembled the French, with the only difference that it was drawn by ten to twelve mules decorated with gay bridles and bells. They were harnessed to the vehicle in pairs and were steered not so much by the reins as by the cries of the *majoral*, which the excellently trained mules obeyed without resistance. In the narrow urban streets, before sharp curves and dangerous sections in general, the *zagal* sprang off the carriage and, running beside the mules, led them by the reins. When the awkward point was passed, he jumped back again into his seat (Fig. 308).

The American post also followed the English example, though the distances it had to cover were considerably longer. Together with the form of the carriage and the organization of the service, the Americans took over the methods of the English post-robbery, too. The favourite targets of the highway attacks were the mail-coaches of the Express Company and the Wells-Fargo Company, which carried valuable mail-bags and packages. When the cry 'Hand down that box!' was heard, the conductor usually obeyed without uttering a word, and the passengers witnessed the scene in silence, if they valued their life.

Travelling by private coach. Comfort-loving Europeans, if they belonged to the court or rich aristocracy, travelled in their own coaches, using only the horse-relay facilities of the post. The passion for travelling, which had been subdued for a long time after the Napoleonic wars, broke out with fresh vigour. The possibilities offered by the re-opened roads were especially appreciated and exploited by the English whose carriages practically swarmed through the Rhineland and France.

Distinguished English families travelled in four-horsed, large and deep coaches. The master and mistress occupied the main seats inside the excellently built and balanced spring carriage, while the footman and maid sat in the *cabriolet*-seats at the back. The children and other members of the family, and the rest of the staff followed the main coach in separate calashes. When William Nightingale, father of Florence Nightingale, decided to cross to the Continent with his family, he had a coach built according to his own plans, in which he could comfortably eat, drink, write, draw, and even sleep, if necessary. The huge structure sheltered Mr. and Mrs. Nightingale, their two daughters, two maids, a footman and a messenger; it was drawn by six horses led by three postilions. A sailing-boat transported the vehicle from Southampton to Havre, whence their route led to Paris,

Bordeaux, Narbonne, Nice, Genoa and Florence, where they stayed for some time before they returned to Paris via Geneva.

Adventurous journeys. In a book entitled *The Recollections of an Old Man from his Youth,* Wilhelm von Kügelgen also gives an interesting and amusing description of a family journey in 1814. The work from which we quote as follows ran to countless editions: —

> The carriage of the indescribable proportions hung inertly on its springs in a state of decay. Its doors were fastened with strings, and the leather curtains which were as dry as parchment could be neither buttoned up nor buckled back. The horses were apparently half asleep or dead; they hung their heads heavily, and nobody seemed to understand how they had come so far. Although the coachman claimed that his horses were good, he received every travelling-chest brought down from the house with a deep sigh.

Then Kügelgen continues to describe the preparations for their departure saying: —

> At last everything was ready. We children could not even move our arms, for we were tightly wrapped up and swathed like cocoons. One after the other we were put in the miserable box, until finally our faithful Rose also appeared and wished to get in. However, in order to protect herself from the cold, and her traps from the dangers of packing, she had put on all the underwear and clothes she possessed and looked like a Heidelberg barrel. The coachman weighed in his mind each passenger boarding the carriage and found everyone heavy, but when he caught sight of this monster of a girl, he broke into dreadful language, swearing that he would be blowed if he took that person in his carriage.
> "Then go to blazes!" cried my father, and he had all the luggage unloaded from the vehicle. Thus our first start was a failure.

The family then hired another coach for the journey, and Kügelgen writes: —

> Though it was a considerably better vehicle, it was far from being perfect. The roads were thawing out, and the carriage kept swaying from one side to the other, like a drunk carouser, until it got stuck in a snow-covered pot-hole near Naumburg. My father and the coachman jumped off. They got wet all through and, although they did their best to encourage the animals with cries and beating, and the horses also pulled at the harness with all their might, the coach stood stock still, as if rooted to the spot.
> Then it almost looked as if fate was going to be merciful to us, for we discovered a group of men shovelling the snow quite near to where we stood. My father appealed to them, but they replied that their job was to clear the snow-filled ditches, lest a carriage should fall in, but nothing else concerned them. Eventually, Russian soldiers who happened to march by helped to pull the carriage out of the pot-hole.

Pushkin tells us the story of a journey he made in Erzerum, in the course of which he joined Count Vladimir Pushkin at Novotserkask in 1829. According to the description given by the poet, Count Pushkin travelled in a "veritable moving fortress", the "northern" part of which contained the food and wines, the "southern", the books, uniforms, pistols and rifles. Travelling in this huge vehicle was not only safe but pleasant, for the contents of the "northern" compartment were produced at every station, and the travellers were not pressed by any public affair or other matters of higher importance.

But when the Russian Tsar Alexander I went to the Viennese Congress, he changed horses every four hours and covered the St. Petersburg–Vienna route in twelve days. (The post required twenty-eight days for the same journey.) La Garde also tells us a story connected with the Viennese Congress. Its 'hero' happens to be the younger brother of Alexander I, the Grand Duke Constantine, an ill-famed despot who was also staying in Vienna at the time of this political event. It appears that he had a nasty quarrel with Prince Alfred Windischgraetz, in the course of which words ran so high that Constantine threatened the Prince with a smack in the face. They would have fought a duel after this, but the Tsar decided otherwise: he bade Constantine leave Vienna for Warsaw, without delay. The Grand Duke started immediately and reached the Czech frontier at dawn the following day. Here he changed his postilion, but the new man in the box drove so slowly that Constantine grew more and more impatient. As all his goading was lost on the driver, and the horses finally reduced their trot to amble, the Grand Duke could stand it no longer: he jumped up, knocked the driver's hat off, and seizing him by his hair, began to hail down blows on the poor devil.

"Do you understand now, you dirty dog!" he howled.

"Perfectly, Sir," answered the driver, "but there seems to be something wrong with the bridle."

Saying this, the driver got off the carriage, and while the Grand Duke wrapped himself up in his cloak and leaned back in the carriage, the man cut the traces with a knife, lashed two of the horses to a gallop and, jumping on the third, rode up to Constantine to 'fix him' with his whip. Having completed the job to his satisfaction, he put the spurs to his horse and rode off.

The Vienna Congress gathered the European sovereigns and political notabilities in the Austrian imperial capital. In autumn 1814, when most of the royalties were already there, the continuous flow of coaches, riders and pedestrians in the alleys of the Viennese Prater presented a marvellous sight. However, the endless stream of vehicles included a large number of coaches perfectly identical in design, for, in order to avoid hurting anyone's feelings and to solve the problems of etiquette, Emperor Francis—who made the vehicles available to his guests from his own coach park—had three hundred coaches built exactly the same.

The Emperor himself and his consort took part in the Prater parades in a simple phaeton; Napoleon's famous adversary, the Archduke Karl, also rode in a coach of bourgeois style. Emperor Alexander, on the other hand, used an elegant and unusual carriage called the *carrick*. The Prussian king mingled in the crowd on horseback; from among the British participants of the Congress, Lord Stewart and Sir Sidney Smith made a veritable show of their splendid carriages, while Lord Castlereagh used a simple coupé. Not only the guests, however, but the aristocrats of the various countries belonging to the Hapsburg Empire, Austrians, Czechs, Poles and Hungarians, also rivalled each other in pomp and revelled in the great variety of coaches, horses, gears and liveries.

Naturally, this kind of luxury was not confined to Vienna. A Frenchman, writing under the pseudonym "A lonely traveller", left us a description of the London city traffic, the mere reading of which is enough to make one giddy. He himself compares the spectacle to a torrent.

The German author Fontane saw Queen Victoria in a London street on 9th December, 1857, as Her Majesty was driving from Buckingham Palace to Westminster Abbey in a coach drawn by four pairs of dapple-grey horses with expensive harness and blue silk tassels. The same author also describes the coach of the French Ambassador which he had an opportunity to see from the drawing-room of St. James's Palace on 9th May, 1858, while the vehicle stood waiting in the park behind the building. Its body was painted dark green and was decorated with the ducal crowns in silver; the green-red-white colouring of the wheels reminded Fontane of a faded French tricolour. Long ribbons of the same colours hung even from the blinkers of the horses.

The following story, although its characters are Germans, fits in here among the London 'snapshots'. The time is 4th May, 1828. It is a little gallant episode between the opera-singer and famous *prima donna* Henriette Sontag who sang in London at that time, and Heinrich Fürst von Pückler-Muskau, writer, cavalier, soldier and a variety of other things. Pückler himself described the day in a letter as follows: —

> Riding, walking, looking at the beautiful scenery and visiting the sights of Greenwich took up the time until dark. Dinner was consumed by candlelight mingled with moonlight which poured in through the open windows overlooking the river. It was only at twelve o'clock that we left for home in a well closed coach. You know my ways: I cannot leave such opportunities unexploited even if I am afraid of being indelicate. Fear and anger were the first reactions to my approaches, but finally these emotions subsided and, though nothing improper has actually happened, all endearments possible under the circumstances were exchanged before we arrived home.

After this anecdote of Parisian flavour, let us return to Paris itself where, naturally, the streets continued to resound from the clatter of splendid equipages. Ehrler, Binder and Farry, and Breilman & Co. were the coach-builders who supplied the finest coaches, but special English ones were often imported from England.

Empress Josephine was an enthusiastic patroness of pleasure-driving, just as all the other ladies of the European courts. But even Louis Philippe, the bourgeois-minded king, used a magnificent coach painted in yellow, blue and white, and bearing the monogram LP with the crown on its door. The Second Empire did not wish to remain behind in splendour either: Empress Eugénie who, with her sumptuous elegance, dictated Paris fashion, had no reason to be modest in respect of pleasure-driving and luxury coaches, of all things. Chroniclers have even recorded for posterity that the slim, silk-stockinged ankles of the beautiful Empress —*horribile dictu!*—showed now and again from under the hem of her skirt which, according to the morals of the time, was about equal to wearing a mini-skirt today. In Paris, this only gave cause to an appreciative but respectful smile, but not so at the Viennese court of Francis Joseph, known for its austere code of morals. When during her visit to Vienna Eugénie drove out with Empress Elisabeth, Francis Joseph was frankly shocked by this display of ankles which he considered bad form for an Empress. He could not let it pass without remark, so when Empress Elisabeth followed Eugénie in the coach, and the groom was arranging her eight-metre train into picturesque folds, the Emperor bent down to her and, in a voice loud enough for Eugénie to hear and in French, that she might also understand, he said: "Mind, my dear, that your legs don't show."

Only a few years later fate forced Eugénie to be content with a modest cab and with less conspicuous toilettes. On 4th September, 1870, when the Republic had been proclaimed at the Paris town-hall and the rioting masses were already pouring in through the gates of the Tuileries, Eugénie at last decided to abdicate and have the imperial flag hauled down. She was led out of the palace through a back door by the Austrian ambassador Prince Metternich, and the ambassador of Piemont, Nigra. There the Empress stood in the street, deeply veiled, in the company of her waiting-maid. A boy, recognizing her, cried out: "Why, it is the Empress!" but nobody paid any attention. The possibility of escape came in the form of a jolting cab that happened to pass by. But hardly were they seated in safe obscurity inside this humble vehicle than they were seized with fresh panic realizing that all the money they possessed was three francs. What if the driver kicks up a row about the fare? They thought it better to alight before it exceeded their funds, in a side-street, at the house of the dentist, Dr. Evans. With his help, they succeeded in escaping to Deauville and thence to the port of Ryde (Isle of Wight).

The Third Republic, interpersed with royalist elements, did not give up the aristocratic luxuries of the preceding regime. The beauty and diversity of the coaches survived the fall of the

Empire, just as many of its customs and formalities: a driver and a *valet de pied* continued to sit on the box of the coaches; both wore cockaded top hats, a dark livery, and boots with their tops folded over; the only difference between them was that, while the first had a whip in hand, the second sat with his arms folded.

A fine carriage was associated with rank, whether as a mark of nobility or social status, or with some outstanding achievement in a given field of activity. The Easter present given by M. de Gramont-Caderousse to the mistress of his heart, a famous Paris beauty, should be glossed as belonging to the latter category. It was indeed a 'huge Easter egg', for when it was 'broken', an elegant pair-drawn victoria complete with coachman and *valet de pied* emerged from it.

In the thirties and forties, the aristocracy of the Prussian capital, Berlin, paraded with their coaches in the Wilhelmstrasse and Unter den Linden, while in the *Tiergarten* they tried to imitate the promenade of the Viennese Prater, with comparatively poor results. According to an eye-witness, the few really splendid coaches of the local nobilities and foreign embassies formed but a miserable minority among the obtrusively tasteless coaches of higher middle-class people and the *Droschkes* of the petit bourgeoisie. Still, Prince Wilhelm, son of King Friedrich Wilhelm III, organized a truly elegant coach parade in the *Tiergarten* in May, 1845, which was watched open-mouthed by twelve thousand spectators. The event was arranged again in 1846 and 1847, but the continuation of this custom was swept away by the revolution of 1848.

In St. Petersburg the distinguished society met in the evenings at the northernmost end of the isles, called the Pointe. It was a queer sort of 'standing-promenade' which may sound paradoxical but still covers the facts; namely, once the coaches arrived on the spot, they just remained standing in one place. The gentlemen alighted and visited the ladies who remained seated in their carriages. If it was a princess, they courted her only to proceed to pay marked attention to some fashionable actress a little further along.

Hired coaches and 'fiacres'. Descending the nineteenth-century social ladder step by step, we come to the hired coaches still much in demand at that time, although the truly typical not 'privately owned' carriage was by then the *fiacre*, *Droschke*, hackney or cab, or whatever name this category of vehicles bore.

The *fiacre*, above all the Viennese *Fiacker*, belongs to the most evocative symbols of the nineteenth century, and as far as the Viennese 'cabby' is concerned, operettas, ditties, cultural-historic works on Vienna and memoirs dripping with nostalgia, have

309

preserved his figure in a more lasting way than any monument could have done. The cabby as a character survived the world wars. Like a relic of old times spreading that mild smell of moth-balls peculiar to a museum piece, he still stands near the Stefans-kirche and at other points frequented by foreign tourists likely to fancy an anachronistic drive. The Viennese *Fiacker* owes its world-wide fame not only to its elegance but also to the skill, witty remarks and pat answers of its driver. It has the fame of a historic past. As early as in 1814, the year of the Congress of Vienna, Karl von Nostitz, a colonel in Russian service, was reproached with practically living in a *Fiacker*. "At any hour of the day, and whether you are in the Graben or in the Prater, at the ramparts or elsewhere, you are bound to come across him driving in a *Fiacker*. He is not human but half man, half carriage, like a Centaur."

In 1836, England developed a typical form of the hired carriage called 'hansom' after its inventor, Joseph Hansom. It was a light, open two-seater, driven from a highly elevated box behind the passengers with whom the coachman communicated through a hole (Fig. 309). These vehicles took over the function of the former hackneys.

In France, after a temporary absence, the *fiacres* reappeared again on the scene in the nineteenth century. Two companies were running them: the one had yellow vehicles, the other, green ones, and the uniform of the coachmen differed, too, but not their language! The cracking joints of the old boxes cautioned the prospective passenger from afar against availing himself of this means of transport, and the unanalysable, suspicious smell that struck him on opening the door of such a vehicle only added to his doubts.

The *fiacre* often figured as the scene of episodes in nineteenth-century French literature. Without going into details we would only refer to Maupassant's *Bel-Ami*, to the fatal *fiacre* drive of Monsieur Duroy and Madame Marcelle, and to Madame Bovary's famous *scène du fiacre*. The well-known French author Armand Salacrou expressed his opinion of the latter at a round-table debate organized by the *Figaro Littéraire* on the subject: *Love, as expressed in films*. He said: "*Eh bien*, this scene does not shock us in the novel but becomes perfectly impossible on the screen."

The first Berlin hackney-coach guild existed only for a short while, but in 1814, that is, soon after its liquidation, *Droschkes* built on the Warsaw pattern (Fig. 310) appeared again in the streets of Berlin.

In two decades their number increased to 236 one-horse and 30 pair-horse vehicles. *An Englishman living in Germany* wrote of the service in flattering terms and found it particularly inge-

309 The London hansom
310 The Berlin Droschke

nious that the coachman had to give the passenger a printed slip bearing the amount of the fare, the licence number of the vehicle and the number of the passengers carried. He ends his report saying that he wished the same system were introduced in England! At first only a single firm was licensed to transport passengers, but after the expiration of this concession in 1857, the number of transport enterprises increased rapidly. Scores of people started to run hackneys. The result was that the level of the service—the appearance of the carriages and the condition of the horses—declined steadily, for the division of the transport business among so many competitors naturally meant a lower income per carriage. The police finally checked the *Droschkes* in service in 1868 and excluded 1,630 out of 2,639 vehicles from the traffic.

310

289

The Omnibus gained ground very fast. After the failure of the *carrosse à cinq sous* in Paris, a similar regular service was established in 1826 in Nantes. It is believed by some that the businessman named Omnes who started the Nantes service coined the term 'omnibus' from his own name. Another, simpler and more generally accepted explication is that the word 'omnibus' is the dative plural form of the Latin adjective *omnis*, meaning 'for all'. A year later Bordeaux followed the Nantes example, and after a further year a number of companies were licensed for the maintenance of omnibus services also in Paris (Fig. 311). The

311

fare was fixed again in five *sous*. The enterprises found it difficult to get going, until one of the concessionaires hit upon an idea which did not fail to attract passengers: he devised a scheme by which the owner of a five-*sous* ticket could change omnibuses at certain junctions. The system, which was called *correspondance*, proved very effective within a short time; the takings of its initiator increased rapidly, and other enterprises also introduced similar facilities. In 1855 the various private omnibus companies of Paris were united into a single organization, the *Entreprise Générale des Omnibus*. Even at the end of the century the Paris omnibus continued to run according to fairly patriarchal rules. Not only did the stops follow each other at short distances, but the vehicles picked up signalling pedestrians also between the

290

stops. The buses were painted yellow, green, chestnut, brown, etc. Among their many archaic features, most of which have long sunk into oblivion, there is an original and practical if primitive one, worth mentioning, namely, that the signalling cord of the conductor was tied to the foot of the driver. (His feet were covered with a rug winter and summer alike.)

311 The Paris omnibus
312 Journey on a Kremser

After modest beginnings in the eighteenth century, omnibus traffic in London was given a fresh start by George Shillibeer on 4th July, 1829. Shillibeer was first a coach-builder in Paris. As such, he was commissioned by a Paris promoter of omnibus services to build two buses of an improved type. Shillibeer carried out not only this order but also his own idea of introducing the well-tried Paris omnibus service into London. The first London omnibus ran between Paddington Green and the Bank. It was a flat-roofed, high-sprung, box-like structure that seated eighteen passengers (Pl. LXIV). The word 'omnibus' was painted in large letters on its sides. Later, when this was imitated by rival proprietors, Shillibeer replaced the inscription by his own name. Like his competitors, he also reduced the number of horses from the initially used three to two. The first omnibuses were single-deck vehicles; the process of accommodating passengers on the roof was gradual. First there was room only for two or three passengers beside the driver; later, a second row was arranged behind this, and, eventually, travelling on the roof became a regular feature. It was fairly difficult to clamber on to these top seats; one had to be young and agile, and belong to the male sex to do it. It was not meant for ladies at all, if but for the steps. Yet one had a fine view from the top. We have it from the great William Ewart Gladstone that "The best way to see London is from the top of a bus." The horse-bus was developed continuously until the end of the century, and by the last days of its era it reached the peak of carriage-building: it was probably the lightest and strongest vehicle of its kind in the whole world.

312

291

The Berlin public service (Fig. 312) bore the name of its founder, Kremser. The first of these vehicles—which could carry ten to twelve passengers—appeared at the Brandenburger Tor in 1825 to run between Berlin and its suburbs. The *Kremser* was used also for organized excursions, called *Kremserfahrt* and gay companies and skittle parties often hired one for their outings. The *Kremser* was usually crowded, and people nicknamed it the 'herring wagon'. The Post maintained a service called *Journalière* between Potsdam and Berlin. It was scheduled to cover this

313

route six times a day there and back, but, as far as it appears from a casual remark of the Postmaster General Nagler, it was not a very successful service, for when Nagler was told around the end of the 'thirties that a railway would be built between these two points, he exclaimed: "Nonsense! I am running six-seater post buses to Potsdam six times a day with nobody sitting in them, and now they want to build a railway!"

In conclusion, let us recall a few carriage types which represented a sort of transition between the farm wagon and the coach.

The Dutch adopted and adapted to their own farm wagons a good many features of the French coach of the eighteenth century. The collections of the Leek National Rijtuigmuseum and the Arnhem open-air museum show that they liked and readily imported ornamented coaches from abroad but built handsome farm wagons also themselves (Fig. 313).

In the German *Stuhlwagen* six seats were suspended on straps. *An Englishman living in Germany* described it in 1834 as a rather terrifying vehicle: he had to hold fast to its side with both hands, lest he be shot out of his seat, while other passengers—apparently more used to this type of conveyance—chatted and tittered as if no such danger existed. The *Stuhlwagen* was fashionable also in Hamburg (Fig. 314). The Hamburg burgher who could afford it spent the week-end 'outside the town-gates', and if a larger party assembled, they hired a *Stuhlwagen* for the occasion.

The English farm wagons were famous for their handsome design. In a letter to C. H. B. Quennel, dated 7th April, 1921, Thomas Hardy wrote about them as follows: — "...the old ones left hereabout—at any rate till lately—are more graceful, the curve being very marked and the floral designs painted on the front and tail-board very ingenious..."

293

Historic associations. In eighteenth- and nineteenth-century paintings, engravings and drawings representing town-scapes or palaces, the carriage appeared, in one form or other, be it a coach, a mail-coach or a carrier's wagon. With historic events the situation is similar: the carriage, though only of secondary importance, always formed part of the picture; sometimes it came to the fore but more often appeared in the background.

As we have already seen from the many examples cited at random in the foregoing, the coach and other types of carriages cropped up as mute witnesses at the most unexpected and surprising places. It would not be too exaggerated to state that the biography of certain historic figures, especially of those of the nineteenth century, could be reconstructed in broad outlines through the rôle the carriage had played in their life. Here is, for example, a short sketch of the life of Napoleon:

If we leave out of consideration such common events as, for example, the accident when the young Buonaparte had to be pulled out through a window of his overturned carriage, we can escape some needless brooding on the 'ifs of history'. Let us rather look at the Emperor at Compiègne, as he hastens to meet the eight-horsed state-coach of Marie-Louise and, burning with excitement and curiosity, throws open the door of the coach to get in, beside the future Empress. Or take the episode the German author Friedrich Förster described to Theodor Körner: On 13th December, 1812, Förster saw Napoleon get out of a rickety carriage fixed on sledge runners. The Emperor had just arrived from Russia, frozen to the bone... Now let us skip again the events of Golf Juan which lead up to Paris and the hundred days' rule, and finish with an idyllic picture: when the 'King of Rome' began to walk, a small children's phaeton, varnished blue and drawn by two lambs, appeared with the child-king, later Duke of Reichstadt, on the terrace of the Tuileries. The vehicle (Pl. LXV), a masterpiece of Tremblay, is now the pride of the Wagenburg at Schönbrunn.

Relations between the carriage and literature could be illustrated by a similar series of instances. Scanning the literature of the nineteenth century, we could cite a host of novelists and poets who had been inspired by the mail-coach, as we have already said. One could select countless episodes in which the carriage played a prominent rôle. A vast number of carriage anthologies could be compiled in this manner.

We are, however, nearing the end of this volume destined to give a selection of facts and episodes of general interest from the incredibly involved history of the carriage. There is little more left to say, for hardly had the new invention, which was to oust the coach from its position within a few decades, unfolded its outlines, when the development of the coach came to a standstill, and was followed by gradual extinction. The spirit prevailing at the end of the century, which tended to create something new and revolutionary in so many other walks of life, seems to have deemed this means of transport antiquated even in the small area still not covered by the railway.

There was a last upswing at the end of the century, with magnificent carriage parades, splendid coaches, rubber tyres and increased comfort (Pl. LXVI). But all this was only a delusive flare. From 1905 on, the courts of Europe began to replace their scrapped state-coaches by motor-cars. Only the Austrian Emperor, Francis Joseph, a living monument of conservatism, stuck to the horse-drawn carriage. The Viennese court kept up its coach park until the death of the old Emperor in 1916.

After this, the coach gradually developed (or deteriorated?) into a museum piece. Now we can practically count the occasions on which it is still used. Only peoples respectful of tradition continue to hold the coach in esteem, but even they confine its use to important state ceremonies, such as coronations, the opening of Parliament, etc.

But before rolling a stone over the grave of this cultural relic with a past of six thousand years let us throw a parting glance at the respectable career it had followed.

It should be borne in mind that, although the animal-drawn vehicle is gradually becoming a rarity in the greater part of Europe, its persisting influence is still manifest in various forms even in our days. The first railway carriages and motor-cars took their form from the mail-coach, the coach and the coupé, and even if the modern express train or racing-car hardly bears the marks of its origin or has any feature in common with its ancestor (except that it also runs on wheels), we must not forget that the early railway carriages were basically mail-coaches on iron wheels, and the early motor-cars differed from the horse-drawn wagonette or coupé only in so far that there was no horse tied to it, a steering-wheel rose high in front of the box, and the wheels were provided with tyres; the resemblance between the ancestors and descendants is plainly apparent from contemporary illustrations.

But apart from this heritage, certain forms of horse-drawn vehicles are still actually visible today. We have already mentioned the state-coach, still used for ceremonies, but old types of carriages appear occasionally also at demonstration drives and shooting-parties even in the most motorized countries. In many places it is customary for newly-married young couples to drive round in an open carriage drawn by white horses; in other regions, country places or less motorized territories, horse-drawn vehicles, inherited from elders, are still used out of tradition or simply lack of money for cars; and finally, in many parts of the world certain persisting forms of wagons and carts are still used in agriculture.

This volume hardly represents more than an appreciative cursory glance, compared to the study which the immense cultural historical cyclorama of the development of the carriage would deserve. However, if the series of fleeting pictures presented herein have flashed a beam of light on the essential points of this fascinating technical, historical and sociological subject, then the present work has succeeded in approaching its aim.

List of Plates

The author would like to express his gratitude to the Science Museum, London, as well as to the other institutions which put illustrations or illustration copyrights at his disposal, and for their kind permission to reproduce objects in their possession in this book.

Acknowledgements to institutions not mentioned here by name are given with the particular illustrations.

I Detail of the 'standard' of Ur. About 2500 B.C. British Museum, London (Ch. Zervos: "L'Art de la Mésopotamie." Cahiers d'Art, Paris. Photo by Coppola.)

II Sumerian king riding a chariot. Fragment of the Stela of the Vultures. Lagash, about 2500 B.C. Musée du Louvre, Paris. (S. N. Kramer: L'Histoire commence à Sumer. Arthaud, Paris, 1952. Photograph by Franceschi.)

III Cylinder seal from Babylon. Kassite, about 1530–1160 B.C. Vorderasiatisches Museum, Berlin. (Staatliche Museen zu Berlin, Photographische Abteilung.)

IV Carrying of Sharrukin's throne-chariot. Relief from the royal palace of Khorsabad. 722–705 B.C. Musée du Louvre, Paris. (Photo by Alinari.)

V Alabaster relief with warriors on chariots. Nineveh, North Palace. Age of Ashur-bani-pal, 668–628 B.C. Musée du Louvre, Paris. (Alinari.)

VI Syrians paying tribute. Relief from a stairway of the Apadana at Persepolis. Age of Xerxes, 484–465 B.C. (F. Altheim: Die Weltgeschichte Asiens im griechischen Zeitalter, Fig. 16.)

VII The work of the carriage-builders. Egyptian wall paintings. About 1475 B.C. (From W. Wreszinsky: Atlas zur altägyptischen Kulturgeschichte. Vol. 2. Leipzig, 1923.)

VIII Detail of a painted wooden chest. From the tomb of Tutankhamen. About 1330 B.C. Egyptian Museum, Cairo. (Bildarchiv Foto Marburg.)

IX Pharaoh Seti I on his war-chariot. Relief of the Amun Temple at Karnak. About 1310 B.C. (Bildarchiv Foto Marburg.)

X Lion-hunters on chariot. Relief from Tell Halaf. 9th century B.C. Vorderasiatisches Museum, Berlin. (Staatliche Museen zu Berlin, Photographische Abteilung.)

XI Coloured clay model of a quadriga carrying a goddess. Cyprus. Museo Barracco, Rome. (Alinari.)

XII Indian state-cart. End of 19th century. (From the Archives of the Museum of Ethnography, Budapest. Gillming bequest.)

XIII Two-storied temple with the 'wheel of the doctrine'. From the stone wall of the Dhammacakka temple at Bharhut. 2nd century B.C. Indian Museum, Calcutta. (Archaeological Survey of India.)

XIV Prince Vishvantara roaming in the forest. Relief from Goli. 2nd–3rd century A.D. Museum, Madras. (Archaeological Survey of India.)

XV A wagon-shaped clay vessel. From Budakalász, Hungary. About 2000 B.C. Hungarian National Museum, Budapest. (Photo by the Museum.)

XVI Remains of a four-wheeled Scythian wagon, as found at Szentes-Vekerzug. About 500 B.C. Hungarian National Museum, Budapest. (Photo by the Museum.)

XVII War-chariot on a carved sardonyx stone. Vaphio, Greece. About 1500 B.C. (Photograph by M. Hirmer.)

XVIII Funeral procession and war-chariots on a geometric vase. Athens. Middle of the 8th century B.C. National Museum, Athens. (Bildarchiv Foto Marburg.)

XIX Hydria with scene of harnessing from Vulci. Antikenabteilung, Staatliche Museen zu Berlin, Charlottenburg (From E. Buschor: Griechische Vasen. Piper, Munich, 1940. Fig. 151.)

XX Attican crater with representation of a quadriga. Museum, Arezzo. (Alinari.)

XXI Garden of the Hesperides with Heracles driving a biga. Painting on a vase. Museo Nazionale, Naples. (Alinari.)

XXII The Trundholm sun-chariot. About 1300–1200 B.C. Nationalmuseet, Copenhagen. (L'Œil, February 1963.)

XXIII Pomeranian face-urn. Grabowo, Poland. Hallstatt period. Poznan. (From Ipek 4, 1928, Pl. 4/5.)

XXIV Pomeranian face-urn. Elzanow (Elsenau), Poland. Hallstatt period. Staatliches Museum für Vorgeschichte, Berlin. (From Ipek 4, 1928, Pl. 4/2.)

XXV Etruscan magistrate on his cart. Side of a Tuscan sarcophagus. 3rd–2nd century B.C. Museo Vaticano, Rome. (Anderson.)

XXVI Race of trigas. Fragment of a sarcophagus from Chiusi. 6th–5th century B.C. Museo Nazionale, Palermo. (From Giulio Quirino Giglioli: L'arte etrusca. Milan, 1935, Pl. CXLVIII/2.)

XXVII Detail of the back of a grave stela. Certosa of Bologna. 4th century B.C. Museo Civico, Bologna. (From L. Goldscheider: Etruscan Sculpture. Phaidon, London, 1941, Vol. 4.)

XXVIII Etruscan heating-pan stand. Musée du Louvre, Paris. (From Massimo Pallottino: Art of the Etruscans. Thames and Hudson, London, 1955.)

XXIX Life and entertainment of children. Relief on a sarcophagus. Museo Kircheriano, Rome. (Alinari.)

XXX Funeral scene with carpentum mortuarium. Museo Archeologico, Firenze. (Alinari.)

XXXI Cybele's processional cart. Bronze. Found in Rome. 2nd century B.C. Metropolitan Museum of Art, New York. (Photo Metropolitan Museum of Art.)

XXXII Street scene: a Roman travelling-wagon. Fragment of the cover of a sarcophagus. Nationalmuseet, Stockholm. (From G. Rodenwaldt: Die Kunst der Antike. Berlin, 1927.)

XXXIII Roman mail-coach on a funeral relief in the wall of the church at Maria-Saal, Carinthia, Austria. (Alinari.)

XXXIV Triumphal march of Emperor Tiberius. Relief on the Boscoreale cup. Musée du Louvre, Paris. Collection Ed. Rothschild. (J. Charbonneaux: L'Art au siècle d'Auguste. Paris, 1948, Fig. 82.)

XXXV Chariot race. Relief. 2nd century A.D. Museo Vaticano, Rome. (Alinari.)

XXXVI Travelling-wagon on a relief from Vaison-la-Romaine. Musée Calvet, Avignon. (Alinari.)

XXXVII Procession of a Byzantine emperor. Scene on an ivory table. 5th–6th century. Domschatz, Trier (Treves).

XXXVIII The Oseberg carriage. Universitets Oldsaksamling, Oslo.

XXXIX Illumination from the "Très Riches Heures" of the Limbourg Brothers. 1410-1416. Musée Condé, Chantilly. (Photo Giraudon.)

XL Woodmen. Detail of a Tournai tapestry. Early 16th century. Musée des Arts Décoratifs, Paris. (Photo Musée des Arts Décoratifs.)

XLI Illumination from Jean Miélot's "Vie et Miracles de Notre-Dame." 15th century. Bibliothèque Nationale, Paris. (Photo Maget.)

XLII Diocesan Philippus returns from the coronation of Queen Kandake. Detail of the Mikuszowice triptych. About 1470. Muzeum Narodowe, Cracow. (Photo Muzeum Narodowe.)

XLIII Miracle of the gold in the stick. Detail of a panel of the Jánosrét Master's St. Nicholas Altar. About 1476. Museum of Fine Arts, Budapest. (Photo Museum of Fine Arts.)

XLIV "Jacob's Journey to Egypt." Illumination from the Weltchronik of Rudolf von Ems. About 1350. Zentralbibliothek, Zurich. (Guide artistique de Zurich. Zurich, 1945, Fig. 23.)

XLV "The Journey of St. Elizabeth of Hungary to the Wartburg." Painted panel from the Lübeck Church of the Holy Ghost. About 1430. (Photo Staatliche Museen zu Lübeck.)

XLVI The Florentine carroccio. Illumination from the Codex Chigiano. 14th century. Rome.

XLVII The state-coach of Emperor Frederick III. About 1450. Joannaeum, Graz, Austria. (Photo: Ernst Matthäus Fürböck, Graz.)

XLVIII Relief of a wheel on the sun- chariot. Temple of the Sun, Konarak, Orissa. About 1240 A.D. From Sylvain Lévi: Aux indes sanctuaires, Pl. 79. (Photograph by Odette Monod-Brühl. Musée Guimet, Paris.)

IL Frieze of the Hoysaleswara temple at Halebid. 13th century A.D. (From Sie und Er, Nr. 7, May 1959.)

L Body of a bridal coach, presented by John Frederick, Prince-Elector of Saxony, to his bride, Sibylle de Cleve, 1527. Kunstsammlungen der Veste Coburg. (Photo Kunstsammlungen der Veste Coburg.)

LI German coach. From a printed book entitled Kurtze gegrundte Beschreibung des Pfalzgrafen bey Rhein hochzeitlichen Ehren Fests, fol. 29. Adam Berg, Munich, 1568.

LII Hungarian Kotschiwagen. Drawing by Jeremias Schemel in the Chunteruet Buoch, 1568. Kunsthistorisches Museum, Vienna. (By courtesy of the Museum.)

LIII Adriaen Pauw van Meenastede, Dutch ambassador's arrival in Münster on Sept. 1st, 1647. Painting of Gerrit de Haen and Gerard Ter Borch. Landesmuseum für Kunst und Kulturgeschichte, Münster. (Photo Landesmuseum für Kunst und Kulturgeschichte.)

LIV Phaeton. Coloured line engraving. Late 18th century. (H. B. Moc: The Highway and its Vehicles. London, 1926, Pl. XXVIII.)

LV Sir George Armitage's phaeton. 1770. The Science Museum, London. (By courtesy of the Museum.)

LVI The Imperialwagen. Vienna. 18th century. Wagenburg, Schönbrunn, Vienna. (Photo Kunsthistorisches Museum, Vienna.)

LVII The British royal state-coach, designed by the architect William Chambers. 1761. The London Museum, Kensington Palace, London. (Photo London Museum.)

LVIII The imperial coronation coach of the Bavarian Prince-Elector Karl Albrecht (Emperor Karl VII). Paris, 1741. Schloss Nymphenburg, Marstallmuseum, Munich. (Photograph by Gunther Schmidt, Deutscher Kunstverlag, Munich.)

LIX 'Egyptian' berline. The bridal coach of Carlo Felice, King of Sardinia. About 1800. Palazzo Pitti, Florence. (Photo by Brogi.)

LX The state-coach of Prince Dietrichstein. Wagenburg, Vienna, Schönbrunn. (Photo Kunsthistorisches Museum, Vienna.)

LXI Victoria. 1890. The Science Museum, London. (By courtesy of the Museum.)

LXII Post-station in Hungary in the middle of the 19th century. Lithograph by Bachmann and Hohmann, 1861.

LXIII Royal mail-coach. The Science Museum, London. (By courtesy of the Museum.)

LXIV Model of Shillibeer's omnibus. 1829. The Science Museum, London. (By courtesy of the Museum.)

LXV The phaeton of the 'King of Rome' (Napoleon's son). Designed by the coachmaker Trembley, Paris, 1813. Wagenburg, Schönbrunn, Vienna. (Photo Kunsthistorisches Museum, Vienna.)

LXVI On the Vienna Ringstrasse. Drawing by Felicia von Myrbach.

298

List of Illustrations

(From a drawing by C. Arriens in A. Fürst: Das Weltreich der Technik. Berlin, 1924, Fig. 64.)

49 Portuguese 'creaking cart'. Early 19th century. (From J. Chr. Ginzrot: Die Wagen und Fahrwerke der Griechen und Römer und anderer alten Völcker ... Munich, 1817.)

50 Reconstruction of King Abargi's funeral at Ur. (L. Woolley: Ur-Excavations. Vol. 2: The Royal Cemetery. Oxford, 1934. Pl. 30.)

51 Ground-plan of the grave of King Abargi. (L. Woolley: Ur-Excavations, Vol. 2: The Royal Cemetery. London, 1934.)

52 Reconstruction of the sledge-chariot of Queen Shub-ad. About 2500 B.C. British Museum, London. (L. Woolley: Ur-Excavations, Vol. 2: The Royal Cemetery. London, 1934. Pl. CXXII.)

53 Detail of the 'standard' of Ur. About 2500 B.C. British Museum, London. (From Ch. Zervos: L'Art de la Mésopotamie. Cahiers d'Art, Paris.)

54 Cylinder seal from Kish. Jemdet Nasr period. Ashmolean Museum, Oxford. (S. Langdon–L.Ch. Watelin: Excavations at Kish. Paris, 1934, Vol. IV, Pl. XXIV/2.)

55 Two wheels of a four-wheeled chariot. Kish. Jemdet Nasr period. (S. Langdon–L. Ch. Watelin: Excavations at Kish. Paris, 1934. Vol. IV, Pl. XXIII/1.)

56 Copper model of the chariot from Tell Agrab. About 2500 B.C. Iraq Museum, Baghdad. (Illustrated London News, 6th Nov., 1937.)

57 Cylinder seal from Cappadocia. About 1900 B.C. (B. Th. Bossert: Altanatolien. Berlin, 1942, Fig. 409.)

58 Cylinder seal from Cappadocia. Kültepe. About 1900 B.C. Collection de Clercq, Paris. (Catalogue méthodique et raisonné de la Collection de Clercq. Paris, 1888, Vol. I, 284.)

59 Clay model of a chariot. Assur, about 2000 B.C. (V. Christian: Altertumskunde des Zweistromlandes. Leipzig, 1940, Pl. 447/7.)

60 Clay model chariot. Susa, about 2500 B.C. Collection Morgan, Louvre, Paris. (Lefebvre des Noëttes: L'Attelage et le cheval de selle à travers les âges. Paris, 1931, Vol. 2, Fig. 3.)

61 Clay model chariot. Susa, about 2500 B.C. Collection Morgan, Louvre, Paris. (Lefebvre des Noëttes: L'Attelage et le cheval de selle à travers les âges. Paris, 1931, Vol. 2, Fig. 4.)

62 Clay model chariot Susa, about 2500 B.C. Collection Morgan, Louvre, Paris. (Lefebvre des Noëttes: L'Attelage et le cheval de selle à travers les âges. Paris, 1931, Vol. 2, Fig. 10.)

63 Clay model chariot. Susa, about 2500 B.C. Collection Morgan, Louvre, Paris. (Lefebvre des Noëttes: L'Attelage et le cheval de selle à travers les âges. Paris, 1931, Vol. 2, Fig. 9.)

64 Cart on a painted vase from Susa. About 2500 B.C. (From Gordon V. Childe: "The First Waggons and Carts from the Tigris to the Severn." Proceedings of the Prehistoric Society, New Series Vol. I, 8.)

65 Nail-studded wheel from Susa. About 2500 B.C. (From Gordon V. Childe: Proceedings of the Prehistoric Society, New Series 17 [1951], 180, Fig. 36.)

66 Bronze model of a 'saddle on wheels' from Susa. About 2500 B.C. Musée du Louvre, Paris.

67 Chariot and driver. Clay model. Kish. Jemdet Nasr period. (S. Langdon–L. Ch. Watelin: Excavations at Kish. Paris, 1934, Vol. IV, Pl. XIV/2.)

68 Covered wagon. Tepe Gawra, Layer VI. About 2500 B.C. Dropsey College, Philadelphia, U.S.A. (E. A. Speiser: Excavations at Tepe Gawra, Vol. I, Pl. XXXV/a.)

69 Offering presented to the weather-god in his chariot. 2360–2180 B.C. Pierpont Morgan Library, New York. (H. Frankfort: Cylinder Seals. London, 1939, Pl. 22/a.)

70 Chariot with representation of god or goddess. About 2500 B.C. (Léon Heuzey: Origines orientales de l'Art, Pl. XVI.)

71 'Incense wagon.' Khafaje, about 3000 B.C. (After a reproduction in the Illustrated London News, 9th June, 1934.)

72 Construction of the Assyrian spoked wheel: hub, spokes and felloe. Original drawing by L. Lakner.

73 Cart from Branosera, Palencia, Spain. 19th century A.D.

74 Mexican ox cart. 1865 A.D. Smithsonian Institution, Washington. (From E. John Long: The Story of Transportation. Washington.)

75 Imprint of a cylinder seal with the representation of a war-chariot. Mitanni, 1750–1500 B.C. Collection de Clercq, Paris. (Catalogue méthodique et raisonné de la collection de Clercq. Paris, 1888, Vol. I, 310.)

76 Lion-hunt of King Ashur-nasir-pal (883–859 B.C.). Limestone relief, Nimrud. Vorderasiatisches Museum, Berlin. (Photo Bildarchiv Marburg.)

77 War-chariot. Bronze relief from Tell Balawat. Age of Shalmaneser III (859–824 B.C.). British Museum, London. (Photo after Pritchard.)

78 Captured women and children carried away in carts. Gypsum relief. Nimrud, Central Palace. Age of Tukulit-pal-E-saria III (745–727 B.C.). British Museum, London.

79 The Sin-Shamash temple with the 'procession of the gods'. (Reconstruction from W. Andrae: Das wiedererstandene Assur. Leipzig, 1938.)

80 Transport of a lammashu (bull colossus). Nineveh, relief in the palace of Sennacherib I (705–680 B.C.). (From A. H. Layard: Monuments of Nineveh.)

81 Transport of ropes and cranes. Nineveh, relief in the palace of Sennacherib I. British Museum, London. (H. R. H. Hall: Babylonian and Assyrian Sculpture in the British Museum. Paris, 1928, Pl. XXX.)

82 Ashur-bani-pal in his state-chariot. Alabaster relief from Nineveh ⚬668–628 B.C.

Musée du Louvre, Paris. (Photo Bildarchiv Marburg.)

83 Ashur-bani-pal in his hunting-chariot. Alabaster relief from Nineveh. 668–628 B.C. British Museum, London.

84 Assyrian soldiers escorting prisoners and transporting women in a cart. Alabaster relief from Nineveh. 668–628 B.C. British Museum, London.

85 Umanaldashi II, King of Elam, is led to prison. Relief from Nineveh. 668–628 B.C. British Museum, London. (Photo by W. Forman.)

86 Elamite prisoners beside carts. Alabaster relief from Nineveh, North Palace of Ashur-bani-pal. 668–628 B.C. Musée du Louvre, Paris. (Photo by Alinari.)

87 Elamites in escape. Relief from Nineveh, palace of Ashur-bani-pal. 668–628 B.C. British Museum, London. (Photo by W. Forman.)

88 Assyrian soldiers crossing a river. Relief from the North-West Palace of Nimrud. British Museum, London. (Photo by W. Forman.)

89 Detail of a bronze helmet. Hill Karmir-Blur near Teishebai. Armenian Soviet Socialist Republic. Age of Arghishti, King of Urartu, 781–760 B.C. Ermitage, Leningrad. (A. L. Mongait: Arheologiya v SSSR, p. 219.)

90 Clay model of a covered cart. Mingechaur, Azerbaidzhan Soviet Socialist Republic. 10th–9th century B.C. (A. L. Mongait: Arheologiya v SSSR, p. 249.)

91 Clay model of a covered cart. Mingechaur, Azerbaidzhan Soviet Socialist Republic. 10th–9th century B.C. (A. L. Mongait: Arheologiya v SSSR, p. 249.)

92 Lion-hunt of Darius I, King of Persia. Seal of the King. 522–486 B.C. British Museum, London.

93 Wall painting from the tomb of Menna. Thebes, Egypt. Age of Thutmosis IV, Dynasty XVIII. 1420–1411 B.C. (W. Wreszinski: Atlas zur altägyptischen Kulturgeschichte. Leipzig, 1935, Vol. II, Pl. 231.)

94 Wall painting from a tomb in Thebes, Egypt. Dynasty XVIII–XIX. After 1400 B.C. British Museum, London.

95 Hunting scene. Relief of the tomb of Ebe. Thebes, Sheh abd el-Gurna. Age of Amenhotep III. About 1375 B.C. (W. Wreszinski: Atlas zur altägyptischen Kulturgeschichte. Leipzig, 1935, Vol. II, Pl. 141.)

96 Relief from the tomb of Kha-em-chet. Thebes, Sheh abd el-Gurna. Age of Amenhotep III. About 1375 B.C. (W. Wreszinski: Atlas zur altägyptischen Kulturgeschichte. Leipzig, 1935, Vol. II, Pl. 191.)

97 Chariot from the tomb of the parents-in-law of Amenhotep III, from the Valley of the Kings. About 1375 B.C. Egyptian Museum, Cairo.

98 State-chariot from the tomb of Tutankhamen. About 1350 B.C. Egyptian Museum,

Cairo. (From P. Fox: Tutanhamon's Treasure. Oxford University Press, London, 1951.)

99 Ostrich feathers fan from the tomb of Tutankhamen. About 1350 B.C. Egyptian Museum, Cairo. (From P. Fox: Tutanhamon's Treasure. Oxford University Press, London, 1951.)

100 War-chariot from Thebes, Egypt. 15th century B.C. Museo Archeologico, Florence.

101 Relief from the tomb of Horonemheb. Saqqara, about 1350. Vorderasiatisches Museum, Berlin. (W. Wreszinski: Atlas zur altägyptischen Kulturgeschichte. Leipzig, 1923. Vol. II, Pl. 386.)

102 Wall painting from the tomb of Huie: a Nubian princess in a carriage drawn by oxen. Thebes, Egypt. Age of Tutankhamen, 1354–1338 B.C. (From N. de G. Davies — A. H. Gardiner: The Tomb of Huy, Viceroy of Nubia in the Reign of Tutankhamun. Theban Tombs Series, Egypt Exploration Fund, London, 1926.)

103 The battle of Kadesh. Detail from a relief of Abydos. Age of Rameses II, 1290–1224 B.C. (From a photograph of the expedition of Eduard Meyer.)

104 Galloping war-chariots. Rock painting on the plateau of Tassili-Ahaggar, Central Sahara. Early first millennium B.C. (H. Lhote: "Le Cheval et le chameau dans les peintures et gravures du Sahara." Bulletin de l'Institut Français d'Afrique Noire, XV, 3.)

105 Detail of a Hittite cylinder seal. About 1375–1110 B.C. (M. Riemschneider: Die Welt der Hethiter. Stuttgart, 1954.)

106 Royal procession. Basalt relief from Arslan Tash. Age of Tukulit-pal-E-saria III, about 730 B.C. Museum, Constantinople. (M. Ebert: Reallexikon der Vorgeschichte. Berlin, Vol. 5, Pl. 84.)

107 War-chariot from a battle scene. Relief from the 'long wall' of Kargamish. Age of Ashur-nasir-pal II, 883–859 B.C. Museum, Ankara. (M. Vieyra: Hittite Art. Alec Tiranti, London, 1955, Pl. 48.)

108 King Sulumeli's sacrifice to the water-god. Malatya, middle of the 8th century B.C. Museum, Ankara. (H. Th. Bossert: Altanatolien. Wasmuth, Berlin, 1942, Pl. 778.)

109 Relief with a lion-hunt. Arslantepe, near Malatya. First millennium B.C. Museum, Constantinople. (M. Vieyra: Hittite Art. Alec Tiranti, London, 1955, Pl. 67.)

110 Relief with warrior and charioteer from Senjirli. Archaeological Museum, Constantinople. (M. de Saint-Pierre: Trésors de la Turquie. Paris, 1959, Fig. 136.)

111 The sun-god comes in his chariot to the help of god Temb in his fight against a lion. Sakça-Gözü, 9th century B.C. Vorderasiatisches Museum, Berlin.

112 Hunt. Gold plate from Ras Shamra. 15th century B.C. Musée du Louvre, Paris.

113 Ivory gaming-chest with relief of a hunting scene. Encomi, Cyprus. About 1200 B.C.

British Museum, London. (A. Murray: Excavations in Cyprus. London, 1900.)

114 Prisoners of war paying homage to a king. Relief on an ivory tablet. Megiddo, about 1350–1150 B.C. Palestine Archaeological Museum, Jerusalem. (G. Loud: The Megiddo Palestine Archaeological Museum Ivories. 1939.)

115 Clay model of a cart (with wooden accessories reconstructed). Mohenjo-Daro, Indus Valley. About 2000 B.C. Prince of Wales Museum, Bombay. (H. Mode: Das frühe Indien. Weimar, 1960, Pl. 2.)

116 Copper model of a carriage-body. (Pole and axes are missing.) Chanhu-Daro, Indus Valley. About 2000 B.C. (E. J. H. Mackay: Chanhu-Daro Excavations 1935–36. New Haven, 1943, Pl. LVIII/2.)

117 India's coat of arms.

118 Grave No. M 020 with the remains of a carriage found at Hiao-t'ung, China. End of the second millennium B.C. (Chungkuo: K'aoku Hsüeh-Pao, Vol. II, Fig. 5.)

119 Ancient Chinese pictographs—the signs for carriages. End of the second millennium and beginning of the first millennium. B.C. (Chungkuo: K'aoku Hsüeh-Pao, Vol. II, Figs. 2–11.)

120 'Ghosts' of chariots at Liu Li Ko. 4th century B.C.

121 Detail of the gate of the San-chi stupa. Early 1st century B.C. Musée Cernuschi. (Lefebvre des Noëttes: L'Attelage et le cheval de selle à travers les âges. Paris, 1931. Vol. 2, Fig. 102.)

122 Battle on the bridge. Detail from a relief. Shantung, China. Han period, around 150 B.C. (From O. Sirén: Les Arts anciens de la Chine, Vol. 3.)

123 Stone relief from a grave. Han period. From a rubbing. (From E. von E. Consten: Das alte China. Stuttgart, 1958, Pl. 93.)

124 Recovery of a so-called Chou Ting, a sacred tripod. Hsiao T'ang Shan. 2nd century A.D. From a rubbing. (L. Bachhofer: A Short History of Chinese Art. London, 1947, Pl. 85.)

125 Cart. Han period. After a rubbing of the Chavannes expedition.

126 Relief from a pedestal. Wei Tartar dynasty, 524 A.D. University Museum, Pennsylvania, U.S.A. (L. Ashton: An Introduction to the Study of Chinese Sculpture. London, 1924, Pl. LIV/b.)

127 Clay model cart and horse. From a Han-period grave of the Si-Chuan province. (After J. V. Avdiev.)

128 Clay model cart. China. Han period. Collection Rousset. (Lefebvre des Noëttes: L'Attelage et le cheval de selle à travers les âges. Paris, 1931, Vol. 2, Fig. 131.)

129 Oxen yoked to two-wheeled cart. Stone slab of Züschen, Hessen-Nassau. German Federal Republic. Before 2500 B.C. (J. Boehlau–F. v. Gilsa: Neolithische Denkmäler aus Hessen. Kassel, 1898, Pl. V, 61.)

130 Ligurian rock drawing.

131 Ancient cart tracks in Malta. (Th. Zammit: Antiquity, Vol. I, 1928.)

132 Plan of kurgan (grave-mount) No. 9 at Tri Brata, near Elista, Kalmyk Republic, U.S.S.R. About 1000 B.C. (I. V. Sinicin: "Pamyatniki predskifskoy epohi v styepyah Nizhnego Povolzhya." Sovetskaya Arheologiya, X [1948], Fig. 14.)

133 Clay model cart found in kurgan No. 9 at Tri Brata, near Elista, Kalmyk Republic, U.S.S.R. (Yoke, pole and wheels reconstructed. From I. V. Sinicin, ibid.)

134 Body of a model carriage. UI, district of Maikop, U.S.S.R. (M. Ebert: Reallexikon der Vorgeschichte. Berlin. Vol. 7, Pl. 87/2.)

135 Stela from Znamenka, near the river Yenisei. About 1000 B.C. (M. P. Gryaznov—I. P. Schneider: "Drevnie izvayaniya Minusinskich stepey." Materiali po Etnografii, Vol. IV [1929].)

136 Drawing on the Shuliek Rock, district of Minusinsk, U.S.S.R. (M. Ebert: op. cit.)

137 Remains of a carriage as found in kurgan No. 5 at Pazirik. 5th–4th century B.C. (A. L. Mongait: Arheologiya v SSSR. Moscow, 1955, p. 173.)

138 The same carriage reconstructed. (T. Talbot Rice: The Scythians. New York–London, 1957.)

139 Nomadic caravan, "as the Kunduran Tartars used it" even in 1817. (J. Ch. Ginzrot: Die Wagen und Fahrwerke der Griechen und Römer und anderer alten Völcker ... Munich, 1817, Vol. 1, Pl. XIII.)

140 Clay model of a four-wheeled caravan from Kerch, Crimea. 3rd century B.C.

141 Drawing of a cart, engraved on the inner wall of a stone chest. Berikey, near Derbent, Daghestan, U.S.S.R. Early 2nd millennium B.C. (Fr. Hančar: "Ein nordisches Streitwagenbild im östlichen Kaukasus." Forschungen und Fortschritte, XIX [1943], Fig. 1.)

142 Carriage found in a grave near Adiaman, Armenian Soviet Socialist Republic. Early 1st century B.C. (After a photograph of the Armenian Academy of Sciences, Yerevan.)

143 War-chariot on a relief at Prinia, Crete. Minoan period. (Lefebvre des Noëttes: L'Attelage et le cheval de selle à travers les âges. Paris, 1931, Vol. 2, Fig. 47.)

144 Terra-cotta tablet with sign of a war-chariot and a horse. Knossos. Late Minoan period, 1470–1420 B.C. (A. J. Evans: The Palace of Minos. London, 1935, Vol. 4. II, Fig. 800/b.)

145 Mycenaean stela representing a war-chariot. 1600–1500 B.C. National Museum, Athens. (Photo Bildarchiv Marburg.)

146 Detail of a Geometric vase. Rape of Helena. Geometric style, 8th century B.C. (E. Buschor: Griechische Vasen. Munich, 1940.)

147 Detail of an amphora from Melos. Apollo and Muses on a chariot. Middle of the 17th century B.C. National Museum, Athens. (G. M. A. Richter: A Handbook of Greek Art. London, 1959.)

148 Detail of the so-called Chigi jug. About 630 B.C. Museo di Villa Giulia, Rome. (Photo Bildarchiv Marburg.)

149 Detail of a red-figured vase. Metropolitan Museum, New York. (G. Richter: Red-Figured Athenian Vases in the Metropolitan Museum of Art. Yale University Press, 1936.)

150 Detail of the so-called François vase. Zeus, Hera and Urania. Chiusi. Crater by Kleitias and Ergotimos. About 560 B.C. Museo Archeologico, Florence. (G. M. A. Richter: A Handbook of Greek Art. London, 1959.)

151 Detail of an amphora by the so-called Rycroft painter. About 520 B.C. Museum of Art, Worcester. (R. V. Schoder: Masterpieces of Greek Art. London, 1960.)

152 Detail of a 'DES' crater by Polygnotos. Nike as driver. Spina. About 440 B.C. (From N. Alfieri–P. E. Arias: Spina. Munich.)

153 Terra-cotta horse-cart with amphorae. Euboea, 7th century B.C. National Museum, Athens. (G. M. A. Richter: A Handbook of Greek Art. London, 1959.)

154 Terra-cotta funeral wagon. Vari, about 600 B.C. National Museum, Athens. (G. M. A. Richter: A Handbook of Greek Art. London, 1959.)

155 Warrior and war-chariot on the crater from Vix. About 575 B.C. Museum Châtillon-sur-Seine. (From a post-card.)

156 Greek wedding procession. From a vase of the 4th century B.C. Cabeiric sanctuary near Thebes. (H. L. Lorimer: "The Country Cart of Ancient Greece." The Journal of Hellenic Studies, XXIII [1903].)

157 Lekythos with wedding procession by the Amasis painter. About 540 B.C. Metropolitan Museum of Art, New York, U.S.A. (G. M. A. Richter: A Handbook of Greek Art. London, 1959, Fig. 437.)

158 Detail of a black-figured vase. Cart carrying wine-jars. 6th century B.C. Musée du Louvre, Paris. (Histoire générale du travail, Vol. 1, Pl. 35.)

159 Funeral scene. Attican terra-cotta slab. Collection Rayet, Paris. (From O. Rayet: Monuments de l'art antique. Quentin, Paris, 1880.)

160 Cart with cross-bar type wheels. Ulyastay Djabhan aymak, Mongolian People's Republic. (Photo by A. Róna-Tas.)

161 Marble relief with war-chariot. Kyzikos near Brussa. Museum, Constantinople. (B. Meissner–D. Opitz: "Betrachtungen zu einem archaischen griechischen Rennfahrer-Bilde." Abhandlungen der Preußischen Akademie der Wissenschaften, Nr. 6, 1943.)

162 Horse-drawn chariot on slab of a stone chest in a tomb. Kivik, Scania, Sweden.

Bronze Age. (H. Leicht: Kunstgeschichte der Welt. Zurich, 1945.)

163 Horse-drawn chariot on a stone. Villfara, South Sweden. (G. Kossinna: Die deutsche Vorgeschichte. 8th edition, Leipzig, 1941, Fig. 238.)

164 Cultic chariot of Dupliaya, Voivodina, Yugoslavia. About 1400 B.C. Museum, Belgrad. (W. Otto: Handbuch der Archäologie. Munich, 1950, Vol. 2, Pl. 11/1.)

165 Cauldron on wheels. Skallerup, Denmark. Bronze Age. (From L'Œil, February 1963, No. 98.)

166 Bronze cauldron on wheels. Peckatel, Mecklenburg, German Democratic Republic. (J. Déchelette: Manuel d'archéologie préhistorique, celtique et gallo-romaine. Paris, 1924, Vol. 2, Fig. 107/2.)

167 Wagon from a rock drawing at Rished, Askum, Bohuslän, Sweden. Bronze Age. (After G. A. Gustafson.)

168 Wagon from a rock drawing at Långön, Tossene, Bohuslän, Sweden. Bronze Age. (After G. A. Gustafson.)

169 Rock drawing resembling a cultic carriage. (Fr. Altheim: Literatur und Gesellschaft im ausgehenden Altertum. Halle-Saale, 1950, Vol. 2.)

170 Rock drawing with representation of carriages and drivers. Rished, Askum, Bohuslän, Sweden. (From H. Reinerth: Vorgeschichte der deutschen Stämme.)

171 Wheel from the Dystrup Bog, Örum, Jutland, Denmark. (S. Müller: "Nye Fund og Iagttagelser fra Sten-, Bronze- og Jernalderen." Aarboger, II, 1907.)

172 Wheel, found at Lilla Mellösa, Södermanland, Sweden. Iron Age (?). (G. Berg: Sledges and Wheeled Vehicles. Stockholm-Copenhagen, 1935.)

173 Wheel of a processional carriage. Bronze. La Côte-Saint-André, Dép. Isère, France. Bronze Age. Museum, Lyon. (J. Déchelette: Manuel d'archéologie préhistorique, celtique et gallo-romaine, Vol. 2.)

174 Wooden three-piece wheel from the peat-bog at Mercurago near Ancona, Italy. (J. Déchelette: Manuel d'archéologie préhistorique, celtique et gallo-romaine, Vol. 2.)

175 Wooden wheel made of several pieces from the peat-bog at Mercurago near Ancona, Italy. (J. Déchelette: Manuel d'archéologie préhistorique, celtique et gallo-romaine, Vol. 2.)

176 Ritual carriage from Strettweg near Judenburg, Austria. Bronze. 7th century B.C. Joannaeum, Graz. (Kunsthistorischer Atlas, Wien, 1889, Pl. XLI.)

177 Ritual carriage from Frög near Rosegg, Austria.

178 Carriage-urn from Kánya. Balogh Ádám Museum, Szekszárd.

179 Incised picture of a carriage on the fragment of an urn. Sopron, Hungary. (From

M. Hoernes–O. Menghin: Urgeschichte der bildenden Kunst in Europa. Vienna, 1925.)

180 Detail of the decoration of the Kuffarn situla.

181 Celtic grave with carriage. Somme-Bionne, Dép. Marne, France. (Read—Smith: Guide to Early Iron Age Antiquities. 1925.)

182 Reconstruction of a carriage found in Bell, German Federal Republic. (W. Rest: "Das Grabhügelfeld von Bell am Hunsrück." Bonner Jahrbücher, 48, 1948.)

183 Wagon found in the bog of Dejbjaerg, Denmark. Reconstruction according to O. Montelius. Nationalmuseet, Copenhagen. (From O. Montelius's article in Prähistorische Zeitschrift, II [1910].)

184 Plan view of the same wagon found at Dejbjaerg. (O. Klindt-Jensen: "Foreign Influences in Denmark's Early Iron Age." Acta Archaeologica, Copenhagen, XX [1949].)

185 Reconstruction of the Celtic chariot found at Llynn Cerrig, Anglesey. Early Iron Age. National Museum of Wales, Cardiff. (C. F. Fox: A Find of the Early Iron Age from Llynn Cerrig Bach, Anglesey.)

186 Four-wheeled wagon with shafts. Region of Sandrio, Italy. (K. Jaberg–J. Jud: Sprach-und Sachatlas Italiens und der Süd-Schweiz. Zofingen, 1935, Vol. VI.)

187 Bronze Etruscan chariot. From Monteleone di Spoleto. 600–550 B.C. Metropolitan Museum of Art, New York, U.S.A. (G. Q. Giglioli: L'arte etrusca. Milan, 1935.)

188 The last journey. Relief on a sarcophagus from Vulci, Italy. (Illustrierte Kultur- und Sittengeschichte. Zurich, 1955.)

189 Model of a bronze Etruscan cart. Metropolitan Museum of Art, New York, U.S.A. (L. H. Parias [dir.]: Histoire générale du travail, Vol. 1.)

190 Plaustra drawn by mules and oxen. Detail of a carved frieze. Ephesos. British Museum, London. (A. H. Smith: Catalogue of Sculptures of the British Museum, II, No. 1285.)

191 A plaustrum mosaic from the baths at Ostia, Italy. End of the 3rd century A.D. (Alinari.)

192 Terra-cotta sculpture of a covered carpentum. Collection Fouquet. (P. Perdrizet: Les Terres-cuites grecques de la Collection Fouquet. 1921, Vol. 2.)

193 Relief representing a cisium with the cisiarius and his passenger. From the mausoleum at Igel, near Trier, German Federal Republic. (After a photograph in the Rheinisches Landesmuseum, Trier.)

194 Medal of Emperor Tiberius, with the representation of a tensa. Bibliothèque Nationale, Paris. (Lefebvre des Noëttes: L'Attelage et le cheval de selle à travers les âges. Paris, 1931, Vol. 2, Fig. 80.)

195 Model of a Roman racing-chariot. Bronze. Rome. British Museum, London.

196 Detail of the relief on the Marcus Aurelius column in Rome.

197 A boy on a carriage with shafts. Detail of a relief on a sarcophagus. Treves (Trier). 3rd century A.D. Musée du Louvre, Paris. (Lefebvre des Noëttes: L'Attelage et le cheval de selle à travers les âges. Paris, 1931, Vol. 2, Fig. 63.)

198 Wagon carrying wine, drawn by three mules. Gallo–Roman relief. Museum, Langres. (L. H. Parias [dir.]: Histoire générale du travail, Vol. I.)

199 Reconstruction of a Thracian wagon. (From I. Venedikov: Thrakische Wagen.)

200 A similar wagon—as excavated. (From I. Venedikov: Thrakische Wagen.)

201 A metope of the Adamklissi memorial, the triumphal memorial of Emperor Trajan. After 100 A.D. Museum, Bucharest. (After a photograph.)

202 War-chariots. Carving on a Byzantine casket. Bone. 9th century. Musée des Thermes et de l'Hôtel de Cluny, Paris. (Lefebvre des Noëttes: L'Attelage et le cheval de selle à travers les âges. Paris, 1931.)

203 Transportation of a relic. Merovingian bas-relief from Vienne, Isère, France. 9th century A.D. (From René Huyghe: L'Art et l'homme. Larousse, Paris, 1957–61.)

204 Miniature from the Pentateuch of Tours. 7th century A.D. (Lefebvre des Noëttes: L'Attelage et le cheval de selle à travers les âges. Paris, 1931, Vol. 2, Fig. 117.)

205 Cart on the base of a cross. Ahenny, Ireland. 8th century. (H. S. Crawford: Handbook of Carved Ornament from Irish Monuments of the Christian Period. Dublin, 1926.)

206 Carruca nutans, carriage with suspended body. Frankish. (Meyers großes Konversations-Lexikon. 6th edition. Leipzig–Vienna, 1906, Vol. 13, Pl. IV, Fig. 12.)

207 Miniature from the Stuttgart Psalter. Early 9th century A.D. Landesbibliothek, Stuttgart. (From N. E. T. de Wald: The Stuttgart Psalter.)

208 Miniature in a Frankish manuscript. 10th century. Bibliothèque Nationale, Paris. (Lefebvre des Noëttes: L'Attelage et le cheval de selle à travers les âges. Paris, 1931, Vol. 2, Fig. 140.)

209 Miniature in a Frankish manuscript. 10th century. Bibliothèque Nationale, Paris. (Lefebvre des Noëttes: ibid., Fig. 142.)

210 Cart with studded wheels from The Romance of Alexander. Illuminated by Jehan de Grise. Bodleian Library, Oxford. (H. Belloc: The Highway and its Vehicles. London, 1926, Pl. V.)

211 Cart with studded wheels, carrying corn uphill. The Luttrell Psalter. About 1338. British Museum, London.

212 French travelling-wagon. From a manuscript Vita sancti Dionysii. About 1317.

Bibliothèque Nationale, Paris. (C. Piton: Le Costume civil en France du XIII^c au XIX^c siècle. Paris, 1913.)

213 Travelling German merchant with his cart. Woodcut from Augsburger Aesop. 1475. (E. Redslob: Vom Römerberg zum Brandenburger Tor. Munich, 1957, p. 13.)

214 Late Saxon country cart. In an Anglo-Saxon calendar prefixed to a treatise on astronomy and chronology. British Museum, London. (H. Belloc: The Highway and its Vehicles. London, 1926, Pl. II.)

215 Cart with shafts. From a psalter. 13th century. Bibliothèque Nationale, Paris. (L. H. Parias [dir.]: Histoire générale du travail, Vol. II.)

216 Detail of the façade of the Cathedral Borgo S. Donnino (Fidenza), Italy. 12th century. (Lefebvre des Noëttes: L'Attelage et le cheval de selle à travers les âges. Paris, 1931, Vol. 2, Fig. 149.)

217 Capital in the crypt of the Cathedral of St-Denis, France. 12th century. (Lefebvre des Noëttes: ibid., Fig. 147.)

218 Detail of the Bayeux tapestry. Part of William's baggage train: a wine cart. About 1080. Musée de la Tapisserie, Bayeux, France. (A. Fürst: Weltreich der Technik. Berlin, 1924, Vol. 2.)

219 Wagon with whipple-trees. Detail of the bronze door of the Cathedral of Novgorod. Third quarter of the 12th century. (From A. Goldschmidt: Die Bronzetüre von Nowgorod in Gnesen. 1932.)

220 Peasant with his carriage. From the Sachsenspiegel. 14th century. (W. Hofstätter–H. Reichmann–J. Schneider: Ein Jahrtausend deutscher Kultur im Bilde, 800–1800. Leipzig, 1929.)

221 On the highway. Miniature from a Hebrew manuscript. 14th–15th century. Germanisches Museum, Nuremberg. (W. Hofstätter–H. Reichmann–J. Schneider: Ein Jahrtausend deutscher Kultur im Bilde, 800–1800. Leipzig, 1929.)

222 Allegory of the foundation of Magdeburg. Woodcut by C. Botho in Cronecken der Sassen. Mainz, 1492. (G. Steinhausen: Der Kaufmann in der deutschen Vergangenheit. Leipzig, 1899.)

223 Woodcut in Peter Attendorn's Directorium statuum. 1489. (Illustrierte Kultur- und Sittengeschichte. Zurich, 1955.)

224 The family of Baron Guitschard travels to Bern. From Diebold Schilling's Amtliche Berner Chronik. 1478. Staatsbibliothek, Bern.

225 Yolantha of Savoyen captured by Burgundian mercenaries. Werner Schodeler: Eidgenössische Chronik. 1476. Bürgerbibliothek, Luzern.

226 Czech (Hussite) stove tile. Prague. 15th century. Museum of Applied Arts, Prague. (After a photograph by courtesy of the Museum.)

227 Wagon fortification (Wagenburg). Pen drawing from the Wolfegger Hausbuch.

228 German 'tank'. Pen drawing from the Wolfegger Hausbuch.

229 "How Pope John Lay in the Snow on the Arlen Mountain." Woodcut from U. von Reichenthal: Das Concilium, so zu Constanz gehalten ist worden. 1483.

230 Entrance of a Princess into Paris. From the Wroclaw (Breslau) manuscript of Froissart's Chronicle. About 1470. (W. Hofstätter–H. Reichmann–J. Schneider: Ein Jahrtausend deutscher Kultur im Bilde, 800–1800. Leipzig, 1929.)

231 Chinese relief. After a rubbing (543) of the Chavannes expedition ('mission').

232 Stone relief with carts from Angkor Thom. 8th century.

233 German carrier's wagons in front of the gate of Lübeck. Woodcut. About 1560.

234 German woodcut of moralizing content: the education of children. From a Fliegendes Blatt. Nuremberg, 1568.

235 March of an army. Detail from a woodcut of Jost Amman. 1572.

236 Paris timber-vendors. Woodcut from Ordonnances de prévosté des marchans de Paris. 16th century.

237 Pie-vendor with his cart. Woodcut from Wie habt an das Concilium zu Constanz. Augsburg, 1536.

238 Ransoming a Swiss village. Woodcut from Stumpf's Schweizerchronik. Zurich, 1548.

239 Cart carrying a condemned woman to the scaffold. French woodcut. 16th century.

240 Siege of Wolfenbüttel. Detail of Lucas Cranach's woodcut. 1542.

241 Detail from a stall in the Cathedral of Amiens. Early 16th century.

242 Covered German travelling-wagon, the so-called German Rollwagen. Woodcut. About 1500.

243 Merchants travelling to the Frankfurt fair. Title-page of Jörg Wickram's Rollwagenbüchlein. Middle of the 16th century.

244 May Day in The Shepheard's Calendar by Edmund Spenser. Woodcut. 1581.

245 The parting of John Frederick, Prince-Elector of Saxony, and Emperor Charles V, September 2, 1552, near Linz. (The Emperor sits in a litter, while the Prince-Elector's travelling-wagon is waiting in the background. Second half of 16th century.)

246 The Pope gives his blessings. St. Peter's Place, Rome. Woodcut. About 1564.

247 'Celestial' carriage. Woodcut by Hans Schäufelein in Leonrodt's Himmelwagen und Höllenwagen. Augsburg, 1517.

248 A state-coach of Veronese origin. Formerly in the Palazzo Serego-Alighieri, Verona. (Lithography by F. Casanova, after a drawing by G. Franco, Bologna, 1862.)

249 Side elevation of the same state-coach.

250 A state-coach body. In the Palazzo Serego-Alighieri, Verona. (Lithography by F. Casanova, after a drawing by G. Franco, Bologna, 1862.)

251 Covered wagons in a carriage parade held at the Augsburg Congress of 1530. Woodcut by Hans Tirol.

252 "The Wedding of the Children." Woodcut of the so-called Petrarch Master. Early 16th century.

253 Travelling-wagon. (A version of the original Hungarian kochy.) Coloured woodcut by A. Guldenmund. 16th century.

254 Landau. The Austrian Archduke Ernst with his escort. Woodcut by Georg Lang. 1593.

255 Wheelwright's shop. Woodcut by Jost Amman, in Das Ständebuch. Eygentliche Beschreibung aller Stände mit kunstreichen Figuren. (With rhymes by Hans Sachs.) Frankfurt on the Main, 1568.

256 Detail of the engraving "The Nuremberg Shooting-Match" by P. Isselburg. 1614.

257 Hackney-coach in Covent Garden. Engraving. 17th century.

258 Fleeing from the plague in London. 1630. From a broadside in the possession of the Society of Antiquaries, entitled "London Soundes a Trumpet that County May Hear It".

259 An English travelling-coach. From an engraving by John Dunstall in the London Prospects Portfolio, Vol. V.

260 Travelling-coach with leather curtains. Drawing by Willem Buytewech. Early 17th century. Kupferstichkabinett der ehemaligen Staatlichen Museen, Berlin.

261 English coach. Line engraving. Second half of the 17th century.

262 Detail from D. Loggan's Oxonia illustrata. 1675.

263 Accident of Henry IV, King of France, 9th June, 1606. Copper-plate engraving.

264 State-coach in which Henry IV was killed. (J. Ch. Ginzrot: Die Wagen und Fahrwerke der Griechen und Römer und anderer alten Völcker . . . Munich, 1817, Vol. 2.)

265 Model of a coach, style Louis XIV. End of the 17th century. Musée de Cluny, Paris.

266 Coach of the Earl of Castlemaine, ambassador of James II presenting his credentials to Pope Innocent XI. End of the 17th century.

267 A landau before the town-gate of Altdorf, Germany. Copper-plate engraving. 17th century.

268 Berline.

269 Halbberline, ancestor of the urban coupé.

270 Hungarian wagon. Etching by Justus van der Nypoort in A. E. B. von Birckenstein's Ertzhertzogliche Handgriffe.

271 Turks carrying the heads of the decapitated in a Hungarian wagon. Copper-plate engraving by Wilheim Peter Zimmermann in Samuel Dilbaum: Eikonographia. Augsburg 1604.

272 Dutch travelling-carriages. Detail of a painting by Jan Brueghel.

273 Open travelling-carriage with two ladies. Pen drawing by Gerrit Claesz Bleker. 1643. Albertina, Vienna.

274 Johann Hautsch's 'automatic' carriage. Copper-plate engraving. 1649.

275 The 'automatic' carriage of Stephan Farfler. Copper-plate engraving. 1649.

276 Execution of a woman for witchcraft in Augsburg on March 23, 1669. Detail of a German Relatio: "Way to the Scaffold." Woodcut by Elias Wellhöfer. 1669.

277 Drawing from "The Coaches Overthrow or a ioviall Exaltation of Diverse Tradesmen and Others, for the Suppression of Troublesome Hackney Coaches." 17th century.

278 English hackney-coach. Detail from W. Hollar's etching. 1646.

279 Coach with a perch. 18th century. After a contemporary coach-builder's design.

280 Coach with a crane-neck. 18th century. After a contemporary coach-builder's design.

281 English town coach. After a design by Herbert Felton.

282 Elegant Spanish travelling-coach, used especially for long journeys. 18th century. Musée du Tourisme et des Voitures, Compiègne.

283 Post-chaise with a straight perch, suspended by leather braces, with additional straps. 18th century. After "Travelling", a drawing by Thomas Rowlandson.

284 Landau. After a design by Herbert Felton.

285 Sociable. After a design by Herbert Felton.

286 "The Runaway." After a drawing by Thomas Rowlandson.

287 The coach of the newly installed Lord Mayor in a London street. Copper-plate engraving by Hogarth. 18th century.

288 The British royal state-coach. (J. Ch. Ginzrot: Die Wagen und Fahrwerke der Griechen und Römer und anderer alten Völcker . . . Munich, 1817, Vol. 2.)

289 Italian Baroque coach. Detail of an etching by Piranesi. 18th century.

290 The state-coach of Empress Maria Theresa. Second half of the 18th century. Wagenburg, Schönbrunn, Vienna.

291 Stage-wagon. After a drawing by Thomas Rowlandson.

292 The criminal Schwarzbeck carried on a cart to Bern. Woodcut. About 1730.

293 Some 18th-century carriages: 1. Travelling-cabriolet with four wheels. 2. Travelling-calash built (according to Mme de la Roche) at Petersburg in 1820, without iron accessories. 3. Travelling-calash on horizontal springs. 4. Country calash. (J. Ch. Ginzrot: Die Wagen und Fahrwerke der Griechen und Römer und anderer alten Völcker . . . Munich, 1817, Vol. 2.)

294 The coronation coach of Napoleon. Musée des Voitures, Versailles.

295 The state-coach of the Empress Josephine, called l'Opale. Beginning of 19th century. Palais de Malmaison.

296 Travelling-carriage from the biedermeier period. About 1830. Deutsches Museum, Munich.

297 Four-horse German Kalesche. 1837. After a contemporary drawing.

298 Tilbury. After a design of Brice Thomas, Paris.

299 Brougham. After a design of E. Bodolló.

300 Five-horse Hungarian farm wagon. About 1890. Drawing by Ákos Garay.

301 Indian cart drawn by a zebu.

302 Rich Indian woman on a carriage drawn by zebus. (Meyers Großes Konversations-Lexikon. 6th edition, Vol. 15.)

303 Bashkir wagon in front of a yurt (felt tent). (Photo by the Archives of the Museum of Ethnography, Budapest.)

304 Mail-coach used in the Swiss Alps (Brig–Gletsch–Göschenen). 1830–1840. Deutsches Museum, Munich. (After a photograph.)

305 English mail-coach at the middle of the 19th century.

306 The dangers of the German mail-coach. After a contemporary cartoon.

307 Express mail-coach at the customs. Beginning of 19th century. Contemporary engraving.

308 Spanish mail-coach. (Woodcut from F. Reuleaux: Das Buch der Erfindungen. Leipzig–Berlin, 1887, Vol. VII.)

309 The London hansom. Lithograph reproduced in Th. Fontane's Bilderbuch aus England.

310 The Berlin Droschke. About 1850. Drawing by Th. Hosemann.

311 The Paris omnibus. About 1860. After a drawing by V. Adam.

312 Journey on a Kremser. About 1830. Drawing by Ludwig Löffler.

313 Dutch farm wagon. Open-Air Museum, Arnhem.

314 A Hamburg Stuhlwagen. About 1830. After a lithograph by Suhr.

Bibliography

The Bibliography includes but a fragment of the material consulted. The degree to which the respective sources have been exploited differs greatly; the majority of them have provided only a few data and illustrations for the author, while others served as a steady source of information during the process of writing.

ADAMA VAN SCHELTEMA, FREDERIK: *Der Osebergfund.* 2nd, rev. ed. Rabitzsch, Leipzig, 1938.

ADAMA VAN SCHELTEMA, FREDERIK: *Die Kunst der Vorzeit.* Kohlhammer, Stuttgart, 1950.

ALBRIGHT, W. F.: "Mitannian Maryannu ['chariot-warrior'] and the Canaanite and Egyptian Equivalents." — *Archiv für Orientforschung,* 6 (1931).

ALFIERI, NEREO–ARIAS, PAOLO ENRICO: *Spina.* Hirmer, Munich, 1958.

ALFÖLDI, A.: "Állatdíszes kerékvető-fejek kelta–római kocsikról." — *Archaeologiai Értesítő,* 48 (1935).

ALFÖLDI, A.: "Chars funéraires bacchiques dans les provinces occidentales de l'Empire romain." — *L'Antiquité classique,* 8 (1939).

ALFÖLDI, A.–RADNÓTI, A.: *Zügelringe und Zierbeschläge von römischen Jochen und Kummeten aus Pannonien.* Serta Hoffilleriana, Zagreb, 1940.

ALMGREN, OSCAR: "Tanums härads fasta fornlämningar från bronsåldern Hällristningar." — *Bidrag till Kännedomen om Göteborgs och Bohuslands Fornminnen,* 8 (1912).

ALMGREN, OSCAR: *Nordische Felszeichnungen als religiöse Urkunden.* Diesterweg, Frankfurt on the M., 1934.

ALTHEIM, FRANZ: *Die Krise der Alten Welt im 3. Jahrhundert n. Zw. und ihre Ursachen.* Vol. 1: *Die ausserrömische Welt.* Ahnenerbe-Stiftung, Berlin-Dahlem, 1943.

ALTHEIM, FRANZ: *Die Weltgeschichte Asiens im griechischen Zeitalter.* Vols. 1–2. Niemeyer, Halle/Saale, 1947–1948.

ALTHEIM, FRANZ: *Literatur und Gesellschaft im ausgehenden Altertum.* Niemeyer, Halle/Saale, 1950.

ALTHEIM, FRANZ: *Geschichte der Hunnen.* Vols. 1–5. De Gruyter, Berlin, 1959–1962.

American Schools of Oriental Research. The Annual of the—. Vol. 16 (for 1935–1936). Ed. by Millar Burrows–E. A. Speiser. American Schools of Oriental Research, New Haven, 1936.

AMIRA, KARL VON: *Die germanischen Todesstrafen. Untersuchungen zur Rechts-*

305

und Religionsgeschichte. Verlag der Bayerischen Akademie der Wissenschaften, Munich, 1922.

AMMIANUS, MARCELLINUS: *Res gestae.* With an English translation by John C. Rolfe. Heinemann, London, 1956.

ANDRAE, WALTER: *Das wiedererstandene Assur.* Hinrichs, Leipzig, 1938.

APOR, PÉTER: *Metamorphosis Transylvaniae.* Eggenberger, Pest, 1863. (*Mon. Hung. Hist. Script.,* 11.)

ARANZADI, TELESFORO DE: "Der ächzende Wagen und Anderes aus Spanien." — *Archiv für Anthropologie,* 24 (1897).

ARBOIS DE JUBAINVILLE: "Le Char de guerre des celtes dans quelques textes historiques." — *Revue Archéologique,* 11 (1881).

ARETZ, GERTRUDE: *Die elegante Frau.* Goethlin und Co., Leipzig–Zurich, without date.

ASHTON, LEIGH: *An Introduction to the Study of Chinese Sculpture.* Ernest Benn, London, 1924.

AVDIEV, VSEVOLOD IGOREVITCH: *Istoriya drevnego vostoka.* 2nd ed. Gospolitisdat, Leningrad, 1953.

AYMARD, ANDRÉ–AUBOYER, JEANNINE: *L'Orient et la Grèce antique.* Preface to the Series by Maurice Grouzet. 2nd, rev. ed. Presses Universitaires de France, Paris, 1955. (*Histoire générale des civilisations,* 1.)

AYMARD, ANDRÉ–AUBOYER, JEANNINE: *Rome et son empire.* 2nd, rev. ed., Presses Universitaires de France, Paris, 1956. (*Histoire générale des civilisations,* 2.)

BABEAU, ALBERT: *Paris en 1789.* Firmin-Didot et Cie., Paris, 1893.

BACHHOFER, LUDWIG: *A Short History of Chinese Art.* Batsford, London, 1947.

BANDI, HANS GEORG–BREUIL, HENRI, etc.: *The Art of the Stone Age. Forty Thousand Years of Rock Art.* Crown, New York, 1961. (*Art of the World,* 5.)

[BARCLAY DE TOLLY]: *Souvenirs d'un voyageur solitaire ou Méditations sur le caractère national des Anglais.* Vol. 2. Brockhaus et Avenarius, Leipzig–Paris, 1853.

BARNETT, R. D.–FORMAN, WERNER: *Assyrische Palastreliefs.* Artia, Prague, without date.

BAYARD, ÉMILE: *Les Styles régence et Louis XV.* Garnier, Paris, without date.

BEAZLEY, J. DAVIDSON: *The Development of Attic Black-Figure.* California and Cambridge Univ. Press, Berkeley–London, 1951.

BELLOC, HILAIRE: *The Highway and its Vehicles.* Ed. by Geoffrey Holme. Studio, London, 1926.

BELLONI, LUIGI: *La carrozza nella storia della locomozione.* Fratelli Bocca, Milan, 1901.

BERG, GÖSTA: *Sledges and Wheeled Vehicles. Ethnological Studies from the View-Point of Sweden.* Stockholm–Copenhagen, 1935. (*Nordiska Museets Handlingar,* 4.)

BERKEBILE, DON H.: "Conestoga Wagons in Braddock's Campaign, 1755." — *Contributions from the Museum of History and Technology,* 9 (1959).

BEYER-FRÖHLICH, MARIANNE: *Selbstzeugnisse aus dem Dreissigjährigen Krieg und dem Barock.* Ed. by —. Reclam, Leipzig, 1930.

BICKNELL, CLARENCE: *A Guide to the Prehistoric Rock Engravings in the Italian Maritime Alps.* Giuseppe Bessone, Bordighera, 1913.

BILLERBECK, ADOLF–DELITZSCH, FRIEDRICH: *Die Palasttore Salamanassars II von Balawat. Erklärungen ihrer Bilder und Inschriften.* Hinrichs-J. Hopkins, Leipzig–Baltimore, 1908. (*Beiträge zur Assyriologie und semitischen Sprachwissenschaft,* Vol. 6, No. 1.)

306

BILLIARD, RAYMOND: *La Vigne dans l'antiquité*. H. Lardauchet, Lyon, 1913.

BING, J.: *Der Sonnenwagen von Trundholm*. Kabitzsch, Leipzig, 1934.

BIRKET-SMITH, KAJ: *Kulturens Veje*. Copenhagen, 1941–1942.

BITTEL, KURT: *Prähistorische Forschung in Kleinasien*. Universum-Druckerei, Istanbul, 1934. (*Istanbuler Forschungen*, 6.)

BLEI, FRANZ: *Die Sitten des Rokoko*. Georg Müller, Munich, 1921.

BLÜMNER, HUGO: *Das Kunstgewerbe im Altertum*. Vols. 1–2. Freytag–Tempski, Leipzig–Prague, 1885.

BLÜMNER, HUGO: *Die römischen Privataltertümer*. C. H. Bock, Munich, 1911.

BODE, WILHELM VON: *Die Meister der holländischen und flämischen Malerschulen*. Rev. and enlarged by Eduard Plietzsch. 8th ed. Seemann, Leipzig, 1956.

BOEHLAU, J.–GILSA, F. VON: *Neolithische Denkmäler aus Hessen*. Kassel, 1898.

BOEHN, MAX VON: *Die Mode. Menschen und Moden im siebzehnten Jahrhundert. Nach Bildern und Stichen der Zeit*. Selected, with commentaries, by —. 3rd ed. Bruckmann, Munich.

BOEHN, MAX VON: *Die Mode. Menschen und Moden im achtzehnten Jahrhundert. Nach Bildern und Stichen der Zeit*. Selected by Oskar Fischel. Text by —. Bruckmann, Munich, 1909.

BOEHN, MAX VON: *Die Mode. Menschen und Moden im neunzehnten Jahrhundert. Nach Bildern und Kupfern der Zeit*. Selected by Oskar Fischel. Text by —. Bruckmann, Munich [1925].

BOROVKA, GREGORY: *Scythian Art*. Translated from the German by V. G. Childe. Ernest Benn, London, 1928.

BOSSERT, HELMUTH THEODOR: *Altanatolien. Kunst und Handwerk in Kleinasien von den Anfängen bis zum völligen Aufgehen in der griechischen Kultur*. Wasmuth, Berlin, 1942.

BRANTÔME, LE SEIGNEUR: *Vies des dames galantes*. Garnier Frères, Paris, 1883.

BREASTED, JAMES HENRY: *The Battle of Kadesh*. University Chicago, Decennial Publ. I. 5. Chicago, 1904.

BREASTED, JAMES HENRY: *Geschichte Ägyptens*. Phaidon, Vienna [1936].

BREASTED, JAMES HENRY: *The Conquest of Civilization*. Harper Bros., New York–London, 1938.

BRODARITHUS, STEPHANUS: *De conflictu Hungarorum cum Turcis ad Mohatz verissima historia*. Cracoviae, 1527.

BRUNHES, JEAN: *La Géographie humaine*. Abr. ed. Presses Universitaires de France, Paris, 1947.

BURCKHARD VON BIRCKENSTEIN, ANTON ERNST: *Ertz-Hertzogliche Handgriffe dess Zirckels und Linials, oder ausserwählter Anfang zu denen mathematischen Wissenschafften*. With appendix by —. Koppmayer, Augspurg, 1689.

BURKE, THOMAS: *The English Inn*. H. Jenkins, London, 1948.

BURNAND, ROBERT: *La Vie quotidienne en France en 1830*. Hachette, Paris.

BURNAND, ROBERT: *La Vie quotidienne en France de 1870 à 1900*. Hachette, Paris, 1955.

BUSCHOR, ERNST: *Griechische Vasen*. Piper, Munich, 1940.

CABANÈS: *Mœurs intimes du passé*. Series 8. *Éducation de princes*. Albin Michel, Paris, 1923.

CAPRINO, C.–COLINI, A. M.–GATTI, G.–PALLOTTINO, M.–ROMANELLI, P.: *La colonna di Marco Aurelio*. "L'ERMA" di Bretschneider, Rome, 1955.

Catalogue méthodique et raisonné de la collection de Clercq. Paris, 1888.

CHAMPDOR, ALBERT: *Die altägyptische Malerei*. 2nd ed. Seemann, Leipzig, 1959.

CHARBONNEAUX, J.: *L'Art au siècle d'Auguste*. Édition de Clairfontaine, Paris, 1948.

307

CHASTENET, JACQUES: *La Vie quotidienne en Angleterre au début du règne de Victoria. 1837–1851.* Hachette, Paris, 1961.

CHELIUS, FRITZ H.: *Intriganten und Diplomaten.* Traditions-Verlag Kolk und Co., Berlin, [1938].

CHILDE, GORDON V.: "Horses, Chariots and Battle Axes." — *Antiquity,* 15 (1941).

CHILDE, GORDON V.: *The Dawn of European Civilization.* 5th ed. Routledge and Kegan Paul Ltd., London, 1950.

CHILDE, GORDON V.: "The First Waggons and Carts from the Tigris to the Severn." — *Proceedings of the Prehistoric Society.* London, N. S. I, 8 (1953).

CHRISTIAN, VIKTOR: *Altertumskunde des Zweistromlandes.* Vol. 1: Text, Vol. 2: Plates. Hiersemann, Leipzig, 1940.

CLARK, JOHN GRAHAM DOUGLAS: *Prehistoric Europe. The Economic Basis.* Methuen, London, 1952.

CONSTEN VON ERDBERG, ELEANOR: *Das alte China.* Klipper, Stuttgart, 1958.

CORNIDES, DANIEL: "Beweis, dass die Kutschen eine ungarische Erfindung, und dass selbst die in allen europäischen Sprachen beynahe ähnliche Benennung dieses Fahrzeugs in Ungarn zuerst erstanden sey." — *Ungrisches Magazin,* 1. Pressburg (1781).

CORNIDES, DANIEL: "Nachtrag einiger Bemerkungen vom ungrischen Ursprunge der Kutschen." — *Ungrisches Magazin,* 2. Pressburg (1782).

CORNIDES, DANIEL: "Nachlese einiger Bemerkungen vom ungrischen Ursprunge der Kutschen." — *Ungrisches Magazin,* 3. Pressburg (1783).

COTTRELL, LEONARD: *The Anvil of Civilisation.* Faber and Faber, London, without date.

COULTON, GEORGE GORDON: *Life in the Middle Ages.* Four volumes in one. MacMillan–Cambridge University Press, New York–Cambridge, 1931. (*The Cambridge Anthologies,* 3.)

COURTHION, PIERRE: *Paris d'autrefois. De Fouquet à Daumier.* Text by —. Skira, Genève–Paris–New York, 1957. (*Le goût de notre temps,* 20.)

CRAWFORD, H. S.: *Handbook of Carved Ornament from Irish Monuments of the Christian Period.* Royal Society of Antiquaries of Ireland, Dublin, 1926.

CREEL, H. G.: *The Birth of China.* Jonathan Cape, London, 1936.

[CROLE, B. E.]: *Geschichte der deutschen Post von ihren Anfängen bis zur Gegenwart.* 2nd ed. W. Malende, Leipzig [1889].

CROME, BRUNO: *Kulturgeschichtliche Miniaturen aus einer alten Chronik.* Vandenhoeck and Ruprecht, Göttingen, 1921.

DANTÍN CERECEDA, JUON: "El carro leonés del concejo de Gordón." — *Anales del Museo de Pueblo Español,* Vol. 1, Quart. 1–2 (1935).

DAVIES, N. DE GARIS–GARDINER, ALAN H.: *The Tomb of Huy, Viceroy of Nubia in the Reign of Tutankhamun.* Egypt Exploration Fund, London, 1926. (*Theban Tombs Series.*)

DÉCHELETTE, J.: *Manuel d'archéologie préhistorique celtique et gallo-romaine.* Vol. 1: Picard, Paris, 1908. Vol. 2.: Picard, Paris, 1924.

DERRY, T. K.–WILLIAMS, TREVOR I.: *A Short History of Technology. From the Earliest Times to A.D. 1900.* Oxford University Press, New York–Oxford, 1961.

DIETZ, JOHANN: *Meister — erzählt sein Leben.* Langewiesche–Brandt, Ebenhausen, 1915.

DIEZ, ERNST: *The Ancient Worlds of Asia. From Mesopotamia to the Yellow River.* Macdonald, London, 1961.

DILBAUM, SAMUEL: *Eikonographia, aller deren Ungarischer Stätt, Vöstunge, Castellen und Häuser, welche von Anfang der Regierung Rudolphi dess andere...*

Gedruckt zu Augsburg bey Christoff Mang in Verlegung Wilhelm Peter Zimmermann, 1604.

Dittmann, K. H.: "Die Herkunft der altägyptischen Streitwagen in Florenz." — *Germania*, 18 (1934).

Domanovszky, Sándor: "Mázsaszekér." — *Emlékkönyv Fejérpataky László életének hatvanadik, történetírói működésének negyvenedik, szemináriumi vezetőtanárságának harmincadik évfordulója ünnepére.* Franklin, Budapest, 1917.

Donner, Kai: "Quelques traîneaux primitifs." — *Finnisch-Ugrische Forschungen*, 15 (1915).

Doppelmayr, Johann Gabriel: *Historische Nachricht von den nürnbergischen Mathematicis und Künstlern, welche fast von dreyen Seculis her durch ihre Schrifften und Kunst-Bemühungen die Mathematic und mehreste Künste in Nürnberg...* Peter Conrad Monath, Nuremberg, 1730.

Dubly, Henry-Louis: *Ponts de Paris à travers les siècles.* Introduction by François Carco. Mondes, Paris, 1957.

Durand, W.: *Das Vermächtnis des Ostens.* A. Francke, Bern, 1942. (*Die Geschichte der Zivilisation*, 1.)

Ebeling, Erich–Meissner, Bruno: *Reallexikon der Assyriologie.* Vols. 1–2. W. de Gruyter, Berlin–Leipzig, 1928–1938.

Enciclopedia universale dell'arte antica classica e orientale, Vol. 2. Enciclopedia Italiana, Rome, 1959.

Evans, Arthur: *The Palace of Minos.* Vols. 1–5. MacMillan, London, 1921–1936.

Evliya çelebi: *Im Reiche des Goldenen Apfels.* 2nd ed. Styria, Graz–Vienna–Köln, 1963.

Excavations at Kish. Vols. 1–4. P. Geuthner, Paris. Vol. 1 (1923–1924): S. Langdon, 1924. Vol. 3 (1925–1927): L. Ch. Watelin–S. Langdon, 1930. Vol. 4 (1925–1930): L. Ch. Watelin–S. Langdon, 1934.

Excavations at Tepe Gawra. Union of Pennsylvania, Philadelphia. Vol. 1 (Levels 1–8.) By E. A. Speiser. (*Publications of the American Schools of Oriental Research.*)

Eyre, Edward: *European Civilisation. Its Origin and Development.* By various contributors, ed. under the direction of —. Oxford University Press, London, 1935.

Fekete, Johann, Graf de Galántha: *Wien im Jahre 1787.* Rikola, Vienna–Leipzig–Berlin–Munich, 1921.

Feldhaus, Franz Maria: *Die Maschine im Leben der Völker. Ein Überblick von der Urzeit bis zur Renaissance.* Birkhäuser, Basel–Stuttgart, 1954. (*Wissenschaft und Kultur*, 7.)

Flacelière, Robert: *La Vie quotidienne en Grèce au siècle de Périclès.* Hachette, Paris, 1959.

Florescu, Florea Bobu: *Das Siegesdenkmal von Adamklissi. Trophaeum Traiani.* Verlag der Akademie der Rumänischen Volksrepublik—Rudolf Habelt, Bukarest–Bonn, 1965.

Foltiny, Stephen: "The Oldest Representation of Wheeled Vehicles in Central and Southern Europe." — *American Journal of Archeology*, 63 (1959).

Fontane, Theodor: *Journeys to England in Victoria's Early Days.* Translated by Dorothy Harrison. Massic Publication Co., London, 1939.

Forestier, G.: *La Roue. Étude paléo-technologique.* Berger-Levrault et Cie., Paris–Nancy, 1900.

Fournel, Victor: *Les Rues du vieux Paris.* Firmin-Didot et Cie., Paris, 1879. (*Galerie populaire et pittoresque.*)

Fox, Cyril: "Sleds, Carts and Wagons." — *Antiquity*, 5 (1931).

Fox, Cyril: *A Find of the Early Iron Age from Llyn Cerrig Bach, Anglesey.* National Museum of Wales, Cardiff, 1946.

Fox, Penelope: *Tutanhamon's Treasure.* Oxford University Press, London, 1951.

Frankfort, H.: *Cylinder Seals.* MacMillan, London, 1939.

Frédérix, Pierre: *Histoire de la Vitesse.* Hachette, Paris, 1961. *(Tout par l'image.)*

Funck-Brentano, Frantz: *Le Moyen Age.* Hachette, Paris, without date.

Funck-Brentano, Frantz: *La Renaissance.* Arthème Fayard et Cie., Paris, 1935.

Fürst, Artur: *Das Weltreich der Technik.* Vol. 2. Ullstein, Berlin, 1924.

Gaul, Károly: "Ókori kocsik helyreállítása." — *Archaeologiai Értesítő*, 1890.

Gerke, Friedrich: *Griechische Plastik in archaischer und klassischer Zeit.* Atlantis, Zurich–Berlin, 1938.

Geschichte des Kunstgewerbes aller Zeiten und Völker. Ed. by Bossert Helmuth Theodor. Vols. 1–4. E. Wasmuth, Berlin, 1928–1930.

Giglioli, Giulio Quirino: *L'Arte Etrusca.* Fratelli Treves, Milan, 1935.

Ginzrot, Johann Christian: *Die Wagen und Fahrwerke der Griechen und Römer und anderer alten Völcker nebst der Bespannung und Verzierung ihrer Zug-, Reit- und Last-Thiere,* von —, Königlich Baierischem Wagenbau-Inspector. Vols. 1–2. Munich, 1817.

Ginzrot, Johann Christian: *Die Wagen und Fahrwerke der verschiedenen Völker des Mittelalters und der Kutschen-Bau neuester Zeiten nebst der Bespannung, Zäumung und Verzierung ihrer Zug-, Reit- und Last-Thiere,* von — Königlich Baierischem Wagenbau-Inspector. Vols. 3–4. Munich, 1830.

Glatzer, Ruth: *Berliner Leben 1648–1806.* Ed. by —. Rütten und Loening, Berlin, 1956.

Gleichen-Russwurm, A. von: *Das galante Europa. Geselligkeit der grossen Welt. 1600–1789.* Julius Hoffmann, Stuttgart, 1911.

Gleichen-Russwurm, A. von: *Die Sonne der Renaissance. Sitten und Gebräuche der europäischen Welt. 1450–1600.* Julius Hoffmann, Stuttgart, 1921.

Götze, Albrecht: *Hethiter, Churriter und Assyrer.* H. Aschehoug–O. Harrasso-with–Les Belles Lettres, Oslo–Leipzig–Paris, 1936. (*Instituttet for Sammenlignende Kulturforskning*, Series A, 17.)

Gräffer, Franz: *Kleine Wiener Memoiren und Wiener Dosenstücke.* Selected, introduced and edited by Anton Schlosser in association with Gustav Gugitz. Vols. 1–2. Georg Müller, Munich, 1918–1922. (*Denkwürdigkeiten aus Alt-Österreich*, 14.)

Granet, Marcel: *La Civilisation chinoise. La vie publique et la vie privée.* La Renaissance du Livre, Paris, 1929.

Grekow, B. D.–Artamonov, M. L.: *Geschichte der Kultur der alten Rus',* Vol. 1: *Die materielle Kultur der alten Rus'.* Akademie-Verlag, Berlin, 1959.

Gryaznov, M. P.–Shneider, I. P.: "Drevnie izvayaniya Minusinskich stepey" — *Materiali po Etnografii*, Vol. 2, No. 4 (1929).

Guide artistique de Zurich. Ed. Syndicat d'Initiative de Zürich. Orell Füssli, Zurich, 1945.

Haenel, Erich–Kalkschmidt, Eugen: *Das alte Dresden. Bilder und Dokumente aus zwei Jahrhunderten.* Collected and published by —. Hanfstaengl, Munich, 1925.

Hahn, Eduard: "Zur Entstehung des Rades und des Wagens." — *Internationales Zentralblatt für Anthropologie*, 8 (1903).

HAHN, EDUARD: *Das Alter der wirtschaftlichen Kultur der Menschheit. Ein Rückblick und ein Ausblick.* Carl Winter, Heidelberg, 1905.

HAHN, EDUARD: *Von der Hacke zum Pflug.* 2nd ed. Quelle und Meyer, Leipzig, 1919.

HALD, KARL: *Alt-Nürnbergs Verkehrswesen seit Mitte des 14. Jahrhunderts.* Published by —. Nuremberg, 1929.

HALL, H. R. H.: *Babylonian and Assyrian Sculpture in the British Museum.* G. Van Oest, Paris–Brussels, 1928.

HALSTEAD, IVOR: *Post Haste.* Lindsay Donald Ltd., London, 1944.

HALTENBERGER, MICHAEL: "Primitive Carriers in Land Transportation." — *Bulletin of the American Geographical Society*, 47 (1915).

HANČAR, FRANZ: "Ein nordisches Streitwagenbild im östlichen Kaukasus." — *Forschungen und Fortschritte*, 19 (1943).

HANČAR, FRANZ: *Das Pferd in prähistorischer und früher historischer Zeit.* Herold, Vienna–Munich, 1956.

HATT, G.: "Lappiske slaedeformer." — *Geografisk Tidskrift*, 22 (1913).

HAUDRICOURT, ANDRÉ G.: "Lumières sur l'attelage moderne." — *Annales d'Histoire Sociale*, 1945.

HAUDRICOURT, ANDRÉ G.: "Contribution à la géographie et à l'ethnologie de la voiture." — *La Revue de Géographie Humaine et d'Ethnologie*, 1 (1948).

HAUDRICOURT, ANDRÉ G.–M. JEAN-BRUNHES, DE LA MARRE: *L'Homme et la charrue à travers le monde.* Gallimard, Paris, 1955. (*Géographie Humaine*, 25.)

HEINEMANN, FRANZ: *Der Richter und die Rechtspflege in der deutschen Vergangenheit.* Diederichs, Leipzig [1900]. (*Monographien zur deutschen Kulturgeschichte*, 4.)

HEISCHKEL, E.: "Die Strasse in der Geschichte der Medizin." — *Technikgeschichte*, 23 (1934).

HEMMEON, J. C.: *The History of the British Post Office.* Harvard University Press, Oxford–University Press, Cambridge (Mass.), London, 1912.

HERBERSTEIN, SIGMUND FREIHERR ZU: *Rerum Moscoviticarum commentarii... quibus Russiae ac metropolis eius descriptio, chorographicae tabulae... continentur. Hic nunc primum accedunt, scriptum recens de Graecorum fide... et commentarius de bellis Moscorum adversus finitimos, Polonos, Lituanos... et alios gestis ad annum usque 71, scriptus ab Ioanne Leuvendaio,* Basilea, Oporinus, 1571.

HERMES, GERTRUD: "Das gezähmte Pferd im alten Orient." — *Anthropos*, 30 (1936).

HILZHEIMER, M.: "Die Anschirrung bei den alten Sumerern." — *Prähistorische Zeitschrift*, 22 (1931).

Histoire générale des techniques. Vol. 1: *Les origines de la civilisation technique* By de LA CAILLE, CASTAGNOL CONTENAU, G., ETC. Vol. 2: *Les premières étapes du machinisme.* By DUBUISSON, M.–AUDIN, M.–DAUMAS, M., ETC. Presses Universitaires de France, Paris, 1962–1965.

Histoire générale du travail. Dir.: Parias, Louis-Henri. Vols. 1–4. Nouvelle Librairie de France, Paris, 1959–1961.

HOERNES, M.–MENGHIN, O.: *Urgeschichte der bildenden Kunst in Europa (von den Anfängen bis um 500 v. Chr.).* 3rd. ed. Vienna, 1925.

HOFSTAETTER, WALTHER–REICHMANN, HANS–SCHNEIDER, JOHANNES: *Ein Jahrtausend deutscher Kultur im Bilde. 800–1800.* Julius Klinkhardt, Leipzig, 1929.

HOLMES, V. I.: *Daily Living in the Twelfth Century.* 2nd print. University Press, Madison (USA), 1952.

HORVÁTH TIBOR: "Pictorial Representation of Han Mural Paintings and Reliefs." — *Az Iparművészeti Múzeum Évkönyvei*, 2 (1955); Képzőművészeti Alap Kiadóvállalata, Budapest, 1956.

HORWITZ, HUGO TH.: "Die Drehbewegung in ihrer Bedeutung für die Entwicklung der materiellen Kultur." — *Anthropos*, 28 (1933), 29 (1934).

HORWITZ, HUGO TH.: "Über das Aufkommen der Kutschen genannten Wagen und ihre Herkunft aus dem Orte Kozce." — *Technikgeschichte* 23 (1934).

HUYGHE, RENÉ: *L'Art et l'homme*. Vols. 1–3. Larousse, Paris, 1957–1961.

Illustrierte Kultur- und Sittengeschichte. After Jakob Burckhardt, Theodor Mommsen [etc.] Revised and enlarged by J. A. v. Bradish, Helmut L. Demel [etc.]. Frei, Zurich, 1955. *(Handbücher der allgemeinen Bildung.)*

JABERG, K.–JUD, J.: *Sprach- und Sachatlas Italiens und der Süd-Schweiz*, Vol. 6. Ringier, Zofingen, 1935.

JOKL, NORBERT: "Die magyarischen Bestandteile des albanischen Wortschatzes." — *Festgabe Josef Szinnyei zum 70. Geburtstag*. Published by the Hungarian Institute of the Berlin University. — *Ung. Bibl.*, I, Series B. Berlin (1927).

KAHRSTEDT, ULRICH: *Kulturgeschichte der römischen Kaiserzeit*. 2nd, rev. ed. Francke, Bern, 1958.

KARAISL, VON KARAIS, FRANZ–SCHMIEDER, EBERHARD: *Die deutsche Strasse*. L. Staackmann, Leipzig, 1940.

KARO, GEORG: *Die Schachtgräber von Mykenai*. Bruckmann, Munich, 1930–1933.

KASTELIC, JOŽE: *Situla Art. Ceremonial Bronzes of Ancient Europe*. With contributions by Karl Kromer–Guido Mansuelli. Thames and Hudson, London, 1965.

KLETLER, PAUL: *Deutsche Kultur zwischen Völkerwanderung und Kreuzzügen*. Athenaion, Potsdam, 1934.

KLINDT-JENSEN, OLE: "Foreign Influences in Denmark's Early Iron Age." — *Acta Archaeologica*, 20 (1949).

KLINKOWSTROEM, CARL: *Knaurs Geschichte der Technik*. Droemer, Munich-Zürich, 1959.

KNIGGE, ADOLF FRANZ FRIEDRICH: *Über den Umgang mit Menschen*. Hann, Hannover, 1788.

KORZENDORFER, ADOLF: "Post, Poststrasse, Postkutsche." — *Technikgeschichte*, 23 (1934).

KOSSINNA, GUSTAV: *Die deutsche Vorgeschichte—eine hervorragende nationale Wissenschaft.* 2nd ed. Kabitzsch, Würzburg, 1914. *(Mannus-Bibliothek, 9.)*

KOTHE, HEINZ: "Verbreitung und Alter der Stangenschleife." — *Ethnographisch-Archäologische Forschungen*, 1 (1953).

KRAIKER, WILHELM: *Die Malerei der Griechen*. Kohlhammer, Stuttgart, 1958.

KRAMER, S. N.: *History Begins at Sumer*. Translated from French. Thames and Hudson, London, 1958.

KREISEL, HEINRICH: *Prunkwagen und Schlitten*. Leipzig, 1927.

KROPF LAJOS: "Még egyszer a kocsiról." — *Egyetemes Philologiai Közlöny*, 21 (1897).

Kulturleben der Strasse vom Anfang bis zur grossen Revolution. Singer and Co., Berlin, without date.

Kunsthistorischer Atlas. Ed. by the K. K. Central Commission for the Research and Maintenance of Art and Historical Monuments. Ed. by M. Much, Vienna, 1889.

Kunsthistorisches Museum. Führer durch die Sammlungen. 9. Sammlung: Auer, Erwin M.: *Historische Prunk- und Gebrauchswagen (Wagenburg–Monturdepot)*. Vienna, 1958.

KUNSTLER, CHARLES: *La Vie quotidienne sous Louis XVI*. Hachette, Paris, 1950.

KUNSTLER, CHARLES: *La Vie quotidienne sous Louis XV*. Hachette, Paris, 1953.

KUNSTLER, CHARLES: *La Vie quotidienne sous la Régence*. Hachette, Paris, 1960.

LA BAUME, WOLFGANG: "Bildliche Darstellungen auf ostgermanischen Tonge-fässen der frühen Eisenzeit." — *Jahrbuch für Prähistorische und Ethnographische Kunst*, 4 (1920).

LA BAUME, WOLFGANG: "Wagendarstellungen auf ostgermanischen Urnen der frühen Eisenzeit und ihre Bedeutung." — *Blätter für Deutsche Vorgeschichte*, 1 (1924).

LA BAUME, WOLFGANG: *Die pommerellischen Gesichtsurnen*. Verlag des Röm. – Germ. Zentralmuseums, Mainz, 1963.

LACROIX, PAUL: *XVIIIᵉ siècle. Institutions, usage et costumes. France 1700–1789*. 2nd ed. Firmin-Didot, Paris, 1875.

LAFFONT, ROBERT–BROSSE, JACQUES–OSTIER, JACQUES: *Cent mille ans de vie quotidienne*. Pont Royal (Del Duca-Laffont), Paris, 1960.

LA GARDE, AUG. DE: *Gemälde des Wiener Kongresses 1814–1815*, Vol. 2. Enlarged with commentary by Gustav Gugitz. Müller, Munich, 1914.

LA MARMORA, ALBERT: *Voyage en Sardaigne de 1819 à 1825, ou Description statistique, physique et politique de cette île, avec des recherches sur ses produits naturels et ses antiquités*. Vols. 1–4. Paris, 1839–1857.

LANE, R. H.: "Waggons and their Ancestors." — *Antiquity*, 9 (1935).

LANG, K.: "Über die Entstehung des Wagens." — *Völkerkunde*, 6 (1930).

LANGDON, S.: "Discoveries at Kish." — *Illustrated London News*, No. 4650, 2, VI (1928).

LAROCHE, MME. [LA ROCHE], MARIE SOPHIE (B. GUTERMAN): *Journal einer Reise durch Frankreich*. Altenburg, 1787.

LAYARD, AUSTEN HENRY: *Nineveh and its Remains*. John Murray, London, 1849.

LECHLER, J.: "Neues über Pferd und Wagen in der Steinzeit und Bronzezeit." — *Mannus*, 25 (1933).

LEE, CHARLES E.: *The Horse Bus as a Vehicle*. British Transport Commission, London, 1962.

LEFEBVRE DES NOËTTES: *L'Attelage et le cheval de selle à travers les âges. Contribu-tion à l'Histoire de l'Esclavage*. Preface by Jérome Carcopino, de l'Institut. Picard, Paris, 1931.

LEHNER, I. H.: "Ein gallorömischer Wagen aus Frenz an der Inde im Kreis Düren." — *Bonner Jahrbücher* 1923.

LEICHT, HERMANN: *Kunstgeschichte der Welt*. Orell Füssli, Zurich, 1945.

LEITICH, ANN TIZIA: *Die Wienerin*. Forum, Vienna–Hannover–Basel [1960].

LÉVI, SYLVAIN: *Aux indes sanctuaires*. 135 photographs selected and com-mented by Odette Monod-Brühl, assistant keeper of the Guimet Museum. Paul Hartmann, Paris [1951].

LHOTE, HENRI: *A la découverte des fresques du Tassili*. Arthaud, Paris, 1958.

LIEBE, GEORG: *Der Soldat in der deutschen Vergangenheit*. Diederichs, Leipzig, 1899. (*Monographien zur deutschen Kulturgeschichte*, 1.)

LINDNER, ARTHUR: *Der Breslauer Froissart*. Festschrift des Vereins für Geschich-te der bildenden Künste zu Breslau zum fünfzigjährigen Jubiläum. Kommissions-Verlag von Meisenbach, Berlin, 1912.

LITSCHAUER, FRANZ: *Spanische Kulturgeschichte*. Vols. 1–2. Bernina, Vienna–Leipzig, 1939.

London on Wheels. Public Transport in London in the Nineteenth Century. British Transport Commission, London, 1962.

313

LONG, E. JOHN: *The Story of Transportation.* Smithsonian Publication, Washington, 1958.

LORIMER, H. L.: "The Country Cart of Ancient Greece." — *The Journal of Hellenic Studies,* 23 (1903).

MACH, ERNST: *Kultur und Mechanik.* Spemann, Stuttgart, 1915.

MACKAY, E. J. H.: *The Indus Civilisation.* L. Dickson and Thompson, London, 1935.

MACKAY, E. J. H.: *Chanhu-Daro Excavations 1935–36.* New Haven, 1943.

MACKENZIE, DONALD ALEXANDER: *Ancient Civilizations.* Blackie and Son, London–Glasgow, 1927.

MAHR, OTTO: "Zur Geschichte des Wagenrades." — *Technikgeschichte,* 23 (1934).

MARCZINKÓ, FERENC: *Bertrandon de la Brocquière utazása Magyarországon át művelődéstörténelmi szempontból.* Budapest, 1909. (*Művelődéstörténeti Értekezések,* 34.)

MARLE, RAIMOND VAN: *Iconographie de l'art profane au Moyen Age et la Renaissance et la décoration des demeures.* Vols 1–2. Rijhoff, La Haye, 1931–1932.

MARSHALL, J.: *Mohenjo-Daro and the Indus Civilization.* London, 1931.

Marstallmuseum im Schloss Nymphenburg. Hofwagenburg und Sattelkammer. Official guide, revised by Luisa Hager. Bayerische Verwaltung der Staatlichen Schlösser, Gärten und Seen, Munich, 1959.

MEISSNER, BRUNO: *Babylonien und Assyrien.* Vols. 1–2. C. Winter, Heidelberg, 1920–1925.

MEISSNER, BRUNO–OPITZ, D.: "Betrachtungen zu einem archaischen griechischen Rennfahrer-Bilde." — *Abhandlungen der Preussischen Akademie der Wissenschaften,* 6 (1943).

MENGHIN, O.: *Weltgeschichte der Steinzeit.* Schroll, Vienna, 1931.

MERCKLIN, EUGEN VON: *Der Rennwagen in Griechenland.* Dissertation. Radelli und Hille, Leipzig, 1909.

METTERNICH-SÁNDOR, PAULINE: *Geschehenes, Gesehenes, Erlebtes.* Wiener Literarische Anstalt, Vienna–Berlin, 1920.

MILDNER, HEINZ: *Eroberung der Ferne.* Neues Leben, Berlin, 1959.

MINNS, E. H.: *Scythians and Greeks.* University Press, Cambridge, 1913.

MODE, HEINZ: *Das frühe Indien.* Böhlau, Weimar, 1960.

MOGEY, J. M.–THOMPSON, G. B.: "Primitive Transport Vehicles in Ulster." — *MAN,* 51 (1951).

MONGAIT, A. L.: *Arheologiya v SSSR.* Izdatelstvo Akademii Nauk, Moscow, 1955.

MONTAIGNE, MICHEL DE: *The Journal of Montaigne's Travels.* Translated from French. John Murray, London, 1903.

MONTET, PIERRE: *La Vie quotidienne en Égypte au temps des Ramses. XIIIe–XIIe siècles avant J.-C.* Hachette, Paris, 1946.

MOORTGAT, A.: "Der Kampf zu Wagen in der Kunst des Alten Orient." — *Orientalische Literaturzeitung,* 1930.

MOREAU, SAINT-MÉRY DE: *Voyage aux États-Unis de l'Amérique. 1793–1798.* Yale University Press—Oxford University Press, New Haven–London, 1913.

MORGAN, JACQUES DE: *La Préhistoire orientale.* Posthumous work published by Louis Germain. Vols. 1–3. Gebthner, Paris, 1925–1927.

MOUSNIER, ROLAND: *Les XVIe et XVIIe siècles. Les progrès de la civilisation européenne et le déclin de l'Orient (1492–1715).* 2nd, rev. ed. Presses Universitaires de France, Paris, 1956. (*Histoire générale des civilisations,* 4.)

MÖTEFINDT, H.: *Der Wagen im nordischen Kulturkreis zur vor- und früh-geschichtlichen Zeit.* Stuttgart, 1917. *(Studien und Fortschritte zur Menschen- und Völkerkunde.)*

MÖTEFINDT, H.: "Die Entstehung des Wagens und Wagenrades." — *Mannus,* 10 (1918).

MÜLLER, SOPHUS: *Nordische Altertumskunde, nach Funden und Denkmälern aus Dänemark und Schleswig gemeinschaftlich dargestellt.* German edition by Otto Luitpold Jiriczek. De Gruyter, Strasbourg, 1898–1905. Vol. 1.: *Steinzeit. Bronzezeit.* Vol. 2: *Eisenzeit.*

MUMMENHOFF, ERNST: *Der Handwerker in der deutschen Vergangenheit.* Diede-richs, Leipzig, 1901.

MUSCHG, WALTER–GESSLER, E. A.: *Die schweizerischen Bilderchroniken des 15/16. Jahrhunderts.* Atlantis, Zurich, 1941.

NACHOD, H.: *Der Rennwagen bei den Italikern und ihren Nachbarn.* Dissertation. Leipzig, 1909.

NAVARRO, RAFAEL: *Les Chars de Branosera.* Paris, 1931. *(Art populaire.)*

NEUBURGER, ALBERT: *Technik des Altertums.* 2nd, rev. ed. Voigtländer, Leipzig, 1921.

NEWLIN, ALICE: "An Exhibition of Carriage Designs." — *Bulletin of the Metro-politan Museum of Art,* 35 (1940).

NUOFFER, OSKAR: *Der Rennwagen im Altertum.* Dissertation. Leipzig, 1904.

[OFFENBACH, JACQUES]: *Offenbach en Amérique. Notes d'un musicien en voyage.* Calman Lévy, Paris, 1877.

OHNESORGE, W.: *Die Deutsche Reichspost in Geschichte und Gegenwart.* R. v. Deckers Verlag, G. Scheuck, Berlin, 1941.

OPPENHEIM, MAX FREIHERR VON: *Der Tell Halaf. Eine neue Kultur im ältesten Mesopotamien.* Bruckmann, Leipzig, 1931.

OPPENHEIM, MAX FREIHERR VON: *Tell Halaf.* Vols. 1–4. Revised and published by Barthel Hrouda. Berlin, 1962.

OZANEUX, GEORGES: *La Vie à Colmar sous la Restauration.* Paul Hartmann, 1929. *(Bibliothèque de la Revue d'Alsace.)*

PALLAS, P. S.: *Sammlungen historischer Nachrichten über die mongolischen Völker-schaften.* St. Petersburg, 1776–1809.

PALLOTTINO, MASSIMO: *Art of the Etruscans.* Thames and Hudson, London, 1955.

PÁRDUCZ, MIHÁLY: "Le Cimetière hallstattien de Szentes-Vekerzug." — *Acta Archaeologica Ac. Scient. Hung.,* 2 (1952).

PARET, OSCAR: "Das Fürstengrab der Hallstattzeit von Bad Canstatt. (6. Jh. v. Chr.)" — *Fundberichte aus Schwaben,* n. S. 8 (1935). Appendix.

PATERSON, JAMES: *The History and Development of Road Transport.* Pitman and Sons, London, 1927. *(Pitman's Transport Library.)*

PAULS, EILHARD ERICH: *Von der Postkutsche zum Flugzeug.* Otto Quetzow, Lübeck, 1926.

PÁVAY, V. FERENC: "Ősegyszerű szállítási mód Erdélyben." — *A Magyar Nem-zeti Múzeum Néprajzi Tárának Értesítője,* 1909.

PERROY, ÉDOUARD: *Le Moyen Age. L'Expansion de l'Orient et la naissance de la civilisation occidentale.* 2nd, rev. ed. Presses Universitaires de France, Paris, 1957. *(Histoire générale des civilisations,* 3.)

PFANDL, LUDWIG: *Spanische Kultur und Sitte des 16. und 17. Jahrhunderts. Eine Einführung in die Blütezeit der spanischen Literatur und Kunst.* Kösel und Pustet, Munich, 1924.

PIGGOTT, S.: *Prehistoric India to 1000 B.C.* Penguin Books, Harmondsworth, Middx., 1950.

PITON, CAMILLE: *Le Costume civil en France du XIIIe au XIXe siècle.* Flammarion, Paris, 1913.

PITTIONI R.: "Über den Ursprung des zweirädrigen Streitwagens." — *Sudeta*, 1929.

POËTE, MARCEL: *Une vie de cité Paris de sa naissance à nos jours.* Vols. 1–2. Picard, Paris, 1924–1925.

POLO, MARCO: *The Book of Ser Marco Polo, the Venetian, Concerning the Kingdoms and Marvels of the East.* Translated and ed. with notes by Henry Yule. 3rd, rev. ed. Vol. 2. J. Murray, London, 1926.

POMMERANZ-LIEDTKE, GERHARD: *Die Weisheit der Kunst. Chinesische Steinabreibungen.* Insel-Verlag, Leipzig, 1963.

POPPLOW, U.: *Pferd und Wagen im alten Orient.* Berlin, 1934.

POWELL, T. G. E.: *The Celts.* Thames and Hudson, London, 1963. *(Ancient Peoples and Places.)*

PRITCHARD, JAMES B.: *The Ancient Near East in Pictures.* (Relating to the Old Testament.) Princeton – New Jersey, 1954.

QUENNELL, MARJORIE–QUENNELL, C. H. B.: *A History of Everyday Things in England.* Vols. 1–4. Written and illustrated by —. B. T. Batsford, London, 1947–1948.

RADNÓTI, A.: "Római igaveret a Gellérthegyről." — *Budapest Régiségei*, 15 (1950).

RAWLINSON, GEORGE: *The Ancient History. From the Earliest Times to the Fall of the Western Empire.* Rev. ed. New York, 1899.

RAYET, OLIVIER: *Monuments de l'art antique.* Vols. 1–6. Quantin, Paris, 1880–1883.

Reallexikon der Assyriologie. With the contribution of experts, ed. by Erich Ebeling, Bruno Meissner. Vols. 1–2. W. de Gruyter, Berlin–Leipzig, 1932–1938

Reallexikon der Vorgeschichte. Ed. by Max Ebert. Vols. 1–14. W. de Gruyter, Berlin.

REDSLOB, EDWIN: *Die Welt vor hundert Jahren. Menschen und Kultur der Zeitwende um 1840.* Philipp Reclam jun., Leipzig [1940].

REDSLOB, EDWIN: *Vom Römerberg zum Brandenburger Tor.* Piper, Munich, 1957.

REICKE, EMIL: *Lehrer und Unterrichtswesen in der deutschen Vergangenheit.* Diederichs, Leipzig, 1901.

REINHARDT, LUDWIG: *Kulturgeschichte der Nutztiere.* Ernst Reinhardt, Munich, 1912.

REINHARDT, LUDWIG: *Kulturgeschichte des Menschen*, Vol. 2.: *Die Erde und die Kultur.* Ernst Reinhardt, Munich, 1913.

REST, WALTER: "Das Grabhügelfeld von Bell am Hunsrück." — *Bonner Jahrbücher*, 48 (1949).

RÉTHEI PRIKKEL, MARIAN: "A kocsi eredete." — *Egyetemes Philológiai Közlöny*, 21 (1897).

RICH, A.: *Illustriertes Wörterbuch der römischen Alterthümer mit steter Berücksichtigung der griechischen.* Translated by C. Müller. Paris–Leipzig, 1862.

RICHTER, GISELA: *Greek, Etruscan and Roman Bronzes.* Metropolitan Museum, New York, 1915.

RICHTER, GISELA: *Red-figured Athenian Vases in the Metropolitan Museum of Art.* Vols. 1–2. Yale University Press–Humphrey Milford–Oxford University Press, New Haven–London–Oxford, 1936.

RICHTER, GISELA M. A.: *A Handbook of Greek Art.* Phaidon, London, 1959.

RIEMSCHNEIDER, MARGARETE: *Die Welt der Hethiter*. Kilpper, Stuttgart, 1954. (*Grosse Kulturen der Frühzeit*.)

RODENWALDT, G.: *Die Kunst der Antike. Hellas und Rom*. Propyläen, Berlin, 1927. (*Propyläen-Kunstgeschichte, 3*.)

ROHR, JOHANNES: *Tausend Jahre deutsches Leben. Eine volkstümliche Kulturgeschichte*. Voegel, Berlin, 1931.

ROSA, ANGELIKA: *Lebensschicksale einer deutschen Frau im 18. Jahrhundert in eigenhändigen Briefen*. With the admission of grand-grandson Victor Kirchner. Crentz, Magdeburg, 1908.

ROSTOVTZEFF, MICHAEL: *Gesellschaft und Wirtschaft im römischen Kaiserreich*. Vols. 1–2. Quelle und Meyer, Leipzig, 1929.

ROSTOWZEW, MICHAEL: *Skythien und der Bosporus*, Vol. 1.: Kritische Übersicht der schriftlichen und archäologischen Quellen. Hans Schwetz und Co., Berlin, 1931.

RÜHLMANN, MORITZ: *Allgemeine Maschinenlehre*. 2nd ed. Schwetschke und Sohn, Braunschweig, 1877.

SAINT-PIERRE, MICHEL DE: *Trésors de la Turquie*. Arthaud, Paris, 1959.

SALONEN, A.: "Die Landfahrzeuge des alten Mesopotamien." — *Annales Academiae Scientiarum Fennicae*, Helsinki, Ser. B, 72/3.

SARRE, FRIEDRICH: *Die Kunst des alten Persien*. Berlin, 1922. (*Die Kunst des Ostens, 5*.)

SAVINE, ALBERT: *Un séjour en France sous Louis XV. Lettres du baron de Pöllnitz*. Louis–Michaud, Paris, 1909.

SCHACHERMEYR, FRITZ: "Streitwagen und Streitwagenbild im alten Orient und bei den mykenischen Griechen." — *Anthropos*, 46 (1951).

SCHADENDORF, WULF: *Zu Pferde, im Wagen, zu Fuss. Tausend Jahre Reisen*. Prestel, Munich, 1959.

SCHÄFER, H.: "Armenisches Holz in ägyptischen Wagnereien." — *Sitzungsberichte d. Preuss. Akad. d. Wissenschaften* (Phil. Kl.). 1931.

SCHEFFERUS, JOANNES: *De re vehiculari veterum. Libri. 2. Accedit Pyrrhi Ligorii De vehiculis fragmentum*. Frankfurt, 1671.

SCHEIDIG, WALTER: *Die Holzschnitte des Petrarca-Meisters zu Petrarcas Werk: Von der Artzney bayder Glück des guten und widerwärtigen* (Augsburg, 1532). Henschel, Berlin, 1955.

SCHERR, JOHANNES: *Deutsche Kultur- und Sittengeschichte*. Vols. 1–3. Revised ed. by Franz Blei. Enck, Berlin–Wilmersdorf.

SCHERR, JOHANNES: *Weib, Dame, Dirne*. Revised and ed. by Max Bauer. Paul Aretz, Dresden, 1928.

SCHMID, WALTER: *Der Kulturwagen von Strettweg*. Kabitzsch, Leipzig, 1934. (*Führer zur Urgeschichte, 12*.)

SCHMIDT, FRIEDRICH: *Das Reiten und Fahren in der altfranzösischen Literatur*. Dissertation. Göttingen, 1914.

SCHMIDT, W.–KOPPERS, W.: *Gesellschaft und Wirtschaft der Völker*. Habbel, Regensburg, 1924. (*Völker und Kulturen, 3*.)

SCHMÖKEL, HARTMUT: *Das Land Sumer. Die Wiederentdeckung der ersten Hochkultur der Menschheit*. Kohlhammer, Stuttgart, 1955.

SCHMÖKEL, HARTMUT: *Ur, Assur und Babylon. Drei Jahrtausende im Zweistromland*. 3rd ed. G. Kilpper, Stuttgart, 1955. (*Grosse Kulturen der Frühzeit.*)

SCHNEIDER, HERMANN: *Die Kulturleistungen der Menschheit*. Vols. 1–2. J. J. Weber, Leipzig, 1927–1932.

317

SCHODER, RAYMOND V.: *Masterpieces of Greek Art.* Text and colour photography by —. Studio Books, London, 1960.

SCHÖNEBAUM, HERBERT: *Aber der Wagen rollt.* Ernst Wunderlich, Leipzig, 1952.

SCHREIBER, HERMANN: *Sinfonie der Strasse.* Econ, Düsseldorf, 1959.

SCHULTZ, ALWIN: *Das höfische Leben zur Zeit der Minnesänger.* Vols. 1–2. S. Hirzel, Leipzig, 1879–1880.

SCHULTZ, ALWIN: *Das häusliche Leben der europäischen Kulturvölker vom Mittelalter bis zur zweiten Hälfte des XVIII. Jahrhunderts.* R. Oldenburg, Munich–Berlin, 1903.

SEURE, GEORGES: "Voyage en Thrace." — *Bulletin de Correspondance Hellénique,* 25 (1901).

SEURE, GEORGES: "Chars thraces." — *Bulletin de Correspondance Hellénique,* 49 (1925).

SINGER, CHARLES–HOLMYARD, E. J.–HALL, A. E.: *A History of Technology.* Vols. 1–4. Clarendon Press, Oxford, 1955.

SINICIN, I. V.: "Pamyatniki predskifskoy epohi v stepyakh Nizhnego Povolzhya." — *Sovietskaya Arheologiya,* 10 (1948).

SIRELIUS, U. T.: "Über einige Prototype des Schlittens." — *Journal de la Société Finno-Ougrienne,* 30 (1913).

SIRÉN, OSVALD: *Chinese Painting. Leading Masters and Principles.* Vols. 1–7. Lund Humphries, London, 1956–1958.

Skizzen über Deutschland und die Deutschen mit Bemerkungen über Österreich, Ungarn, Polen und die Schweiz, von einem in Deutschland wohnenden Engländer. Vols. 1–2. Literarisches Museum, Leipzig, 1837.

SMOLIAN, JÜRGEN: "Zur Frage der Entwicklung der Wagenfederung." — *Blätter für Technikgeschichte,* 24 (1962).

SMOLIAN, JÜRGEN: "Vehicula religiosa. Wagen in Mythos, Ritus, Kultus und Mysterium." — *Numen,* 10 (1963).

SMOLIAN, JÜRGEN: "Studien zur Entstehung und Ausbreitung des Wagens." — *Abhandlungen* (EAZ), 1964.

SMOLIAN, JÜRGEN: *Zur Lenkung vierrädriger Wagen in alter und neuer Zeit.* Teubner, Leipzig, 1965. (*Schriftenreihe für Geschichte der Naturwissenschaften, Technik und Medizin,* 2, No, 5.)

SOPRONI, SÁNDOR: "A budakalászi kocsi." — *Folia Archaeologica,* 6 (1954).

SOURDEVAL, CH. DE: *Le Cheval à côté de l'homme et dans l'histoire.* J. Hetzel et Cie., Paris, without date.

SPEISER, E. A.: "Ancient Mesopotamia: A Light that Did Not Fall." — *The National Geographic Magazine,* 99/1 (1951).

SPENGLER, O.: *Der Streitwagen und seine Bedeutung für den Gang der Geschichte.* Stuttgart, 1937. (*Die Welt als Geschichte,* 3.)

STEFAN, S.: *Hundert Jahre in Wort und Bild.* Pallas, Berlin, 1899.

STEINHAUSEN, GEORG: *Der Kaufmann in der deutschen Vergangenheit.* Diederichs, Leipzig, 1899. (*Monographien zur deutschen Kulturgeschichte.*)

STERN, BERNHARD: *Geschichte der öffentlichen Sittlichkeit in Russland,* Vol. 1. Hermann Barsdorf, Berlin, 1907.

STUDNICZKA, F.: "Der Rennwagen im syrisch-phönikischen Gebiet." — *Jahrbuch des Kaiserl. Deutschen Archäologischen Instituts,* 22 (1907).

TAKÁTS, SÁNDOR: *A régi Magyarország jókedve.* Athenaeum, Budapest, 1921.

TALBOT-RICE, TAMARA: *The Scythians.* Thames and Hudson, London, 1957.

THIÉBAULT, DIEUDONNÉ: *Mes souvenirs de vingt ans de séjour à Berlin du Frédéric le Grand...* Bertrand, Paris, 1813.

318

THRUPP, G. A.: *The History of Coaches.* Kerby and Endears, London, 1877.

TOCILESCU, GRIGORE G.: *Das Monument von Adam-Klissi. Tropaeum Traiani.* Hoelder, Wien, 1895.

TÓTH, BÉLA: *Magyar ritkaságok.* 2nd ed. Athenaeum, Budapest, 1907

TÓTH, BÉLA: *Mendemondák.* 3rd ed. Athenaeum, Budapest, 1907.

TREUE, WILHELM: *Der Wandel der Lebenshaltung. Ein Spiegel der Zeiten und Völker.* Volksverband der Bücherfreunde, Berlin, 1939.

TREUE, WILHELM: *Vom Lastträger zum Fernlastzug.* F. Bruckmann, Munich, 1956.

TREUE, WILHELM: *Achse, Rad und Wagen. Fünftausend Jahre Kultur- und Technikgeschichte.* Publishing commissioned by Kotz and Sons Axle Works, Wiehl. Bruckmann, Munich, 1965.

TREVELYAN, GEORGE MACAULAY: *Illustrated English Social History.* Vols. 1–2. Longmans, Green and Co., London–New York–Toronto, 1951.

TSCHUDI, YOLANDE: *Les Peintures rupestres du Tassili-n-Ajjer.* La Baconnière, Neuchâtel, 1956.

TSUI CHI: *Histoire de la Chine et de la civilisation chinoise.* Payot, Paris, 1949.

TYLOR, E. B.: "On the origin of plough and wheel-carriage." — *Journal of the Anthrop. Inst. of Great Britain and Ireland,* 10 (1884).

UNGER, ECKHARD: "Tierbilder aus der Königsnekropole in Ur." — *Kosmos,* 11 (1929).

UNGER, ECKHARD: "Der Obelisk des Königs Assurnassirpal I. aus Ninive." — *Mitteilungen der Altorientalischen Gesellschaft,* 6 (1932).

UNGER, ECKHARD: *Altindogermanisches Kulturgut in Nordmesopotamien.* Harrassowitz, Leipzig, 1938.

VAILLÉ, EUGÈNE: *Histoire générale des postes françaises,* Vol. 2. Presses Universitaires de France, Paris, 1949.

VAUSSARD, MAURICE: *La Vie quotidienne en Italie au XVIIIᵉ siècle.* Hachette, Paris, 1959.

VEHSE, EDUARD: *Hofgeschichten aus Rokoko und Biedermeier.* Duncker, Weimar, without date.

VENEDIKOV, IVAN: *Trakiyskata kolesnitza.* Izd. Bulg. Akad. Naukite, Sofia, 1960.

VERNES, FRANÇOIS DE: *Le Voyageur sentimental en France sous Robespierre.* Vols. 1–2. Geneva, 1796.

La Vie parisienne au XVIIIᵉ siècle. By BERGMANN, H.–CAHEN, L., etc. Alcan, Paris, 1914.

VIEYRA, MAURICE: *Hittite Art.* Alec Tiranti, London, 1955.

VITZTHUM, CARL FRIEDRICH: *St. Petersburg und London in den Jahren 1852–1864. Aus den Denkwürdigkeiten des damaligen k. sächsischen ausserordentlichen Gesandten und bevollmächtigten Ministers.* Vols. 1–3. Cotta, Stuttgart, 1886.

VOS, H. B.: *Rijtuigen.* C. A. J. van Dishoeck, Bussum, 1961.

WACKERNAGEL, RUDOLF H.: *Der französische Krönungswagen von 1696–1825. Ein Beitrag zur Geschichte des repräsentativen Zeremonienwagens.* W. de Gruyter, Berlin, 1966. (*Neue Münchner Beiträge zur Kunstgeschichte,* 7.)

WARD, WILLIAMS HAYES: *The Seal Cylinders of Western-Asia.* Colombia-Carnegie Institution, Washington D.C., 1910. (*Publications of the Carnegie Institution of Washington,* 100.)

WÄSCHER, HERMANN: *Das deutsche illustrierte Flugblatt. Von den Anfängen bis zu den Befreiungskriegen.* Verlag der Kunst, Berlin, 1955.

WATELIN, L. CH.–LANGDON, S.: "Discoveries at Kish." — *Illustrated London News,* 2 June, 1928.

WATSON, WILLIAM: *Archaeology in China*. Max Parrish, London, 1960.

WATSON, WILLIAM: *China before the Han Dynasty*. Thames and Hudson, London, 1961. *(Ancient Peoples and Places.)*

WEBER, OTTO: *Altorientalische Siegelbilder*. Leipzig, 1920.

WEIDNER, E. F.: "Weisse Pferde im alten Orient." — *Bibliotheca Orientalis*, 9.

WEIGLIN, PAUL: *Berliner Biedermeier. Leben, Kunst und Kultur in Alt-Berlin zwischen 1815 und 1848*. 2nd ed. Velhagen und Klasing, Bielefeld–Leipzig, 1942.

WEITZMANN, KURT: *Ancient Book Illumination*. Harvard, Cambridge (Mass.), 1959. *(Martin Classical Lectures*, 16.)

WEULE, K.: *Die Urgesellschaft und ihre Lebensfürsorge*. Stuttgart, 1912.

WEYERSBERG, M.: *Felsbilder im Val Camonica*. Supplement 11 for — *Mitt. d. Forschunginst. für Kulturmorphologie, vorgesch. Kunst Südeuropas*. Frankfurt on the M., 1938.

WEYRICH, EDGAR: *Alt-Wien. (Kulturbild aus Wiens Glanzzeit.)* Deutscher Verlag für Jugend und Volk, Vienna–Berlin–Leipzig–New York, 1927.

WHITE, LYNN T.: *Medieval Technology and Social Change*. Clarendon Press, Oxford, 1962.

WIESNER, JOSEPH: "Fahren und Reiten in Alteuropa und im alten Orient." — *Forschungen und Fortschritte*, 15 (1939).

WIESNER, JOSEPH: "Frühzeitliche Tierbilder in Alteuropa und im Alten Orient." — *Forschungen und Fortschritte*, 17 (1941).

WILHELM, RICHARD: *Geschichte der chinesischen Kultur*. F. Bruckmann, Munich, 1928.

WILLIAMSON, GEORGE C.: *Curious Survivals*. Corr. and rev. ed. Herbert Jenkins, London, 1925.

WOLFF, M.–OPITZ, D.: "Jagd zu Pferde in der altorientalischen und klassischen Kunst." — *Archiv für Orientforschung*, 10 (1935–36.)

WOLFF, THEO: *Vom Ochsenwagen zum Automobil. Geschichte der Wagenfahrzeuge und des Fahrwesens von ältester bis zu neuester Zeit*. J. A. Barth, Leipzig, 1909.

WOOLLEY, L.: *Ur-Excavations*, Vol. 2.: *The Royal Cemetery*. Oxford, 1934.

WRANGEL, C. G.: *Das Buch vom Pferde*. 6th, completely rewritten and rev. ed. by F. W. Kurt Plessing. Vols. 1–2. Schickhardt und Ebner, Stuttgart, 1927–1928.

WRESZINSKI, WALTER.: "Löwenjagd im alten Ägypten." — *Morgenland*, 23 (1932).

WRESZINSKI, WALTER.: *Atlas zur altägyptischen Kulturgeschichte*, Vol. 2. Hinrichs, Leipzig, 1923.

ZAMMIT, THEMISTOKLES: "Prehistoric Car-Tracks in Malta." — *Antiquity*, 1 (1928).

ZERVOS, CH.: *L'Art de la Mésopotamie*. Cahiers d'Art, Paris.

ZETTLER, O.: *Alt-Münchener Bilderbuch. Ansichten aus dem alten München aus der Monacensia*. Müller, Munich, 1918.

ZILLIACUS, LAURIN: *Mail for the World. From the Courier to the Universal Postal Union*. The John Day Co., New York, 1953.

Index

Wrangel, C. G., 272
Wu, 97
Württemberg, 234
Wu Wang, 93

Xaza'el, 56
Xenophon, 66–67
Xerxes (Xshayarsha, Ksajarus),
  67

Yangtze, 95
Yelizavetina Stanitza,
  106
Yellow River, 95
Yenisei, 102–103
yoke, *see* harnessing
York, 234
Yorkshire, 133
Yu, 92

Yugoslavia, 123, 155
yurt, 274

Zagros, 44
Zammit, Th., 100
Zillen, 264
Znamenka, 102
Züschen, 99–100
Zyryans (Komis), 13